A Cycle of Adams Letters

Copyright 1920 Worthington C. Ford
Reprinted by Ross & Perry, Inc. 2002
© Ross & Perry, Inc. 2002 on new material. All rights reserved.

Protected under the Berne Convention.

Printed in The United States of America

Ross & Perry, Inc. Publishers
216 G St., N.E.
Washington, D.C. 20002
Telephone (202) 675-8300
Facsimile (202) 675-8400
info@RossPerry.com

SAN 253-8555

Library of Congress Control Number: 2002105347
http://www.rossperry.com

ISBN 1-932080-03-1

Book Cover designed by Sapna. sapna@rossperry.com

The paper used in this publication meets the requirements for permanence established by the American National Standard for Information Sciences "Permanence of Paper for Printed Library Materials" (ANSI Z39.48-1984).

All rights reserved. No copyrighted part of this publication may be reproduced, stored in a retrieval system, or transmitted, in any form or by any means, electronic, photocopying, recording, or otherwise, without the prior written permission of the publisher.

A Cycle
of
Adams letters

1861-1865

Volume 1

Edited by

Worthington Chauncey Ford

With Illustrations

Ross & Perry, Inc.
Washington, D.C.

TO
MARY OGDEN ADAMS

Possum donata reponere laetus.
                    HOR.

INTRODUCTORY NOTE

THE series of letters printed in these volumes, individual in themselves, make an almost unique combination. The time of writing, the crisis through which not only the nation but republican institutions were passing, the inheritance and position of the writers, and the personal characteristics of each as shown in the letters and as developed in later days, unite to give interest to the subjects treated and the manner of presentation. They are family letters, written in all the freedom of family intercourse, selected from what would fill many volumes; they are much more than family letters, for the description of social conditions, the discussion of public questions, and the wide relations held by the writers, make them a contribution to the social, military and diplomatic history of the War of Secession, unequalled in scope and concentrated interest.

For nearly a century the Adams family of Massachusetts had filled high public office, a succession of students of government, of able administrators, whose independence and upright character commanded recognition. The third generation had as its representative Charles Francis Adams, the favored son of John Quincy Adams. On the election of Lincoln to the Presidency Mr. Adams was nominated to be Minister of the United States to Great Britain and was at once confirmed by the Senate. He sailed for his post in

May, 1861, and reached England only to be met by the Queen's proclamation recognizing the South as belligerents. The act, justified in international law, was interpreted as unfriendly, and seemed in fact to represent the feeling of suspicion and hostility of the ruling class in England towards the American republic, a feeling that found expression in sympathy for the South, in the wish for its success and in a hope that a divided people would remove anxiety on the growth of a democracy that could not be confined to present bounds, and the influence of which on old institutions of Europe was already felt.

The almost complete isolation of the Minister for months after his arrival in London is a strange phenomenon. The requirements of official etiquette were fulfilled, but little beyond that came to welcome the strangers. Mr. Adams himself was, indeed, no stranger in England. When his father held the same office, immediately after the close of the War of 1812, the son had been in an English school. This experience served him well in 1861. He knew the English characteristics, he had been trained in their methods, he could divine how the English mind would think, and so forecast the resulting action. The English reserve and self-restraint were no greater than his own. He could anticipate the manner of expressing a difference of opinion, and provide against surprise by an unexpected performance. He was thoroughly grounded in the history of the United States, in the relations which had subsisted between the United States and Great Britain, and in republican government, with its ever-present longing to improve the world according to its own beliefs. No man in American public life was by inheritance, training and matured convictions, so well fitted to occupy this office at so delicate and critical a time. The seven years of service in London mark the highest point of Mr. Adams' career. Facing perils where a misstep would have involved catastrophe, ruin to himself and destruction to his country, he made no mistake, no surrender to temporary advantage, no concession of right or principle. Against public clamor at home, at times against the instructions of his superior, the Secretary of State, and against the pressure of Americans and plotting Southerners in Europe, he calmly pursued his course. His abilities, prescience and acts have been fully justified by time and events. Never had American diplomacy in Europe been at as low an ebb as in 1861; never had American policy, domestic as well as foreign, stood as high as in 1868, and nowhere higher than in England. To Mr. Adams the country largely owed this change; it was a great achievement, the greater because of the difficulties overcome.

The son, Charles Francis Adams, Jr., had graduated from Harvard College in 1856, and was now in the office of Richard Henry Dana studying law but gradually becoming aware that law was not his proper vocation. He had the same distaste for its practice that had repelled his grandfather, John Quincy Adams. He had grown up in an atmosphere of political discussion, had been accustomed to consider public questions, and was forming connections in journalism as a possible future field for public service. Already he showed the inquiring mind which took nothing for granted, discussed everything and recognized no lines of disciplined obedience to party or to creed. Restive under the inaction of a law office, he chafed under the idea of confinement, of wasted energy and little promise of improvement. His father's service in Congress interested him far more than anything that Kent or Blackstone could offer, and in his communications to the newspapers he was no more blind to the rapidly approaching crisis in the contest between the North and the South than were his older contemporaries. Conscious of a certain capacity of expression he believed the career of publicist offered him better expectations than any other calling, and subsequent events proved him in this to have been correct.

Thus situated when actual war began, only the responsibilities imposed by his father's absence prevented the son from at once entering the army. His older brother, John Quincy Adams, was on the staff of Governor Andrew, proving his capacity and aiding in despatching to the front the regiments so speedily sent from Massachusetts. He saw his college and social companions eagerly enrolling their names and as eagerly accepted for service. The most available member of the family for the army, his strong sense of duty to his father kept him back, until he felt that his duty to his country overshadowed all other calls. Of his service in the war he has given a bare outline in his "Autobiography"; but his letters are far more detailed, and describe, as is nowhere better described, the daily life of a cavalry officer.

The development of character under discipline and experience, the ripening of mind and opinions by close contact with his fellow men and with the questions of army administration, and the growing richness of observation and expression, appear in his letters. He entered the army a restive, unformed youth, without settled ambition or recognized powers; he left it a man of strengthened mind, of broadened views, and with a defined future and true calling. The younger Adams of 1865 was a far different being from the younger Adams of 1861, and he always looked back with interest on his military service as contributing to his later success. It is rare to find a soldier capable of giving an interesting account of his routine duties, of narrating in a logical manner successive events, of speculating justly on a summary of facts, or of sketching in a few words a man's character so as to present a vivid likeness. He is usually inarticulate, or expends the little gift he has in minor details without the needed binding relation. Mr. Adams formed the exception. He could write and he had, though unknown to himself, the best qualities of the historian.

In his "Education" Henry Adams has given a self-drawn representation of himself as a "failure," and in a manner that awakens astonishment and challenges examination. To have been successful in everything that he attempted — teaching, science, history, fiction and criticism — would have satisfied an ordinary mortal. But that was exactly what he was not, and the various readings given to his confessions prove how exceptional he was. He also passed through Harvard

College, had thoughts of studying law, but believed that some years in Europe would round out his education. What those years did for him may be traced in his later writings. Before their effects could be felt he passed the winter of 1860–61 in Washington, a keen observer of passing events, forming independent judgments upon them, while enjoying to the full the advantage of his father's opinions and relations with public men. The months thus spent trained his powers of observation and analysis, so fruitful when applied to his English experience. For he became confidential secretary to his father in London, a position unrecognized, as it was also unpaid, by the government. He used the opportunity wisely and with advantage to the father.

His early letters are in tone very like his "Education." There is the same detachment, the same quality of critic under the guise of philosopher, the same persistent note of irony, the same apparent indifference to results, the same, though less defined, gift of expression. It has been said that it was a "pose" and the man was insincere, but those who were closest to him in later life knew that such a charge was not true. He was keenly interested in running a problem to earth; once apprehended, he turned to other things, looking upon the achievement as rather futile, unworthy of the effort made to master it. In the wealth of his ability he could afford to take such a position, and his letters show that in this respect his whole life was consistent. He had tasted of newspaper correspondence and believed he could cultivate the taste when in London.

A few weeks of experience proved its dangers. This threw him much upon his own resources and the result is reflected in his letters and later writings. It cultivated an independence of utterance, and strong as must have been the influence of the father, it is not the "official" aspect that is the more interesting.

The letters open with the Minister on his way to London, with his son Henry as secretary; with Charles on temporary garrison duty at Fort Independence in Boston harbor; with the war opened and the North partially aroused. They close with the Minister's great triumph in diplomacy accomplished and with the son's retirement from the army, broken in health. The letters require no annotation. The history of the War of Secession has been told and retold in its every phase, and no letters could relate the old story in a connected manner. Yet in the contemporary record which follows will be found no little new history, much untold detail, much discussion, many rumors and predictions, expressed with individuality and in a literary form. The progress of the great conflict supplies the background, against which stand prominently personal experiences, hopes and fears. It is an old story, but the manner of telling it is new, all the more remarkable because unstudied and spontaneous.

The writing of autobiography has its dangers, the greatest of which is the almost inevitable misjudgment of motives and relations viewed after years of riper attainment. It must be partial, biassed, or lose the very quality that should be its strength or justification. The degree of error depends upon the generosity or the narrowness of the writer. Each of the two sons has related his life history. The defect of partial appreciation is evident in each instance, but there is no trace of narrowness associated with it. Disinterestedness, magnanimity and self-control are shown in the letters now drawn from one common source. These qualities will not correct the impression gained from a true reading of the "Autobiography" and the "Education," but they will develop other and deeper attributes natural to the writers, yet concealed almost to suppression in their self-accusing memoirs.

WORTHINGTON CHAUNCEY FORD

Boston, September, 1920

ILLUSTRATIONS

CHARLES FRANCIS ADAMS	*Photogravure frontispiece*
LIEUTENANT-COLONEL HORACE BINNEY SARGENT	24
CHARLES SUMNER	54
CASPAR CROWNINSHIELD	80
JOHN BRIGHT	112
No. 5 UPPER PORTLAND PLACE, LONDON, OCCUPIED BY THE AMERICAN MINISTER	138
GENERAL ROBERT WILLIAMS	156
GEORGE BRINTON MCCLELLAN	194
SURGEON LUCIUS MANLIUS SARGENT	218
MAJOR HENRY LEE HIGGINSON	248
THE DUKE OF ARGYLL	252

A CYCLE OF ADAMS LETTERS
1861

A CYCLE OF ADAMS LETTERS

CHARLES FRANCIS ADAMS TO HIS MOTHER

Fort Independence, May 12, 1861

. . . .

THE truth is that in garrison life, with guard duty three times in two weeks, five hours drill a day and the necessity of waiting on oneself, it is difficult either to write or read much in a room about the size of our bed-room in Boston in which eleven other men are quartered — that is live, eat and sleep — besides myself. Yet I like the life very much and am getting as rugged and hearty as an ox, passing all my time in eating, drilling, sleeping and chaffing. Our mess is made up of very good fellows indeed, all friends of mine, such men as Clark and Pratt, the two celebrated rowers, Tom Motley, Jr., Caspar Crowninshield, Fred d'Hauteville, etc. Our life is one of rigid garrison duty: réveillé at half past five with breakfast at six; dress parade at seven; a squad drill at eight and a company drill at ten; at twelve dinner and at three a battalion drill which lasts until half past five, when we have an evening dress-parade, which finishes work for those off guard for the day. At six we have tea and amuse ourselves till half past nine, when tattoo beats and we go to bed and after a little sky-larking quickly to sleep. When on guard, which every man is about twice a week, it is rather restless, as for twenty-four hours we are on guard two hours and off four, day and night, and properly can't leave the guard room; but as our mess are especial friends of the sergeants rules are rather relaxed in our favor. Food is tolerable, coarse but enough, though devilish unclean at times. In our mess each man takes his turn in washing up the dishes and keeping the quarters of the mess clean. So once in ten days or so visitors see the best blood in America, in the person of your son, washing dishes, sweeping floors, wheeling coal, etc., like a family servant. Meanwhile health is superb and I never looked so browned and hearty in my life. . . .

Outside we hear a good deal of a raging military ardor. A good many young men we know are getting commissions, especially in Gordon's regiment, and from our mess three men went up in one day, among them George R. Russell's son Henry; but two of them came back, Hal only staying. Sam Quincy they say is a Captain. Elliot Parkman has a commission of some sort in the navy and Dick Goodwin, George Bangs, Rufus Choate, Greely and Pelham Curtis and others with Gordon. . . .

CHARLES FRANCIS ADAMS, JR., TO HIS FATHER

Quincy, May 27, 1861

I GOT out here last Saturday evening, having that day been relieved at Fort Independence by the 4th Battalion of rifles. We would like to have stayed there longer, and were certainly arriving at a state of very considerable proficiency in drill, but our being kept there was beginning to create some hard feeling and the

Governor was obliged to yield to the pressure. What will be done with us now, if any thing, no one seems to know. I hardly think they will leave such an efficient body of men alone just now, and yet I do not see how we can be profitably employed. That we shall not be sent out of the State is certain; but the rumors seem to tend towards our being sent to the State camp to serve as a model and to furnish instructors, and ultimately to be used as a supply of officers. Meanwhile I find that I have not returned a day too early, and that my presence is necessary in Boston for some time to come. To me things look pretty bad. Money is plenty, but lenders are very timid. Business is wholly dead and the business community seems to be calculating as to whether they can live out the war or had better go down now. For myself, I see little to change the views I have entertained all along. We are going into this war too heavily to have it last long, but it will be an awful drag while it does last, and all who are not under short sail must go down. I do not believe in getting alarmed or in the eternal ruin of the country; but a great deal of money has got to be lost and all who have, have got to lose some, be it more or less. . . .

Of course all this does not at all add to the pleasure of a reluctant return. I have become fond of military life and I feel ashamed that I am here at home when so many of my friends have already gone, and gone in such a way. I do not wish to boast of what I should do under other circumstances, but I feel, as I look at these tedious and repulsive details [of business], that I should tonight sleep perfectly happy if tomorrow I could hand them all over to anyone who would take them, and for myself go and join my friends in camp. I could get a commission and a good one, for only today Dana evidently wanted to advise me to go and told me I ought to have a majority if I wished it. . . .

CHARLES FRANCIS ADAMS, JR., TO HIS MOTHER

Boston, June 3, 1861

. . . .

THE war affords them [of Quincy] some diversion for their thoughts and the clash of arms is heard even among the Quincy exempts, who hail John Captain. I drilled them the other evening and a funnier sight I don't want to see. Imagine a line of pot-bellied, round-shouldered respectabilities of fifty or thereabouts standing in two rows and trying to dance, and you have a fair idea of this justly celebrated corps. I was infinitely delighted when on glancing down the ranks, as I came the heavy military on them. I saw Mr. Robertson and Captain Crane side by side in the front rank, with Mr. Gill and poor old Flint vainly struggling to cover them in the rear. That was too much and I almost smiled right out loud. The only man I saw who could by any possibility be converted into a soldier was, unfortunately, our worthy pastor, Mr. Wells, who however in case of emergency would probably have other duties to perform. There he was, however, with his musket in his hand and it was so refreshing to see a man who seemed able to bend his back that I asked John to make him a sergeant and I believe he promised that he would. By the way, I really do believe we have drawn quite a prize in Wells. He seems to have pleased every one and you don't know how strange it seems to have some one here who really takes an interest in and means to manage the Parish. I had a short talk with him the other evening and was much pleased. He evidently understands the people here and is going to make his mark, and I have little doubt that if he lives, you'll find the Parish a very different thing when you come home from what it was when you went away. . . .

CHARLES FRANCIS ADAMS TO HIS SON

London, June 7, 1861

. . . .

FOR after all that may be said, there is not and cannot be any assimilation of manners and social habits between Americans and English people. All intercourse with the aristocratic class is necessarily but formal. We are invited everywhere, and dine out almost every day, but this brings us no nearer. Everybody is civil, but each one has his interests in England, so that a stranger is but an outsider at best. . . .

You may be more interested to know a little about the House of Commons. My diplomatic privilege gives me the entrée there, and I have used it twice. The last time was at the close of the debate on the budget, when it was generally understood that the fate of Mr. Gladstone, if not of the whole Cabinet hung on the decision. More than six hundred members were present, and the array showed great equality on the two sides of the House. I had attended on the Monday before and had made up my mind that if the division should follow, the opposition would prevail by a decided vote. The ministry however had influence enough to command an adjournment, and on Thursday the case stood differently. The attack was neither so vigorous nor so confident, whilst the defence was bolder and more strenuous. The first effective stroke came from Lord John Russell, which I did not get in time to hear. The next was from Mr. Cobden, which was plain, direct and evidently telling on the House. The decisive blow came, however, from Mr. Gladstone, who stood like a bull in the arena surrounded by dogs. He began by tossing the very last one who had attacked him, and he went on with every one in turn, until he had them all sprawling on the ground. He is by all odds the best speaker I have heard, and though I cannot think him a very great man, I must award him the palm as a skilful debater. Lord Palmerston is evidently powerful more from his character, talents and position, than from any oratorical qualities. The ministry triumphed by fifteen majority only.

The characteristic of the House is that it is in essence a real deliberative body, whilst our House has ceased to be one. We speak to the people and not to the audience. Hence we make orations and not speeches. I know not how this can be remedied in America. Some members of Parliament tell me that this is perceptibly growing even here. So it must be, in proportion to the control which the people exercise over their representatives. . . .

CHARLES FRANCIS ADAMS, JR., TO HIS FATHER

Boston, June 10, 1861

. . . .

I AM sorry to see what you say of the possibility of your demanding your passports. Stocks rose in New York on Saturday owing to the reported tenor of your despatches, which must however have been of a tone very different from your letter to me. Still I can't help thinking that the tenor of the news from this country must create an improvement in England. Now, however, the feeling here is very bitter, and significant intimations fall from some of the leading papers that the July Congress, while it modifies the Morrill tariff so as to assist and help France to the utmost of our power, will indulge in no friendly legislation to England. This is the tone of the Evening Post, a free-trade journal. If England wants to break down the Morrill tariff, her only course is to take the back track and conciliate our good will. . . .

About this war business. A great change has come over my feelings since you left, as I have told you, and I now feel not only a strong inclination to go off, but a conviction that from many points of view I ought to do it. I am twenty-six years old and of course have a right to do as I choose; but I acknowledge, as I have done all along, that great regard is due in this matter to you and your feelings, and now, as heretofore, I shall not go without your consent; but I think you ought to give that consent, if, under certain circumstances, I ask for it. Undoubtedly a further levy will soon be demanded in this war and when it comes there will be an effort made in this state to send forth a model regiment, and already John Palfrey is spoken of as its colonel. I saw Governor Andrew the other evening and he promised me that, in that or any other regiment to be sent from Massachusetts, if I would apply, he would give me a company. Now if such a regiment is raised, I wish to go in it, and I think I have a right to almost demand your assent to my doing so. How does the case stand? I cannot see that in a business point of view I am very necessary to you. Your property and mine would be just as safe and probably better managed in the hands of a man of business, or Sam Frothingham under John's supervision, than in mine; and of this you must be aware. So how is my presence here necessary to you, which is the only ground on which I think you ought to object? If you say it is, I will give up the idea still, but before saying so I earnestly hope you will consider the matter fairly. You will say there is small glory in a civil war, and this is generally true; but in the civil war in England or in the Revolution here, what should we now think of a man who, in the hour of greatest danger, sat at home reading the papers? For years our family has talked of slavery and of the South, and been most prominent in the contest of words, and now that it has come to blows, does it become us to stand aloof from the conflict? It is not as if I were an only son, though many such have gone; but your family is large and it seems to me almost disgraceful that in after years we should have it to say that of them all not one at this day stood in arms for that government with which our family history is so closely connected. I see all around me going, but I sit in my office and read the papers, for I have nothing else to do. I see great events going on, and a heroic spirit everywhere flashing out, and you ask me for no sufficient cause to stifle my own and, when sitting here at home, I am convinced of my failure as a lawyer, to quietly sink into a real estate agent. I hope you will let me go, for if you should and I return, it will make a man of me; and if I should not return — am I likely to live to a better purpose by going on as I have begun? Perhaps the occasion will not demand it. Perhaps no such regiment will be raised. If it should so happen, however, I earnestly hope for our own credit and that of our name, that you will make no objection to my taking this commission which now I have but to ask for, and going forth to sustain the government and to show that in this matter our family means what it says. . . .

CHARLES FRANCIS ADAMS TO HIS SON

London, June 14, 1861

. . . .

MY position here thus far has not been difficult or painful. If I had followed the course of some of my colleagues in the diplomatic line this country might have been on the high road to the confederate camp before now. It did not seem to me to be expedient so to play into the hands of our opponents. Although there has been and is more or less of sympathy with the slaveholders in certain circles, they are not so powerful as to overbear the general sentiment of the people. The ministry has been placed in rather delicate circumstances, when a small loss of power on either extreme would have thrown them out. You can judge of this by the vote on the Chancellor's budget which was *apparently* carried by fifteen, but *really* by the retirement of opponents from the division. The difficulty seems now to be removed. No farther test vote is expected at this session. I think they are at heart more friendly to the United States than the Conservatives, though the question is not raised between them. I am therefore endeavoring to establish such relations with them as may re-establish the confidence between the countries which has been somewhat shaken of late. Circumstances beyond my control will have more to do with the result for good or for evil than any efforts of mine. I wait with patience — but as yet I have not gone so far as to engage a house for more than a month at a time. . . .

CHARLES FRANCIS ADAMS, JR., TO HIS MOTHER

Boston, June 18, 1861

. . . .

BEFORE this reaches you, you will have heard of the miserable affair at Great Bethel which has made so much noise here. You see a Quincy man was killed — young Souther, a brother of our one-armed friend. Our flags out there were hung at half mast for a day and loud swearing, there as elsewhere, was heard at and about Brigadier General Peirce. It was a bad affair and John Palfrey writes that two companies of regulars would have carried the battery with ease, but this is the beginning of our militia generalship and, alas, that this should have been a Massachusetts man. In fact our good old State, which began this war so well, is likely after going up like a rocket to come down like a stick, and she is now rapidly falling behindhand. While other states have sent out from one to twenty regiments of three year men, she has sent out her first only last week and that one under the command of Colonel Cowdin, a notorious incompetent. In fact Gordon's regiment is the only decent one, so far as I can hear, yet organized in Massachusetts and the others are so wretchedly officered and so thoroughly demoralized already that it will be almost a miracle if the State is not soon disgraced. In fact Andrew does not show that capacity which he gave promise of and his selections of men so far have, I should say, been wretched. I hope the next batch from here which will probably be called for and organized in July and August will show an improvement, and that we shall then send out some superior men, those whom we are now sending out having previously demonstrated their incompetence. . . .

CHARLES FRANCIS ADAMS TO HIS SON

London, June 21, 1861

. . . .

WITH respect to his [Sumner's] language about Governor Seward I very much regret it for the sake of the public interest. He is sowing the seeds of discord where we ought to have a more perfect union. He is disseminating distrust in our Government when it depends upon confidence. I am surprised to find how very general the dislike of the Governor is in society here. The English express fear of his intentions towards them and intimate suspicions of his duplicity, whilst among Americans he finds only here and there a defender. In one or two cases I have already traced these impressions to their source in America, and I think I see the channels through which they are conducted. How much harm they may be doing cannot yet be appreciated. But if by means of them we should be plunged into a war solely from misunderstandings of our reciprocal intentions, we might come to conceive an idea of it. I believe that events are gradually working us out of this danger. But I suspect that the mischief has been considerable, and that we shall feel the effect of it in our future relations with this country for a good while to come. So far as I can, I have done my best to counteract it.

The general impression here is that there will be no war, and a little apprehension is expressed lest the reunion may be the signal for a common crusade against Great Britain. People do not quite understand Americans or their politics. They think this a hasty quarrel, the mere result of passion, which will be arranged as soon as the cause of it shall pass off. They do not comprehend the connection which slavery has with it, because we do not at once preach emancipation. Hence they go to the other extreme and argue that it is not an element of the struggle. With the commercial men the wish is father to the thought. They look with some uneasiness to the condition of the operatives at Manchester, to the downfall of Southern State stocks, to the falling off of the exports of goods and the drain of specie, to the exclusion from the seaports by the blockade, and to the bad debts of their former customers, for all which their sole panacea is *settlement*, somehow, no matter how. If it be by a recognition of two governments, that is as good a way as any other. On the other hand I now look to something of a war. We are in it and cannot get out. The slaveholding politicians must go down or there will be no permanent peace. I confess that in this sense I look with some anxiety to the meeting of Congress. I know not who there is now to give a right tone to its proceedings. Possibly some of the new men may come in and contribute to help on the work. Judge Thomas has a reputation as a lawyer, and he has also been a little of a legislator as long ago as when I was with him, but this is a new field. I hope and trust he may do well. . . .

CHARLES FRANCIS ADAMS, JR., TO HIS FATHER

Boston, July 2, 1861

. . . .

THERE is little news politically, for I am no longer in the way of getting it. There is a marked improvement in the general feeling and in the tone of the press towards England and my apprehensions of trouble would have entirely subsided but that I cannot but fear future trouble on account of this blockade. I fear that it is not effective and that some blundering British admiral will undertake to raise it for that reason, and this will surely lead to trouble. Neither do I believe that our blockade is likely to be effective in less than a hundred days. There are rumors, and pretty well authenticated, that Seward is losing ground in Washington and in New York very fast. Sumner has been here fiercely denouncing him for designing, as he asserts, to force the country into a foreign war, and Mr. George Morey tells me that to checkmate this, Sumner intends on the opening of Congress to make a speech on our foreign relations in which he will declare his entire satisfaction with the position of England and France. . . .

HENRY ADAMS TO CHARLES FRANCIS ADAMS, JR.

London, Tuesday, July 2, 1861

. . . .

MY letters in the [New York] Times will give you pretty much all I have to say about politics. They are very correctly printed; at least the three first which are all that have reached me. There is no doubt in my mind that all the trouble with England arose from a mere blunder of the Ministry resulting from the suddenness of the change in affairs with us. Here it seems to have been thought with reason that the dissolution of the Union would go as it were by default, without much resistance, and the Ministry and even our warmest friends thought that this would be best for us as well as for themselves. The English are really on our side; of that I have no doubt whatever. But they thought that as a dissolution seemed inevitable and as we seemed to have made up our minds to it, that their Proclamation was just the thing to keep them straight with both sides, and when it turned out otherwise they did their best to correct their mistake. America seems clean daft. She seems to want to quarrel with all the world, and now that England has eaten her humble-pie for what was, I must say, a natural mistake from her point of view, I cannot imagine why we should keep on sarsing her. It certainly is not our interest and I have done and shall do all I can, to bring matters straight. As a counterpart to my letters in the Times, I am looking round here for some good paper to take you as its American correspondent. I don't know that I can get one, but certainly it will be a good while before a fair chance is likely to happen. When it does I will let you know.

Seward's tone has improved very much since that crazy despatch that frightened me so. If the Chief had obeyed it literally, he would have made a war in five minutes and annihilated our party here in no time at all. As it is we have worried through safely and are not likely to have much more trouble. There is nothing in the way of particulars to give you so far as I know, for there has been no great scene nor have I met with any very remarkable event. Our presentation was only memorable to my mind from having caused a relapse for me, which frightened me nearly to death.

As to your going to the war, I will tell you plainly how the case seems to me to stand. The Chief is unwilling to do anything about it. His idea is that the war will be short and that you will only destroy all your habits of business without gaining anything. If you will take my advice you will say no more about it; only make arrangements so as not to be taken by surprise, and when the time comes, just write and notify him. He will consent to that as a fait accompli, which he cannot take the responsibility of encouraging himself. . . .

Send us maps of the seat of war — the best ones.

CHARLES FRANCIS ADAMS, JR., TO HIS MOTHER

Boston, July 9, 1861

. . . .

YESTERDAY we [the Battalion] went out to escort Gordon's regiment off — the one raised by the subscription of the Boston gentlemen. There were, as I have told you, lots of my friends in it, and I should have been sorry not to have bid them good-bye; but not till they were gone did I find that the one I should most wished to have seen was gone, and I did n't even see him as the train went off. For Stephen Perkins joined as a Second Lieutenant at the last minute, and I did n't know the fact till he was on his way to Virginia. It made me feel quite badly and I have n't got over it yet. Off they all went, however, and apparently in good spirits and full of life and hope, and the last I saw of the train, Wilder Dwight, rapidly disappearing on its last platform, was waving his hat and dancing a saraband at me, which I returned from the pile of gravel on which we were drawn up, with my whole heart. Sam Quincy was swept by me as he stood on the lower step of a platform looking at his old friends in the cadets, but I did not catch his eye. He looked much as usual. When Hal Russell passed he caught my eye and went through a war dance, with that eager look on his face which a man has when bidding good-bye to old friends on his way to the wars, and when he only recollects pleasant things about them; but Stephen Perkins I did n't see, even as the train went by. They're on their way now and I certainly envy them very much. Next comes Frank Palfrey and then there is n't much of any one to go after that. John Palfrey has come home, by the way, sick — a typhoid fever, but the symptoms are said to be mild. He was over-worked in the sun, surveying, but they do not seem to be apprehensive. Caspar Crowninshield has got home from Washington and expects a commission in the regular army, and, I have little doubt, will get it. . . .

CHARLES FRANCIS ADAMS TO HIS SON

London, July 18, 1861

. . . .

I HAVE engaged a house[1] which will I hope be more convenient. It is not in quite so fashionable or so noisy a situation, but it is amply and in some respects richly furnished, and is in a very good neighborhood. My engagement is only for a year, and even that may be shortened if the Earl of Derby should come into the ministry. For my landlord, who is in Parliament, hopes to get back to the same place he had before, Under Secretary for Foreign Affairs, in which contingency he will want his house in May next. In the exact condition of our affairs I have not considered the arrangement so bad as I might otherwise have done. Our relations with this country are now in a promising

[1] No. 5 Mansfield Street, belonging to Sir William Robert Seymour Vesey Fitzgerald.

condition. I have no idea that anybody means war. But a blockade which shuts up the cotton crop is not unlikely to try the nerves of our friends a little, and to elicit causes of difference that may prove difficult to settle. . . .

I think I have attained a tolerable idea of the texture of London society. I have seen most of the men of any reputation, literary or political. The conclusion is not favorable, so far as the comparison with other periods is concerned. Lord Palmerston, Mr. Gladstone, Lord John Russell and Lords Derby and Ellenborough are the orators. Mr. D'Israeli perhaps might be included. Thackeray, Senior, Monckton Milnes, Grote, Lord Stanhope, and Mr. Reeve, the editor of the Edinburgh Review, constitute pretty much the literature. Perhaps I should include Milman. Gladstone and Cornewall Lewis are the scholar politicians. Intermixed with all these are men of education, if not of eminence, who contribute a share to the common stock of society. But I have not yet been to a single entertainment where there was any conversation that I should care to remember. This is not much of a record as compared with the early part of the present or the close of the last century, with the days of Queen Anne, or of Elizabeth. The general aspect of society is profound gravity. People look serious at a ball, at a dinner, on a ride on horseback or in a carriage, in Parliament or at Court, in the theatres or at the galleries. The great object in life is social position. To this end domestic establishments are sustained to rival each other. The horses must be fine, the carriage as large and cumbrous as possible, the servants as showy in livery as anybody's, the dinners must be just so, the china of Sèvres and the plate of silver, the wines of the same quality and growth, not because each person takes pleasure in the display, but because everybody else does the same thing. And so it is through all the economy of social life. The difference is only in the amount of wealth applicable to each particular instance. Yet with all this there is a studied avoidance of all appearance of ostentation. It is not the fashion to parade titles, scarcely even to use them. I do not think I have heard even the most ordinary forms of address to the nobility resorted to more than a dozen times or so. At one dinner I was surprised to hear a lady spoken to several times as "Duchess" rather than "your Grace." But etiquette is rigid. A white cravat at dinner is indispensable, as well as patent leather shoes, and each person has his distinct place according to the rules which are laid down in the books, in which he must fulfil all his duties to every other person in every, the most exact particular.

Some people say this is true of the London season only. When these same people go to their estates in the country the case is altered. There they are easy and sociable. It may be so, but I doubt it. The Englishman is formal by nature, and he is made so by education. The only question with him is upon the greater or the less. His kindness is all according to rule. If he invites you to his house, he does not think it any part of his duty to put you at your ease there. You must work your own way to acquaintance. He will not help you unless you ask him to do so, and if you do, you subject yourself to a chance of being repelled, unless your situation is such as to make your acquaintance deemed desirable. This is the reason why strangers make so little headway in incorporating themselves into society, and why they seek other countries to dwell in. I know of many Americans in London, but I see scarcely any in the places I am invited to, and these owe their admission to some exceptional recommendation rather than civility or good will. . . .

CHARLES FRANCIS ADAMS, JR., TO HIS FATHER

Boston, July 23, 1861

. . . .

I DON'T see any good in my saying anything of the disgraceful and disastrous battle of yesterday. The impression here is very general that Scott's policy was interfered with by the President in obedience to what he calls the popular will and at the instigation of Sumner, Greeley and others, and the advance was ordered by Scott only after a written protest. The result was a tremendous and unaccountable panic, such as raw troops are necessarily liable to on a field of battle in a strange country, and it all closed in the loss of guns, colors, equipage, and even honor. Almost the first idea that occurred to me was the disastrous effect of this affair on you in your position. I do not see how foreign nations can refuse to acknowledge the Confederacy now, for they are a government *de facto* and this result looks very much as though they could maintain themselves as such. In any case I no longer see my way clear. Scott's campaign is wholly destroyed and he must now go to work and reconstruct it. While our army is demoralised, theirs is in the same degree consolidated. Their ultimate independence is I think assured, but this defeat tends more and more to throw the war into the hands of the radicals, and if it lasts a year, it will be a war of abolition. Everything is set back for at least six months and just now, though not at all discouraged or disheartened, we feel here much as if we had been knocked over the head and had not yet recovered the use of our senses. . . .

HENRY ADAMS TO CHARLES FRANCIS ADAMS, JR.

London, July 26, 1861

. . . .

You say that you wanted to go off with Gordon's regiment. I tell you I would give my cocked hat and knee-breeches to be with them at this moment. I don't understand being sorry for them. I have no doubt that barring a few lives and legs and arms lost, they'll all like it and be the better for it. And as for the lives and legs, if they estimate theirs as low as I do mine, the loss won't amount to much. Pain is the only thing I should fear, but after all, one's health is just as likely to be benefitted as to be hurt by a campaign, bullets and all, so that this does n't count. My own task however lies elsewhere and I should be after all hardly the material for a soldier; so that I do my own work and resign the hope of becoming a hero.

My good old Nick Anderson is a Lieut. Colonel, I see. How I'd like to see him. I suppose Rooney Lee has some command also, so it's as likely as not that he and Nick may come in contact. There never was any friendship between them. Indeed they always hated each other, so that the collision would not be so painful to either of them as it might be. There are so many of our friends in the army now and under fire, that I watch with curiosity the lists of casualties. It won't be long before something happens, I suppose. . . .

HENRY ADAMS TO CHARLES FRANCIS ADAMS, JR.

London, August 5, 1861

WE received yesterday the news of our defeat at Bull's Run, and today your letter and John's with some papers have arrived. Though I do not see that this check necessarily involves all the serious consequences that you draw from it, I am still sufficiently impressed by it to decide me to take a step that I have for some time thought of. If you and John are detained from taking part in the war, the same rule does not apply to me. I am free to act as I please, and from the taste I have had of London life, I see no reason for my sacrificing four years to it. . . .

I wish you, then, on the receipt of this to go to some one in authority and get a commission for me, if you can; no matter what, second, third Lieutenant or Ensign, if you can do no better. They ought to be willing to let me have as much as that. If you can induce the Governor to promise this, see if you can find some fellow I know for a Captain. They say Horace Sargent is going home immediately to raise a regiment. I would serve under him and perhaps other Boston fellows

LIEUTENANT-COLONEL HORACE BINNEY SARGENT

would be mustered under him so as to make it pleasant. If you decide ultimately to go in as Captain, I could serve under you. At any rate I wish to have a commission, and if you succeed in arranging it, let me know at once, by telegraph, if you can. I can be on the way home in three weeks from this time, almost. A day's notice is ample for me here, and as I know nothing of war or drill and don't care to learn a drill here that I might have to unlearn, it will be necessary for me to begin at once. I don't know that I should n't start tomorrow and march in on you with this letter, if it were n't that I don't like to be precipitate, and that I want to watch things here for a while. I presume there will be restlessness here, though I still believe that England will prove herself more our friend than we suppose. . . .

I wish you to understand that I am in earnest and that if you can get me the place and don't, I shall try to get it by other means. As for reasons for it, your own arguments apply with double force to me. Until now I have thought it my duty to do what I have done. But as the reasons why I should stay decrease, the reasons for going into the army increase, and this last battle turns the scale. It makes no difference whether you go or not. I am the youngest and the most independent of all others, and I claim the right to go as younger son, if on no other grounds.

You need not apprehend difficulty on this side. . . . If [your reply] is favorable I shall leave here in the first steamer, and the first positive knowledge they will have of it here, will be simultaneous with my departure. Papa will not interfere. He never does, in cases where his sons choose to act on their own responsibility, whatever he may think. Mamma has been preaching the doctrine too long to complain if it hits her at last.

We are going on as usual here except that we have got into our new house which is a great improvement. I have two large rooms on the third story which I have been making comfortable. Braggiotti is here; dines with us tomorrow.

P.S. August 26. After studying over the accounts of the battle and reading Russell's letter to the Times, I hardly know whether to laugh or cry. Of all the ridiculous battles that ever were fought, this seems to me the most so. To a foreigner or to any one not interested in it, the account must be laughable in the extreme. But the disgrace is frightful. The exposé of the condition of our army is not calculated to do us anything but the most unmixed harm here, though it may have the good effect at home of causing these evils to be corrected. If this happens again, farewell to our country for many a day. Bull's Run will be a by-word of ridicule for all time. Our honor will be utterly gone. But yesterday we might have stood against the world. Now none so base to do us reverence. Let us stop our bragging now and hence-forward. Throw Bull's Run in the teeth of any man who dares to talk large. In spite of my mortification, I could not help howling with laughter over a part of Russell's letter. Such a battle of heels. Such a bloodless, ridiculous race for disgrace, history does not record. Unpursued, untouched, without once having even crossed bayonets with the enemy, we have run and saved our precious carcasses from a danger that did not exist. Our flag, what has become of it? Who will respect it? What can we ever say for it after this?

My determination to come home is only increased by this disgrace. I cannot stay here now to stand the taunts of every one without being able to say a word in defence. Unless I hear from you at once, I shall write myself to Governor Andrew and to Mr. Dana and to every one else I can think of, and raise Heaven and earth to get a commission. If we must be beaten, and it looks now as though that must ultimately be the case, I want to do all I can not to be included among those who ran away. Our accounts say nothing of the Massachusetts regiments. So far as we have learned, the Pennsylvania and foreign regiments are the only ones known to have disgraced themselves, and the Rhode Island ones stood well. Hurry up and send me my commission quick.

CHARLES FRANCIS ADAMS TO HIS SON

London, August 16, 1861

. . . .

WE have now gone through three stages of this great political disease. The first was the cold fit, when it seemed as if nothing would start the country. The second was the hot one, when it seemed almost in the highest continual delirium. The third is the process of waking to the awful reality before it. I do not venture to predict what the next will be. I hope anything but distraction. Thus far the favorable feature has been union. Maintaining that, we can bear a great deal. But unless we can have a principle to contend for, the money question will infallibly shake us to pieces. I am for this reason anxious to grapple with the slave question at once. I wish to settle it in the District of Columbia, to dispose of it prospectively in Maryland, and wherever else we have a hold in the slave states. Money spent in smoothing that road is far better used than in war. It will spread our real strength which mere military supremacy will not. . . .

CHARLES FRANCIS ADAMS, JR., TO HENRY ADAMS

Boston, August 23, 1861

I DID N'T get your letter of the 5th until the steamer of the 21st was gone, so I telegraphed to Mr. Motley at Halifax, as I did n't want to have you come blundering home under the impression that I had been ordered off, and now I will at once answer your letter. If you insist upon coming home and getting a commission, of course you are of age and no one can gainsay you. I don't favor the idea myself for reasons which I will give you presently; but still if you insist I shall be glad to aid you and will do so. In this war some things are getting clear every day and one is that volunteers won't do, and another that haste makes waste. If you insist on going, Ritchie advises that you should get a commission in the regular army and go into that. It will be cut down at the end of the war and meanwhile you'll escape the curse, nuisance and danger of volunteers. If your mind is made up I will apply for you and you can doubtless get your commission and be ready for a winter campaign. Meanwhile you'll gain nothing but blunders by rushing ahead so like the devil.

So much for that; and now allow me to state some considerations which should prevent your coming home at all. I have three in my mind, and first one relates to myself. I am trying, as well as I may, to do what strikes me as my first duty at home. It is very hard for me to stay here, and no one gives me credit for doing it for any cause save fear; but the truth is the Governor is abroad in the public service, and property was never so difficult of management as it now is. . . . Under these circumstances I concluded very reluctantly I ought to stay at home if I could, and I think you'll agree I was right.

Have n't I difficulties enough without your piling up new ones? If you insist on this step, I have no election but, at any sacrifice, must go too. The reason is obvious, for while I am single and robust and John remains at home, the world cannot go into these domestic questions, and your coming home in a hurry to get a commission, while I remained in Boston, would be regarded as a most decided implication on my courage. You can't but see this, and as for your taking a commission under me, it's bad enough to have a hundred men you don't care for to look after; but when it comes to looking after a brother and having your attention taken up by what may be occurring to him, it would be intolerable. Besides I expect drafting will have to begin before long and then I have made up my mind to go, and if I go, I think the family in supplying two out of four to the public service does enough, and you ought to stay at home.

In the next place I think decidedly you ought to stay abroad and remain with your father and mother. No one knows what may happen in these days — a foreign war is possible, even an English war — and difficulties you do not now see may any day spring up, and for one I think most decidedly that while times are so troubled our father and mother have got to an age when they ought not to be deserted abroad by all of their children.

Finally, the most weighty consideration to my mind I reserve for the last. Of course you make this a question of usefulness and duty. You are not particularly well fitted for the army and your object is to be of service to your country. As for distinction and all that sort of thing, when the whole country is rushing into the army it is hardly the place to look for a chance. Where can you be most useful in this emergency? The answer is to my mind too clear to admit of discussion. The rush for commissions is tremendous and you can only get one by shoving somebody equally capable with yourself aside, and you can really do no service, if you get one, which would not be equally well done if you were away. Where you now are you are useful to the whole country and, like a coward, you want to run home because our reverses make the post abroad into which fortune has thrown you very uncomfortable. You fight our battle in England and let us alone to fight it here. There are men enough here, but there your place, if you leave it, must remain empty.

You'll say, you can't do anything and have no opening. What could a second lieutenant in an infantry regiment do that would be so immense? Is that a prodigious opening? Go to work at once in England with all your energy and force your way into magazines and periodicals there and in America, so that you can make yourself heard. For there is going to be difficulty about this blockade and much bad feeling, though, God grant, no blows. For heaven's sake try to influence that and don't throw yourself away by rushing into this mob of bruisers. Try to raise people up a little. Look into the cotton supply question and try to persuade the English that our blockade is their interest. If they raise it and transfer it to our coasts, they have the power to do so, but they ally themselves with slavery — give it the victory, give the lie to their own protestations and secure to the South for years with the advantage of their system of labor and production that monopoly of cotton under which England groans. If the blockade lasts and forces supply, England will purchase, at the price of one year's suffering, freedom and plenty for ever. Touch England through her pocket and help your country that way.

Then write to the Atlantic of the way fighting America appears in English eyes, of her boasting and bragging, her running and terror; tell us of the pain she causes her children abroad and how foolish her angry threats sound, and help your country that way. Here is your field, right before your nose, in which you could be of real service, and you want to rush away to do what neither education nor nature fitted you for —

what others could do as well or better, and get your head knocked off without doing the least good. If you have any energy use it where you are and where it can be of value. If you have n't any keep out of the army. Talk of backing the Governor up in the Times in these days! We've got beyond all that, I hope. For God's sake take a broader view and make yourself heard where a voice is wanted. Don't talk of your connection with the legation to me; cut yourself off if necessary from it and live in London as the avowed Times correspondent and force your way into notice of the London press that way. Wake up and look about you and make yourself useful and don't jog on in this cart horse way, or brag over your harness and wish yourself a blood-horse, with McClellan, instead of a jackass who can't break his traces. There, I have blown my blast and have done, and you can do as you see fit. Free from the legation you could earn a living by your pen in London and be independent, busy, happy and eminently useful. If you come home you won't be of the slightest use to any one, and you will have deserted your post. Now if you want a commission let me know and I'll do my best for you; but have nothing to say to Horace Sargent. He is n't the man and I know him.

We've had a bad panic, but it seems to be over now and I think they were wise in refusing the battle.

CHARLES FRANCIS ADAMS, JR., TO HENRY ADAMS

Quincy, Sunday, August 25, 1861

. . . .

IN my letter I begged you to go to work and try to make the two countries understand each other, for to my eye our foreign relations look very formidable. Why, when England and France are collecting fleets in our southern waters, do we all of a sudden hear rumors of a joint Mexican protectorate? It would be a blessing to mankind, but how will it complicate our relations? This cotton question is beginning to pinch and soon, if ever, if you have any desire to be useful to your country, backed by any energy, you can be useful where you are.

In my letter I asked you to touch England through her pocket. For some time past I have been turning over in my mind an elaborate article on this cotton supply question, but necessarily to be of any good to any one it must be directed more to English eyes than to ours. I touched on it in my last letter, and now I should like to hand it over to you, to see if you can do anything with it. I would write it for the Edinburgh or some really influential review or magazine, but to have effect it should appear in November, when the cotton-shoe will begin to pinch dreadfully, and I would force it into print by laying the plan of it before Mr. Motley or the Governor, or any other person likely to have influence on editors. That done throw your soul into your work and write as if you meant what you said. You always affect in writing too much calmness and quaint philosophy. That will come to you in time, but you do it now at the price of that fresh enthusiasm which is the charm of young writers. If you write now, write as if you were pleading a cause and too much interested to be affected. Throw your soul into your work and say what you feel. If you don't check it, your mannerism will ruin your style in less than five years.

However now for the subject. The books you ought to review, or rather hang your subject on, are Mann's Manual of Cotton, a book of about one hundred pages; the third annual report of the Manchester Cotton Supply Association and the numbers for May and June of the Cotton Supply Reporter of Manchester, and any new book dealing of the troubles in this country. If you accept the subject I have many curious facts collected, which I will send you at once. Start at once with the paradox that, instead of desiring to break this blockade, England should pray it might last for two years and if necessary assist in enforcing it, as if enforced its inevitable result must be, after one or at most two years of high prices, to forever break down the price of cotton to a reasonable profit over the cost of its cheapest possible production. This opens the whole question of supply. Two things are necessary to the production of cotton — an abundance of labor and a cotton soil. Look into the question of soil first. A semi-tropical heat, with a distribution of rain, are the only essentials. India has not the last and will not do; but Central and South America, all Africa (which is not desert), Australia and the Fiji Islands are better than our cotton states and need only organized labor. This with all the necessary material of ships, channels of trade, custom and experience, our planters have to such a degree that while they would furnish a fair supply of cotton on moderate terms, they could kill competition. Now is England's chance to free herself from what has been her terror for years. In India, in Egypt, in Abyssinia and in South Africa, there is an unlimited amount of cotton land of the finest quality and labor is abundant, costing almost nothing, but unorganized. Two years' competition will organize it and once organized it can sell the South. In Australia, the South Sea islands and Central America, there is no labor and here the cooley question rises. Properly regulated the trade would be a blessing, for the Chinese amalgamates and California is in point as well as Dana's reflections on Cuba. The books I have mentioned will give you all the information necessary on these points. This would bring cotton down to the cost, with a profit, of its production in cheap labor countries, say three pence a pound. But it would also lead to immense indirect advantages. As a missionary scheme Africa would be opened up and Livingstone's discoveries made of use; slavery in America would be killed and the slave-trade closed for ever, as the African would be more useful at home than abroad. You will find in the first few pages of a new book called Social Statics more curious facts and reflections on England's efforts at the suppression of the slave-trade, and this leads to the amount yearly expended in its suppression in this way, and which the consequent withdrawal of the fleet would save that government, and the amount England could thus afford to pay to promote the enterprise. Finally it would open the untold tropical fertility of Africa to the commerce of the world and these advantages cannot be estimated. Thus cotton would be produced on both sides of the equator all the year round in unlimited quantities, and England would have by two years' suffering cut the meshes which she could never have broken.

On the other hand England breaks the blockade, or the South is victorious, England may then as well hug her chains, for she must wear them. The Southern confederacy will be aggressive and more slaves and more cotton will be the cry. In spite of England the slave-trade will flourish and their system will spread over Mexico and Central America. Then with the advantages of their organization, slave labor will win the day and England may look for competition in vain. The cotton monopoly will stifle her in the end. They will pretend in Parliament that the recognition of the Confederate States will not extend the area of slavery and all that humbug. Expose this, for it will be a victory of slavery. Recognition will mean war and the prostration at the feet of slavery of free society in America. England can do this if she chooses, but let her not deceive herself and let the results of her action be patent.

Finally the importance of this struggle cannot be overestimated. On the inviolability of the blockade and the consequent cotton pressure throughout the world hangs the destruction of American slavery, the eternal suppression of the slave-trade, the emancipation of England from a thraldom under which her great industrial interest has groaned for fifty years, and finally the civilization and awakening from Barbarism of the great continent of Africa. Even America, deprived of her monopoly, would reap advantage from the result, and this I tried to show in my article in the Atlantic of last April. Are not these results worth the agony of two years of half labor in Lancashire? Are they not worth fighting for? Can England hesitate as to which side her interest favors — as to what course she will adopt?

Here is a general sketch of my idea. I think it would be of service in England and if written as a man should write who is writing for his country at such a time as this, it would surely command attention. Any assistance I can give you I gladly will; but I earnestly beg you, even if this subject does not please you, to make yourself useful in your present position in some way of this kind. You can't tell how much effect here a sympathetic word from England has now, and you can be of the greatest use if you only will. . . .

CHARLES FRANCIS ADAMS, JR., TO HIS FATHER

Boston, August 27, 1861

. . . .

YOUR tone is too dull in your letters and I feel for you sincerely in your Bull-run panic in England. Here things certainly look much better and people feel much better. The money market is easy and our exportation of breadstuffs seems likely to continue.

Finally, this steamer will advise you that at least the government is thoroughly in earnest and that spies and traitors can no longer enjoy immunity. Nor is this all. Last week we were in a terrible panic and Monday was the blackest day I ever saw; but now the Government is working for its life. McClellan has the complete confidence of the people, government securities are rising, money is plenty, and finally the indications are strong that the confederates are being ground to atoms by the very weight of their defensive preparations. Bull-run was a blessing to us, for it startled the people from the conceit, arrogance and pride which must have proved their ruin. There is a universal feeling of confidence abroad, and England may refuse our loan if she chooses to; but I don't think she will for seven and three-tenths per cent is too much of the flesh-pots not to be longed for, and our securities must drift to England. . . .

CHARLES FRANCIS ADAMS, JR., TO HIS FATHER

Boston, September 3, 1861

· · · · · · · · · ·

I PERSUADED Hale to insert a leading article about Russell in the Advertiser, which I send to Henry. The folly of our press in assaulting so savagely an agency so formidable as Russell has troubled me, and I'm glad to see that McClellan is wiser and spares a few civil words where they can be so useful. In fact I think McClellan is showing a tact and power of managing men which reminds me of Seward. For already, even at this distance, I see that he has moulded Russell, Wilson and

Sumner like wax in his fingers. This is very important and I expect before this reaches you McClellan's finger will have been seen and wondered at in the columns of the Times. . . .

CHARLES FRANCIS ADAMS TO HIS SON

London, September 7, 1861

. . . .

THE feeling here which at one time was leaning our way has been very much changed by the disaster at Bull's run, and by the steady operation of the press against us. Great Britain always looks to her own interest as a paramount law of her action in foreign affairs. She might deal quite summarily with us, were it not for the European complications which are growing more and more embarrassing. There are clouds in the north and in the south, in the east and in the west, which keep England and France leaning against each other in order to stand up at all. The single event of the death of Napoleon, perhaps even that of Lord Palmerston, would set everything afloat, and make the direction of things in Europe almost impossible to foresee. Hence we may hope that these two powers will reflect well before they inaugurate a policy in regard to us which would in the end react most fatally against themselves. . . .

HENRY ADAMS TO CHARLES FRANCIS ADAMS, JR.

London, September 7, 1861

YOURS in answer to mine written after the Bull's Run arrived last night and I answer it at once. Whatever weight your arguments might have had on me in ordinary times, just now they are entirely superseded by the new turn things have taken since that letter was written. I could not go home now if I would, nor would if I could. Work has increased to such an extent since our return from our excursion that I am absolutely necessary here. Things have taken a turn which makes it every day more probable that we must sooner or later come into collision with England, and of course with that prospect I can't leave the Chief and the family in the lurch. So you need not at present feel any alarm about my blundering home, as you call it, for I promise you fair warning so that you may be down at the wharf to receive me with the towns-people.

Warning you to preserve it a profound secret, I will disclose to you some of the horrors of the prison-house. Remember, your finger ever on your lip.

You may or may not be informed that among the first instructions to the Chief from the Department was one directing him to offer to the British Government the adhesion of the United States to the four articles of the Treaty of Paris. They related as you know to privateering, neutral goods, neutral flags and blockades. The Chief obeyed instructions and ever since we have been here this matter has dragged its slow length along through strange delays, misunderstandings, and discussions that in so simple a matter were very curious and inexplicable. At last the Chief acting under repeated instructions, broke through all objections and brought it to such a point that he and Mr. Dayton were agreed to sign the Convention on the same day at

Paris and London, with Earl Russell and with Mr. Thouvenel. The day alone remained to be fixed.

Such was the condition of the negotiation when we went off on our excursion. Before we had returned a note was received from the Foreign Office suggesting a convenient day for signing, but transmitting also the draft of a declaration outside the treaty itself, which Earl Russell proposed to read before signing. It ran as follows:

"In affixing his signature to the Convention of this day between H. M. the Queen of Great Britain and Ireland and the U.S. of A. the Earl Russell declares by order of H. M. that H. M. does not intend thereby to undertake any engagement which shall have any bearing direct or indirect on the internal differences now prevailing in the United States."

On receiving this Note the Chief sat down and wrote an elaborate reply. It was in his best style and was certainly an admirable paper. After tearing the whole thing up and placing, as it seems to me, the British Government in a very awkward and untenable position, he ended by breaking off the negotiation until further instructions from home should command him to resume it. This Note Earl Russell has never replied to. A few days after he sent an answer which sounded to me rather like an apology than anything else, but in this Note he said that he should defer the answer to another time.

So that passed away, but only to give place to a greater excitement. Last Monday a special messenger arrived from Seward bringing the package taken on

Mure, directed to Lord Russell. But besides this, which was legitimate, or might be, as coming from the British Consul at Charleston, a great quantity of letters were found on Mure, and among others one that very gravely compromised the British Government. It seems that the British and French Consuls at Charleston have acted *in concert* in making a treaty with Jeff Davis, and that treaty nothing less than this very Convention of Paris.

Here was a pretty to-do. Whatever we might suspect, there was no direct proof against England or France nor was it our interest to make a quarrel. So the Chief sits down and writes a long despatch to Lord Russell complimenting very highly the perfect confidence to which the British Government were entitled, and returning to them the bag of despatches. In another short Note he quoted the letter I have mentioned, and demanded the Consul's recall.

To these Notes no answer has yet been returned. No doubt the graveness of the matter will make a Cabinet meeting necessary, and just now every one is out of town. Lord John however was in Paris on Sunday. Was it to consult with the French Government? You see what a dreadfully tight place they're in and how inevitably the inference of bad faith of a very gross nature is against them.

These are the signs of the times and will no doubt alarm you enough. I am myself more uneasy than I like to acknowledge in my public letters, but hope we shall worry through yet. They won't like the idea of our privateers here when it gets near them.

As for your recommendation to set up here as letter-writer to the Times, you know not what you say. In the first place, all that I know comes from my position and without it I were nothing. In the second place, there are few beings lower in the social scale in England than writers to newspapers. I should destroy myself beyond a hope of redemption.

No, I am very well as I am. I shall gradually make way and worry along. London does not satisfy all my longings, but *enfin* it is an exciting, hard-working life here, and the Chief and I are as merry as grigs, writing in this delightful old study all day long, opposite to each other. When I say delightful I stretch a point, but it is not bad. . . .

HENRY ADAMS TO CHARLES FRANCIS ADAMS, JR.

London, September 14, 1861

YOUR last letter containing principally suggestions on the cotton matter, reached me this week. Also a bundle of newspapers. At present I am busy in another direction, so that I can't yet take up the subject you recommend, but when my immediate bubbles have burst, or have expanded brilliantly, I mean to see what I can do here. Yet I confess I do not promise myself much from the effort. The main principles which you aim at demonstrating, that the American monopoly of cotton is in fact a curse both to America and to Great Britain, and its destruction might be made the cause of infinite blessings to the whole range of countries under the torrid zone, this principle is and has always been an axiom here. It needs no proof, for the cotton-merchants themselves are the most earnest in asserting it. The real difficulty with regard to cotton does not lie there. It is never the hope of a future good, however great, that actuates people, when they have immediate evils such as this want of cotton will produce right before their eyes. Nor should I answer any real question by proving that in two years the world will be infinitely benefitted by our war, when what they alone ask is whether meanwhile England will not be ruined. My own belief is that she will be ruined. This next winter will, I fear, be a dreadful one in this country. in any case, nor will it be bettered if they make war on us. It is not as if the cotton manufacture alone suffered, but the tariff and the war have between them cut off the whole American trade, export and import, and the consequence has been a very bad season, with a prospect of frightful pressure in the winter. Whole counties will have to be supported by subscription.

This is my idea of the real cotton problem in this country. I have no doubt that the suffering interests will make a violent push to solve it by urging the Government to attack our blockade. But that is merely the last struggle of a drowning man. The Government will not do it, I think, and most Englishmen speak of the idea as preposterous. If they did, it would only complicate matters still more and I doubt whether even then they got their cotton. The winter over, the new era will dawn on us; that cursed monopoly will be broken and with it the whole power of the South; the slave-trade will then be ended and slavery with it, for the negro will be of no use; and we may expect sunnier days and renewed prosperity. This is the only view that I could advocate, and this, a generally acknowledged truth, is at best but small comfort to a starving people.

Meanwhile we are getting on in these parts. Lord Russell has just answered the Chief's Note, by *refusing* to dismiss Bunch; acknowledging that he acted under instructions; justifying the step as one which implied nothing and in which even pirates might be admitted to join (i.e. the neutral flag matter); accepting the responsibility for its acts and the consequences; but at the same time declaring that the Ministry has no present intention of recognizing the Southerners, or of leaving their old position.

Of course Seward will revoke Bunch's exequatur, but that need make no trouble. But it is by no means so clear what also may result from this. By a pure accident it was discovered that the British Government were *secretly* entering into connections with the insurgents, and they are now compelled to acknowledge that they have really been acting *behind our backs*. This is no pleasant acknowledgment to make, for evidently secrecy was their object, and the implication is direct against their good faith. They feel that they have been *found out*, and this for an Englishman is anything but pleasant. The affair will hardly end here.

I have been lately hunting up the newspapers. The other day I called on the editors of the Spectator and had a long talk with them. I mean to call on or write to Hughes, the Tom Brown man, who has vigorously taken our side. The Star too we are in with. Miss Martineau writes for the News and she is an invalid, not to be seen. I may very likely myself turn up some of these days in the lists. . . .

CHARLES FRANCIS ADAMS, JR., TO HENRY ADAMS

Boston, Tuesday, September 17, 1861

As I hear nothing more of your coming home I hope you have forgotten that folly. The few of your friends in the army here, like Billy Milton and Howard Dwight, opened their eyes wide with astonishment at the suggestion. Just now I certainly hope that you have n't left, as I send you by this mail a couple of copies of yesterday's and today's Courier, in which you will find two leaders headed "English Views," written by me and which, if you have any opening yet in the English press you may turn to advantage as extracts from the American. The letter of the Times correspondent of 30th August printed in last Saturday's Times (N.Y.) seemed to intimate that the wind now lay in this quarter and American views to the point might, I thought, be of use. These articles were written, however, before I saw that letter, or the Times (London) editorials in the same direction. I offered these articles to Charles Hale who declined to publish them editorially, and so I sent them to the Courier; but Hale remembered my line of thought and reproduced it in his leader of last Monday, which I also send you. So, for once, the Courier and the Advertiser were brought close together on the same day.

Here we feel immeasurably better and not only are

things outwardly more encouraging, but I am informed from private correspondents of military men in Washington that the appearance is not deceptive, an immense improvement has taken place and military men are most sanguine of the future.

I wait anxiously to hear from you. By the way, in case you think favorably of my suggestion of an English article on the American press, did you notice a few days ago an article in the N.Y. Times about the Herald, in which Bennett was called "the old liar," "a skunk," a "stink-pot," etc., etc. How would the two read if the editorial of the celebrated Potts in the Eatanswill Gazette about the "buff-ball in a buff neighborhood" and that were put side by side? Which would be the caricature? . . .

CHARLES FRANCIS ADAMS TO HIS SON

London, September 20, 1861

. . . .

I DEEPLY sympathise with you in your trials about the part you ought to play in the war. Much as I value your assistance during my absence on this side, I should be very reluctant to continue it at the cost of your own convictions of your duty. If you feel that the crisis demands it, I pray that you set aside every other consideration at once. . . . Whichever way you determine, you will know that I appreciate your motives, and that you will have under every circumstance my sympathy and my prayers.

The late modicum of good news has helped us here a good deal. People were beginning to believe that the slaveholding generals were demigods, on Aristotle's or Longinus's principle (I forget which), that mystery is a source of the sublime. The London Times at last frankly admits that if split up we shall no longer be a terror to Europe so that there is no need of going any farther for a reason to explain its crooked policy. Mr. Russell's last letter went far to justify your inference. He has seen a little light and is willing to admit that we are not so badly off after all. . . .

HENRY ADAMS TO CHARLES FRANCIS ADAMS, JR.

London, September 28, 1861

TIME goes precious fast and yet seems to leave very little behind it. I have been very busy for the last three weeks but now am at leisure again though I have some ideas of beginning a new tack. Papa got back late last night from a visit to Lord Russell's in Scotland. I must say I think Lord Russell was rather hard in making him take all the journey, but as it could n't well be helped I am glad it has happened, and especially so as it will have an excellent effect on the relations of the two countries. When I last wrote things looked threatening if I recollect right. Since then they have wonderfully cleared away. Lately, except for the Bunch affair and the negotiation business, England has behaved very well. The Southerners were refused recognition and we are no longer uneasy about the blockade. Lord Russell has explained the Mexican business very satisfactorily and it appears that England is trying to check Spain, not to help her. Lord Russell was very open and confidential towards the Chief and showed him confidential despatches proving the truth of the matter with regard to Spain, besides treating him in every way extremely kindly and confidentially. You know that these are state secrets which no one knows out of the immediate circle here, so you must be very careful not to let it out, even to write back here that you know about it, as it might shake confidence in me. . . .

I have no news for you beyond what I've told. We are all right here, strong and confident. If you win us a victory on your side, the thing's finished. Rosecrans seems to be a good deal of a man, if I understand his double victory over Floyd and Lee. The Lee business has not wholly reached us yet, but seems to be a first-rate thing, as he was one of their great guns.

I occasionally worry a newspaper writer, but advance slowly. Called on Tom Brown Hughes the other day but he was out of town and won't be back for some time. No one is in London, but in about a month I suppose the country visiting will begin and then one may make a few more acquaintances. . . .

We are settling down into the depths of a London autumn. The fogs are beginning and the streets look as no streets in the world do look out of England. Berlin was never so gloomy as London. Every now and then, when things go wrong, I feel a good deal as though I would like to cut and run, but on the whole my position is much better than it was three months ago. I saw a little article of yours (I suppose) in the Transcript a short time ago, and I hope that you will see in some of the London newspapers if not my writing, at least my hand. They need it, confound 'em.

I enclose an order on the Times. I did n't know precisely how to word it for I don't know how many of my letters he has published. Fourteen or parts of fourteen I know of, but there may be more. I wish you could manage to get the money from Raymond without letting the subordinates into the matter. I doubt if I can carry it on much longer without being known.

HENRY ADAMS TO CHARLES FRANCIS ADAMS, JR.

London, October 5, 1861

YOUR letter and your articles in the Courier arrived last Monday. I sent one set of them down to Lucas, the editor of the London Star, and received a complimentary note in return which I will enclose to you. The other set I sent down to the editor of the Spectator, and from him I have not heard. There was one article to the Star which was partly drawn from your's, without quoting it, but there has been no reprint. The Spectator never reprints, but if it notices you, I will send you the notice. Your Manchester paper I have made unavailing efforts to find, but London seems to despise anything provincial, and I can find the paper nowhere. London papers go to Manchester but Manchester ditto don't seem to return the compliment.

This week I have no news for you. Everything seems to be getting along well and the Government here behaves itself very fairly. I don't know whether my last letters will appear or not, but if they do you can form some judgment as to my inventive powers. The truth is that I've lately told so much in that way which was not generally known, that my position began to be too hot and I thought I'd try a little wrong scent. The facts are all invented therefore, but the idea is carried out as faithfully as I could, of quoting the state of English opinion.

We have been overrun by visitors this week. My friend Richardson goes in the Arabia to Boston, if he can, but I'm not sure that he won't have to make Halifax his terminus. He was in a horrible position. His family and property are in New Orleans and he has a brother in the Virginian army. He is himself a good Union man, I believe; at all events he talks so; but he does not want to do anything which will separate him from his family or make them his enemies. So he could not make up his mind to take the oath, and determined rather to run his risk without a passport. I believe he means to pass the winter in Boston. He told me all about his troubles and I strongly advised him not to think of ever living in New Orleans again; at least as an architect.

Sohier and Charley Thorndike have been here this week. Both leave for Paris this morning. Sohier was quite amusing, and dined with us twice. But the trouble about London is that no one ever stays here and I can't keep a companion. As for Englishmen I don't expect to know any of my own age for at least six months more, as this club business has got to be settled and the season to come round again first. We see no English people now, or very few, and the fogs are thick almost every morning. Hooroar! Can you find out (*not* through Sumner, who seems to have distorted even your ideas of Washington affairs) what ground Seward takes on the slave question?

I need n't say that the articles are devilish good and made me blue for a day, thinking of my own weak endeavors in the same way.

CHARLES FRANCIS ADAMS, JR., TO HENRY ADAMS

Quincy, Sunday, October 6, 1861

I RECEIVED your letter of the 7th some ten days ago and not a word from London since; so that as I have seen no signs of trouble in the press, I presume the little flurry you there mention has passed away. In fact I cannot say I share your apprehensions, though I must confess I think the government's cards, *so far as the public sees them,* are played badly enough both here and in England. While the agents of the Confederates are abroad working the whole time at public opinion and at the foreign mind, influencing papers and thinkers and undermining us the whole time, our press at home does but furnish them the materials they need and our agents abroad apparently confine their efforts to cabinets and officials and leave public opinion and the press to take care of themselves. This may not be so in fact, but if it is not, all that can be said is that the Southern emissaries are far more efficient than ours. We have money and the command of the sea, so that Europe can know nothing except through us, and yet, from the beginning, so much more active and efficient has the South been, that we have done nothing but lose ground. Why is this? I may be all wrong, but to me our policy in England seems as plain as noon-day, but I see no signs of its operation on the press, though I hope it is working secretly. England is made up of large interests. Some of those are in our favor and some opposed to us; but why are they not played off against each other? This war promises immense results to India, and has already carried up the Indian bonds. That interest is immensely powerful in England and can only reap benefit from the war; but I have not noticed that its organs were particularly friendly to us. The shipping interest derives great benefit from the war, but their organs are opposed to us. Why is this? What are our agents doing? Why is not India played off against Manchester and London against Liverpool? Why do the Southern agents have it all their own way? Why are not a few American papers sufficiently under the control of government to enable some expression of good sense to go abroad? Why is everything so utterly left to take care of itself? Remember I only ask these as questions, for I do not know but what a profound plan and ceaseless activity under-runs it all; but if it does, the State department certainly keeps its own councils much better than the war. So much for these things.

I wait curiously for the next development from abroad and chuckled amazingly over the tight place in which the Governor had got Lord John. Meanwhile, if there is to be trouble, for Heaven's sake give me a few days' notice. . . .

Tuesday, 7th

I send the *corrected* copy of Sumner's speech herewith. Did you ever see anything like the classical exposure in the Advertiser? How can it be accounted for? What can Sumner mean by perpetrating historical frauds so sure of detection? The speech has been made the subject of most severe criticism and that too from men hitherto Sumner's friends. Dana tore it to shreds for my edification in a most substantial manner, and Sumner has done himself no credit. For myself I'm glad the speech was made, though I think very differently from most in these matters. The education is going on and the fallacies lie hid. I agree with it, however, neither in theory or results, and if we had a Juvenal, would not the celebrated author of a certain 4th of July peace oration, now become the leading advocate for a *savage* SERVILE war, catch particular jess. Sumner is a humbug! There's no doubt about it. He's been a useful man in his day, but he's as much out of place now as knights in armor would be at the head of our regiments.

The convention was managed and its results brought about by Dana, and it was to him a great personal triumph as he had all the old party associations to contend with. You never saw a man chuckle over anything as he did over his doings at Worcester. Sumner, I imagine, is offended with him and will evince it in the usual way. There is, of course, no political contest. The position of the country is now very curious and my strong conviction is that everything is ready and one good victory would start everything. Politics are so dead that a little success would lead to an era of good feeling in the North. Business is, in New England, all ready to rise under the tariff to a state of activity, unusual even in time of peace. Everything that is left

CHARLES SUMNER

is strong and the present feeling of depression is wholly unfounded. I am convinced that one victory would make an almost incredible change, but we shall not see it for a long time without a victory.

CHARLES FRANCIS ADAMS, JR., TO HENRY ADAMS

Boston, October 14, 1861

. . . .

MY impression is that we are on the eve of great movements and the naval expedition, if successful, will open the ball. We can see little in the papers, but it looks to me as if the correspondents were at fault. But in truth McClellan is coiling himself up for a spring on Manassas immediately after a coast success. If he succeeds, and in him alone have I any confidence, the loan will be at a premium in twenty-four hours and all over Europe in six weeks. For those who have confidence now is the time to buy and sell in the victory. . . .

Let me call your attention to the article on England and America in the Examiner I send the Governor by this bag. It is said to be written by Dr. Hedges and is one of the ablest papers I have read for a long time. . . .

By the way, I had almost forgotten what I most wanted to say. In his last letter the Governor hinted that it would be a good thing if I could get a connection as American correspondent with some London paper, as the correspondents from this side as a whole were beneath contempt. I will leave this to you. Of course I demand no pay and only desire to influence public opinion abroad. If any respectable London paper will print my letters, I will let them hear from me as often as there is anything of interest to let them hear about. I am not anxious about it at all, but at this crisis I am anxious to do everything in my power.

HENRY ADAMS TO CHARLES FRANCIS ADAMS, JR.

London, October 15, 1861

IN your last letters I am not a little sorry to see that you are falling into the way that to us at this distance seems to be only the mark of weak men, of complaining and fault-finding over the course of events. In mere newspaper correspondents who are not expected to have commonsense or judgment, this may be all natural, but you ought to know better, for you have the means for hitting the truth nearer. For my own part I tell you fairly that all the gossip and senseless stories that the generation can invent, shall not, if I can help it, shake for one single instant the firm confidence which I feel in those who are guiding our affairs. You are allowing your own better judgment and knowledge to be overruled by the combined talk of a swarm of people who have neither knowledge nor judgment at all; and what is to be the consequence, I would like to know, if you and men like you, who ought to lead and strengthen public opinion in the right path, now instead of exercising your rights and asserting your power for good, give way to a mere vulgar discouragement merely because the current runs for the moment in that direction. Call you that backing of your friends? A plague upon such backing. Every repetition that is given to these querulous ideas tends to demoralize us worse than a defeat would, and certainly here abroad is sure to counteract every attempt to restore confidence either in our nation or her institutions.

Even if I believed in the truth of the sort of talk you quote, I would suspend the moral habeas-corpus for a time and deny it. But I don't believe it; and more than that, in all the instances which you quote about which I know anything at all, I know it to be false. You, like a set of people with whom you now for the first time agree, seem to have fallen foul of the President and Cabinet and in fact every one in authority as the scapegoats for all the fault-finding of the day, simply because their positions prevent them from showing you the truth. Now so far as military and naval affairs go, I know nothing at all, but one fact I have noticed and this is that our worst misfortunes have come from popular interference with them. Croaking is just as likely to bring another defeat, as that ridiculous bravado which sent our army to Bull Run. But your troubles don't end with the army and navy; if they did, I might perhaps think that your informants really knew something about a matter on which you and I know nothing. You go on to find fault with the President and the Secretary of State, or at least to quote others who find fault, as though there might be something in it. Here I am willing to make a direct issue with your authorities, and you may choose between us which you will believe and whose information you think best entitled to credit. They say that the Secretary of State's education and train of mind are not adapted for these times; that his influence is no longer such as it once was; that you can no longer discern under the surface of events that firm grasp and broad conception that we once admired and bent to, in the founder of the republican party; and finally you quote an old calumny, thirty years ago as common as it is today; a year ago as virulent as his prominence could make it; a calumny which you knew then from the testimony of your own eyes and ears to be utterly and outrageously false; and you seem now to suppose that mere repetition is going to shake my own knowledge of facts; my own certainty of conviction; and that too because men who are really ignorant attempt to make you believe that you are so.

You say that Mr. Seward's hand is not evident in the course of events. I disagree entirely to any such idea. I think it is very evident and so much so that, feeling perfect confidence in him, I have come to the conclusion that our ideas are wrong and that his are right, at least on one question. I am an abolitionist and so, I think, are you, and so, I think, is Mr. Seward; but if he says the time has not yet come; that we must wait till the whole country has time to make the same advance that we have made within the last six months, till we can all move together with but one mind and one idea; then I say, let us wait. It will come. Let us have order and discipline and firm ranks among the soldiers of the Massachusetts school.

But apart from this, when you say that you do not see the hand of the Secretary of State in the course of events, I tell you plainly that you do not know that whereof you speak. I do assure you, and I do pretend to knowledge on this point, that his direction of the foreign affairs of the nation has been one of very remarkable ability and energy, and to it we are indebted now in no small degree; in a very large degree, rather; to the freedom from external interference which allows us to give our whole strength to this rebellion. Never before for many years have we been so creditably represented in Europe or has the foreign policy of our country commanded more respect. They will tell you so in Paris and they will tell you so here, if you don't go to such authorities as the Times for your information. The high tone and absolute honor of our country have been maintained with energy and lofty dignity, but are we not on good terms still with foreign nations? Have not the threatening clouds that were hanging over our relations with this country a few months since, been cleared away by an influence that no man of common experience would imagine to be accident? And what of Spain? And Mexico? Trust me, when you come to read the history of these days at some future time, you will no longer think that the hand of the Secretary of State has been paralysed or his broad mind lost its breadth, in a time of civil war.

Now let me read you a lesson in history. When the English nation in the year 1795 were struggling with revolutionary France, their armies were beaten, their allies conquered and forced to sue for peace; every military effort failed the instant it was put forth; famine was in the land; revolution raised its head boldly within the very hearing of Westminster Hall;

ill-success of every kind, infinitely greater than our own, dogged their foot-steps at every move; and their credit sank under their enormous subsidies to Austria, and eternal draughts on the money market. But did the English people hesitate to give a firm and noble support to Pitt, their Prime Minister, in spite of his gross failures? Not a bit of it. His majority in Parliament and throughout the nation was firmer than ever, and when he threw open a loan at last to the people, even in such a dark hour as that after Bull Run was to us, noble and peasant, King and Commoner, snapped it up in a single week, at a rate at which the money-market would have nothing to do with it. The English have the true bull-dog's grip, and that is what we must have if we expect to do anything either in victory or in defeat.

If you think the above worth printing, send it to Charles Hale. If not, no matter.

CHARLES FRANCIS ADAMS TO HIS SON

London, October 25, 1861

. . . .

OUR American news comes much in the old way, always of a chequered character. First, we are compelled to blow away a great deal of froth on the top of the cup, and then we find the liquor more or less muddled beneath. The impression is that "some one has blundered." Our Navy does not look as it did in the last war. *Then* the land expeditions indicated as much incapacity as they do now. Now our ships do nothing but catch fishing schooners. The Alliance, the Goudar, the Thomas Watson, the Bermuda, the Fingal, the Amelia, have all taken quantities of clothing, and military equipment of every description from here, of which we have had notice beforehand. But I do not see a sign of their capture in any quarter. Yet to my mind this is a greater triumph than twenty such results as that at Bull's Run. The latter at least had the effect of seriously crippling the victor. The former supplies the material for carrying on the war indefinitely and gives to all Europe the idea of an ineffective blockade — the most dangerous thing of all to our ultimate success. . . . I cannot sympathise with Mr. Sumner's speech, because the tone is purely vindictive and impracticable. But I do not the less feel that we must ultimately embrace the military necessity as a basis for the reconstruction of a stable government.

HENRY ADAMS TO CHARLES FRANCIS ADAMS, JR.

London, October 25, 1861

. . . .

You complain of the manner in which England has been allowed to wheel round. I mean to write a letter to the Times on that matter some day. Do you know the reason why it is so? How do you suppose we can make a stand here when our own friends fail to support us? Look at the Southerners here. Every man is inspired by the idea of independence and liberty while we are in a false position. They are active, you say. So they are, every man of them. There are no traitors among *them.* They have an object and they act together. *Their* merchants and friends in Liverpool have been warm and vigorous in their support from the beginning. *Ours* have been lukewarm, never uttering a hearty word on our side, and the best of them, such as Peabody and the house of Baring's invariably playing directly into the hands of our opponents. They have allowed the game to go by default. Their talk has been desponding, hesitating, an infernal weight round our necks. How can you suppose that we should gain ground with such allies.

But we might nevertheless have carried the day if the news from home had been such as to encourage our party, which was once strong and willing. You know how much encouragement we have had from your side. Every post has taken away on one hand what it brought of good on the other. It has by regular steps sapped the foundations of all confidence in us, in our institutions, our rulers and our honor. How do you suppose we can overcome the effects of the New York press? How do you suppose we can conciliate men whom our tariff is ruining? How do you suppose we can shut people's eyes to the incompetence of Lincoln or the disgusting behavior of many of our volunteers and officers.

I tell you we are in a false position and I am sick of it. My one hope is now on McClellan and if he fails us, then as I say I give it up. Here we are dying by inches. Every day our authority, prestige and influence sink lower in this country, and we have the mournful task of trying to bolster up a failing cause. Do you suppose I can go among the newspapers here and maintain our cause with any face, with such backing? Can I pretend to a faith which I did once feel, but feel no longer? I feel not seldom sorry in these days that I did n't follow my first impulse, and go into the army with the other fellows. Our side wants spirit. It does n't ring as it ought.

These little ups and downs, this guerila war in Missouri and Kentucky, amount to nothing but vexation. Oh, for one spark of genius! I have hopes of McClellan for he does n't *seem* to have made any great blunders, but I don't know.

We are all in a lull here. The English Government is perfectly passive and likely to remain so. . . .

CHARLES FRANCIS ADAMS, JR., TO HENRY ADAMS

Boston, November 5, 1861

BY the last mail I got a letter from you intended for the press. I have not however used it as intended. . . . The great facts of the case stand out. Six months of this war have gone and in them we have done much; and by we I mean our rulers. But if we have done much with our means, the rebels have performed miracles with theirs. At the end of six months have we a policy? Are traitors weeded out of our departments? Is our blockade effective? Is the war prosecuted honestly and vigorously? To all these questions there is but one answer. The President is not equal to the crisis; that we cannot now help. The Secretary of War is corrupt and the Secretary of the Navy is incompetent; that we can help and ought to. With the rebels showing us what we can do, we ought to be ashamed not to do more. But for me I despair of doing more without a purification of the Cabinet. With Seward I am satisfied, and so is the country at bottom, for our foreign affairs are creditable. Chase will do and to Blair I make no objection. But all the rest I wish the people would drive from power. Your historical examples are not good. When was England greatest? Was it not when an angry people drove the drivellers from office and forced on an unwilling King the elder Pitt, who reversed at once the whole current of a war? I want to see Holt in the War Department and a New York shipowner in that of the Navy, or else Mr. Dana. I am tired of incompetents and I want to see Lincoln forced to adopt a manly line of policy which all men may comprehend. The people here call for energy, not change, and if Lincoln were only a wise man he could unite them in spite of party cries, and with an eye solely to the public good.

Herewith you will receive three Independents, in each of which you will find an article by me for your delectation. They answer at some length your suggestion that I am an "abolitionist." I am also assured that they met with favor in the eyes of Wendell Phillips, which indeed I do not understand. I imagine they will not meet your and my father's views, but on the whole I am not dissatisfied with the two last in general and the last in particular. . . .

Please notice the leader in the Independent of the 24th. I did more than I expected in influencing the editorials of the Independent.

HENRY ADAMS TO CHARLES FRANCIS ADAMS, JR.

London, November 7, 1861

WE have just received the account of the disaster to the 20th, and I tell you, I feel bad. That there was a blunder somewhere I have no doubt, and I am inclined to believe that it was Baker and that he paid for it with his life. But to lose Lee and Paul Revere and to have your friends wounded and defeated is not atoned for by the fact of its being a blunder. Thank God it was no worse and that no one was killed. You can imagine I trembled when I ran down the list of losses.

The anxiety with which we are waiting now for the struggle that is coming is not pleasant to bear. A general battle must come before the month is over, and on its result everything will turn. I shall wait to hear of it before I discuss anything about what is to follow.

Affairs here remain in the old position and promise to remain so until there is something decisive on your side. There is no danger of any movement from England, of that you may be sure, and I have done my best to induce the New York press to change its tone towards this country, but they *are* damned fools, and they will *remain* damned fools, I suppose, and make our difficulties as great as they possibly can be. The English Government are well disposed enough, at least so far as actions are concerned, and now we hate each other too much to care a brass farthing what our *opinions* may be, on either side. Last May was the time for the contest of opinions. Now it is the most wretched folly to waste a moment over what this or any other country *thinks*. We must induce them not to *act*, but as for their thoughts, I, for one, have been thoroughly satisfied that America can expect no sympathy or assistance in Europe from any Government. They all hate us and fear us, even the most liberal. We must depend wholly on ourselves, and so long as we are strong all will go on, but the instant we lose our strength, down we shall go. The New York press are playing into the hands of the party here which is organized on the basis of anti-blockade.

As for me, I am not wholly lazy. A few days ago I called again on Townsend, the editor of the Spectator. He says that the present Ministry will stand and that there will be no interference with us even in the case of another defeat. But he doubts about France. Then I called on "Tom Brown" Hughes and had a long talk with him, but not about politics entirely. He is a regular Englishman and evidently one who prides himself on having the English virtues. He is to ask me to dine with him next week.

But my great gun is the Manchester one. Tomorrow evening I start with a pocketful of letters for Manchester to investigate that good place. With such recommendations I ought to see everything that is to be seen and learn all that is to be learned. I am invited to stay with a Mr. Stell, an American there, and have accepted. My present plan is to report with as much accuracy as possible all my conversations and all my observations, and to send them to you. Perhaps it might make a magazine article; except that it should be printed as soon as possible. If I find that I can make it effective in that form, I shall write it out and send it to you for the Atlantic. If not, I shall contract it and send it to you for the Advertiser or Courier.

As for the matter of your becoming a correspondent of some paper here, I have had it always in my mind, but the difficulty is that every paper here has already one or more American correspondents. I intend to suggest it to Townsend, and should have done so earlier but that I do not think the Spectator cares for correspondents. As for papers against our side, of course I could n't get you onto one of those, nor would I if I could. George Sumner is writing weekly vile letters in the Morning Post. I wish you would put the screws on him to stop it. He does more harm than his head's worth. So does Charles, here and at home. They're both crazy, and George, at least, unprincipled. Charles, though I believe him to be honest, is actuated by selfish motives. . . .

CHARLES FRANCIS ADAMS TO HIS SON

London, November 8, 1861

. . . .

IT may be my predilection that biasses my judgment, but I think I see in my father the only picture of a full grown statesman that the history of the United States has yet produced. By this I mean that in him were united more of all the elements necessary to complete the character than in any other man. I weigh very deliberately the substance of what I affirm. Neither am I disposed to detract from the merit of the many distinguished persons who have likewise run a brilliant career in America. In single points they may have shown a superiority. The mind of Jefferson, or Hamilton, or Webster may when directed to a special object have given indications of more positive power. Marshall may have developed a more disciplined professional intellect. All this may indeed be true. But that does not touch the question. Compare the figures from the foundation to the apex, look at them all round and you will not fail to note deficiencies of a most striking kind in those cases which you will not see in him. Read the writings of Hamilton. You see ability, sagacity and penetration, but you will find it hard to keep awake. Webster is strong in logic and forcible in exposition, but very imperfect in his bases of reasoning. Calhoun is subtle and keen in ratiocination, but never true to any consistent theory of morals. All of them are equally bold in resources for illustration and the philosophy of generalization.

The first and greatest qualification of a statesman in my estimation, is the mastery of the whole theory of morals which makes the foundation of all human society. The great and everlasting question of the right and wrong of every act whether of individual men or of collective bodies. The next is the application of the knowledge thus gained to the events of his time in a continuous and systematic way. It is in this last particular that the greatest number of failures are observed to occur. Many men never acquire sufficient certainty of purpose to be able to guide their steps at all. They then become the mere sport of fortune.

Today they shine because they have caught at a good opportunity. Tomorrow, the light goes out, and they are found mired at the bottom of a ditch. These are the men of temporary celebrity — the Charles Townshends, the John Randolphs, the George Grenvilles, the Harrison Gray Otises of their day. Every civilised nation is full of them. Other men, more favored by nature or education, prove their capacity to direct their course, at the expense of their fidelity to their convictions. They sacrifice their consistency for the sake of power, and surrender their future fame in exchange for the applause of their own day. The number of these is Legion. They crowd the records of all governments. The feebleness of perception and the deliberate abandonment of moral principle in action are the two prevailing characteristics of public men.

In my opinion no man who has lived in America had so thoroughly constructed a foundation for his public life as your grandfather. His action always was deducible from certain maxims deeply graven on his mind. This it was that made him fail so much as a party-man. No person can ever be a thorough partisan for a long period without sacrifice of his moral identity. The skill consists in knowing exactly where to draw the line, and it is precisely here that it seems to me appears the remarkable superiority of your grandfather over every man of his time. He leans on nothing external. He derives support from every thing he can seize. But if circumstances force it out of his hands, he is still found standing firm and alone. . . .

CHARLES FRANCIS ADAMS, JR., TO HIS FATHER

Boston, November 10, 1861

. . . .

I AM very anxious to hear news from Europe, for I cannot believe that it was my "letter" which caused you "a sleepless night." I fear the despatches had something to do with it. In most perfect confidence, will you tell me, does Seward want or intend to make a foreign war? He is too profound a man to brag the country into a war by simply being over-confident and overbearing; and if he does it, I know him well enough to know he means to and has a design, and just now it looks surprisingly like it. As you know I have the highest faith in Seward and would surrender it as late as any one; but a policy so comprehensive and immense, and so evidently doing evil that good might come of it puzzles me strangely. However my faith is abiding that the world will not come to an end this time.

P. S. On reading the foreign files I am annoyed to see the rumpus created in England by the Harvey Birch affair. We again present the ludicrous aspect of two people scared, the one at the other. While Englishmen are trembling over the Harvey Birch, we have been quaking over the seizure of Slidell and Mason. The Harvey Birch, I am told, belonged to secession owners in New York, and all New York is chuckling over their loss, which they most richly deserve. The public at large, so far as I can see and hear, feel no indignation, but merely a sense of intense relief at such a Godsend having just now turned up in the moment of our greatest need. . . .

CHARLES FRANCIS ADAMS, JR., TO HIS FATHER

Boston, November 19, 1861

. . . .

WE have had a little run of luck on this side this last week, and Dupont and Wilkes have bolstered up the reputation of our navy, and indeed not before it was time, as you say. I suppose the seizure of Mason and Slidell reached you before the Beaufort news and made that additionally acceptable. Here it created quite a stir and immense delight, though at first every one thought that it must be a violation of national law; but Dana crowed with delight and declared that if Lord John made an issue on that, you could blow him out of water. I don't think people cared much for Mason, except that his arrogance has made him odious; but of Slidell every one stands in great terror, and to have him safe in Fort Warren is an immense relief. Of the Beaufort affair you can judge as well as I, and if the handling of that fleet does n't please the English, they must be fastidious. As a whole the news is for the moment better, but the symptoms are still bad. We evidently cannot follow up our successes, and the army is perfectly unwieldy. This time and more disaster will cure, but for myself, I by no means partake of the immense elation of our press. I still think that nothing of importance will be done before the spring. . . .

CHARLES FRANCIS ADAMS, JR., TO HIS FATHER

Quincy, November 26, 1861

. . . .

I DON'T know whether you will be surprised or disgusted or annoyed or distressed by the information that I have gone into the army, but such is the fact. Before this reaches you I shall be an officer of the 1st Mass. Cavalry and probably in Carlisle Barracks. You know it now and I am glad of it! You ask what has impelled me to this unadvised and sudden step. Many reasons, I answer; a few of which I will now give you. But in the first place let me say that I have not felt sure of my appointment until within the last five days and that I would have notified you of it before had not former false alarms made me timid of present ones. Now I feel reasonably sure and will give you the reasons of my actions. You will say, of course, that the arguments which were decisive against my going two months ago are decisive now in no less degree; but this is not so. I have all along felt that it was my place to represent our family in the army in this struggle, but a higher sense of public duty kept me at home while I was useful to you; and when that usefulness was gone, the argument which had justified my staying at home became one for my going away. I can be of little future use to you here. . . .

For going I have many reasons. I do not think myself a soldier by nature. I am not sure I am doing that which is best for myself; but I feel that, if I go, I shall be better satisfied with myself, and, as I said to you before, I do not think it right that our family, so prominent in this matter while it is a contest of words, should be wholly unrepresented when it has grown to be a conflict of blows. You say there is neither glory nor honor to be won in civil strife. I answer, that it cannot be otherwise than right for me to fight to maintain that which my ancestors passed their whole lives in establishing. These however are general arguments which I have advanced to you before, but there are others nearer home. I have completely failed in my profession and I long to cut myself clear of it. I have indeed derived an income this summer from my office, but not from the law, and that I have made up my mind to give up. This mortifies me and the army must cover my defeat. My future must be business and literature, and I do not see why the army should not educate me for both, for its routine is that of business and it will go hard if my pen is idle while history is to be written or events are to be described. Thus my decision not only closes one career in which I have failed, but it opens others in which experience teaches me I can succeed if at all. . . .

CHARLES FRANCIS ADAMS, JR., TO HIS MOTHER

Boston, November 29, 1861

. . . .

WHAT is known of Seward in the Legation? Here his fall has been tremendous. Few men are now more violently attacked on all sides. There is a very prevalent rumor that his mind is at all times befogged with liquor; that he drinks half the time, and people won't believe me when I laugh at the idea. Then many of his oldest friends here — myself in the number — are utterly perplexed as to what he is doing. We don't see his mind in the policy of the government anywhere. In fact, we don't see any policy of the government. He seems not equal to the occasion. He may be overruled in the cabinet and devoting himself to his department; but that is not the popular impression and, though the cabinet is unpopular, if any of it went out he would go. I don't understand it and my only solution is that Seward's is one of those calm, philosophic minds which need peaceful times to operate in, when he can study cause and effect and mature his plans for gradually approaching events; but he lacks the energy, decision and "snap" for days like these. . . .

We had a Fast-day the other day and I went to church. I found it fuller than I ever saw it before on a fast-day and Mr. Wells gave us a fast sermon which made some people stare. It was hard on the war and stiff enough, but in laying down his position on slavery his Mississippi life stuck out strong, so strong, in fact, as to lead him to assert that for himself he "did not consider negro servitude as necessarily a wrong." Some people were a little astonished, but as it was an occasional sermon it will not hurt him any. . . .

Of war news there is none, though what the steamer will carry out I can't say. The Lexington affair is bad and Frémont has his choice of a series of successes or removal. The real difficulty with him seems to be extravagance. He spends money like water and one draft on the Secretary of the Treasury from him was for $5,800,000, I am told. Still he has an immense hold, which I cannot understand, on the West, and if successful can maintain himself. . . .

HENRY ADAMS TO CHARLES FRANCIS ADAMS, JR.

London, November 30, 1861

IF I thought the state of things bad last week you may imagine what I think of them now.[1] In fact I consider that we are dished, and that our position is hopeless. If the administration ordered the capture of those men, I am satisfied that our present authorities are very unsuitable persons to conduct a war like this or to remain in the direction of our affairs. It is our ruin. Do not deceive yourself about the position of England. We might have preserved our dignity in many ways without going to war with her, and our party in the Cabinet was always strong enough to maintain peace here and keep down the anti-blockaders. But now all the fat's in the fire, and I feel like going off and taking up my old German life again as a permanency. It is devilish disagreeable to act the part of Sisyphus especially when it is our own friends who are trying to crush us under the rock.

What part it is reserved to us to play in this very tragical comedy I am utterly unable to tell. The Government has left us in the most awkward and unfair position. They have given no warning that such an act was thought of, and seem almost to have purposely encouraged us to waste our strength in trying to maintain the relations which it was itself intending

[1] After the Trent affair.

to destroy. I am half mad with vexation and despair. If papa is ordered home I shall do as Fairfax did, and go into the war with "peace" on my mind and lips.

Our position here is of course very unpleasant just now. We were to have gone to Lord Hatherton's on Monday, but now our visit is put off, and I am not without expectations that a very few weeks may see us either on our way home or on the continent. I think that the New Year will see the end.

This nation means to make war. Do not doubt it. What Seward means is more than I can guess. But if he means war also, or to run as close as he can without touching, then I say that Mr. Seward is the greatest criminal we've had yet.

We have friends here still, but very few. Bright dined with us last night, and is with us, but is evidently hopeless of seeing anything good. Besides, his assistance at such a time as this is evidently a disadvantage to us, for he is now wholly out of power and influence. Our friends are all very much cast down and my friends of the Spectator sent up to me in a dreadful state and asked me to come down to see them, which I did, and they complained bitterly of the position we were now in. I had of course the pleasure of returning the complaint to any extent, but after all this is poor consolation.

Our good father is cool but evidently of the same mind as I am. He has seen Lord Russell but could give him no information, and my Lord did not volunteer any on his side. You will know very soon what you are to expect. . . .

No news of importance has yet reached my ears, but you will see my views as usual in the Times. We are preparing for a departure, though as yet we have taken no positive steps towards making future arrangements.

Beaufort was good. It gave me one glowing day worth a large share of all the anxiety and trouble that preceded and have followed it. Our cry now must be emancipation and arming the slaves.

CHARLES FRANCIS ADAMS, JR., TO HENRY ADAMS

Boston, December 3, 1861

. . . .

YOUR letters were written under the cloud of Balls Bluff, and it is hard for us just now when every one is getting elated again to go back and appreciate the bitterness of which you speak. Yes, every one is in the clouds again, but I must confess my confidence has been too much shaken to be suddenly restored. I am oppressed by a combined sense of ill-luck and incompetence. A few words of Balls Bluff affair and then let us try to forget it. I am informed by Harrison Ritchie, who has been to Washington for the Governor recently and is in "possesshun of certing infamashon," that there is no doubt that the advance was ordered by General Scott without McClellan's knowledge, and the advance on Romney was ordered by him at the same time. The last succeeded and the first failed, and within ten days Scott resigned. The results of the reverse were however fatal, and much in the way that I imagined, the plans of the campaign were frustrated, and here we now are with a disconnected series of successes and reverses leading to little and effecting in themselves still less. So affairs now stand, and soon we must go into winter quarters, for today it has set in bitter cold. Still there are signs of promise in the sky and the blockade promises us far greater results than our arms bid fair to win. The South already is evidently starving, and if it is so in November what will it be in April? They are wild with terror at our naval expeditions and, in despite of all and everything, I never felt so confident of crushing them in time, if no foreign force intervenes, by sheer weight, as I now do. I have lost all confidence in our skill or courage, for the present; but passing events make it pretty clear to my mind that we are learning fast and that brute force is all with us.

Every one is fearfully anxious to hear from England of the reception of Mason and Slidell's capture, and your letter in which you mention that the James Adger was watched created a good deal of uneasiness. The English precedents so clearly justify us that I cannot fear difficulty from that cause; but I do fear very much a popular clamor and feeling of hatred towards us which will make the occurrence of future difficulty very easy. However, every day gained is a great thing now and I think there will be a Southern collapse within four months, if only we can hold over that time.

But I have talked enough of politics. How do they like my going into the army in London? Did they expect it? Were they pleased or disgusted? As for me

I have nothing new to tell you in that regard. The regiment is still here, but I do not expect to be ordered to join until they move to Carlisle barracks, which will probably be very soon, for winter has set in in earnest. . . .

CHARLES FRANCIS ADAMS, JR., TO HENRY ADAMS

Boston, December 10, 1861

YOURS of the 23d of last month reached me yesterday. . . . If we are going to have such a storm as you intimate, I should have to go, so anyhow, and if indeed "all that remains is to drop gracefully," it will not do me or any one else any good for me to anxiously hang on here a few days longer. Yet it does make me feel terribly. We have blundered all summer long and now we have capstoned our blunders by blundering into a war with England. So be it. While there's life there's hope; but I go into the army with a bitter feeling against those under whose lead we have come to this pass, and amid all the shattered idols of my whole life I don't feel as if I cared much when my turn came. I suppose now I shall go into the field against a foreign enemy and I ought to rejoice at that. Still, I don't. Against the rebels I could fight with a will and in earnest. They are traitors, they war for a lie, they are the enemies of morals, of government, and of man. In them we fight against a great wrong — but against England, we shall have forced her into war when she only asked for peace; we shall have made that a cause of quarrel which a few soft words might have turned away. It will be a wicked and causeless war wantonly brought about by us and one in which I most unwillingly would go to my death.

As for Seward I cannot comprehend his policy and so I cannot judge of it, and most slowly and reluctantly will I surrender my faith in him. His policy has been to keep a firm front, and in this it was wise; but I think he might have made himself less offensive to foreign powers in doing it, and I somewhat doubt the expediency of bragging yourself out of the game, as you tell me he has done. Still we have made our bed and now we must lie on it.

I shall probably have joined my regiment this week or early next. You will be surprised to hear that I shall probably regularly enlist and make my début as a simple sergeant in Caspar Crowninshield's company. The truth is they have so backed and filled, and hesitated and delayed, that, having determined to go, I have lost my patience, and have signified to them that I am ready to wait in the ranks until they are ready to give me a commission. Caspar got his company as a promotion for his behavior at Balls Bluff, and I shall get mine, I suppose, at some indefinite future period, when Sargent ceases to be a gas-bag and Williams feels the regiment under his thumb. Meanwhile I shall rough and fight it out with the rest, sleep fifteen in a tent with stable-boys, groom horses, feed like a hog and never wash, and such is my future! Well, it is better than my present, for I shall at least, by going into the army, get rid of the war.

Your last letter, and your statement that there was nothing left but a suspension of relations with England,

CASPAR CROWNINSHIELD

came peculiarly unpleasantly just now. I had again begun to hope. Our blockade has become so effective and we are developing such enormous strength, that in spite of blunders, the confederates seemed likely to be crushed by brute force and starved to death, while we are really more prosperous than we have been for a year, and our poor more comfortable than they have been for four years. The confederates already, before winter begins, are regulating by law the profit on "articles of prime necessity," and what would it have been before spring? I had begun to hope yet to see this rebellion collapse. Of course a war with England exactly reverses positions. It will be short and desperate, and end in the establishment of a confederate government, I suppose. However, a glorious indifference is coming over me. I can live on my pay, the world will not come to an end this time, and if I do, I shall doubtless be very comfortable in my grave. But I do hate to be blundered out of existence and, before a foreign war just as we were getting the whip-hand. Even Balls Bluff will hide a diminished head; it will stand forth in all history as the Koh-i-noor of blunders. . . .

CHARLES FRANCIS ADAMS TO HIS SON

London, December 12, 1861

. . . .

IT has given us here an indescribably sad feeling to witness the exultation in America over an event which bids fair to be the final calamity in this contest. We wonder that there has been so little of comprehension of the nature of the struggle here in public opinion not to jump at once to the conclusion that it would be turned against us by such an act. Putting ourselves in the place of Great Britain, where would be the end of the indignation that would be vented against the power committing it? Yet it seems everywhere to have been very coolly taken for granted that because she did outrageous things on the ocean to other powers, she would remain quiet when such things were done to her. A little observation of her past history ought to have shown that she never sees the right until half a century after she has acted wrong. She now admits her error in our revolution, and in the last war. Now she is right in principle and only wrong in point of consistency. Our mistake is that we are donning ourselves in her cast-off suit, when our own is better worth wearing. And all for what? Why to show our spite against two miserable wretches, twenty thousand of whom are not worth a single hair in the head of any of the persons on both sides of the controversy whose lives and happiness are endangered by the quarrel. . . .

HENRY ADAMS TO CHARLES FRANCIS ADAMS, JR.

London, December 13, 1861

YOUR letter to papa announcing your metamorphosis took us as you may suppose a good deal by surprise. I endorsed it at once. As you say, one of us ought to go, and though of the three as a mere matter of accidental position I might have preferred that it should be John, still, as a question of greater or lesser evil perhaps it's best that it should be you. If we come home, perhaps I may try it myself a little, but if we stay abroad, or if I come home alone, I do not suppose I shall be compelled to do so. At the same time, as a personal matter, I'm sorry you're going, especially as I have, since the last shock, become satisfied that we must sooner or later yield the matter. As a mere question of independence I believe the thing to be settled. We cannot bring the South back. As a question of terms and as a means of thoroughly shaking the whole southern system, I'm not sorry to see the pressure kept up. . . .

You can imagine our existence here. Angry and hateful as I am of Great Britain, I still can't help laughing and cursing at the same time as I see the accounts of the talk of our people. What a bloody set of fools they are! How in the name of all that's conceivable could you suppose that England would sit quiet under such an insult. *We* should have jumped out of our boots at such a one. And there's Judge Bigelow parading bad law "at the cannon's mouth," and Governor Andrew all cock-a-hoop, and Dana so unaccustomed confident, and Mr. Everett following that "Great authority" George Sumner into a ditch, "blind leader of the blind"! Good God, what's got into you all? What do you mean by deserting now the great principles of our fathers, by returning to the vomit of that dog Great Britain? What do you mean by asserting now principles against which every Adams yet has protested and resisted? You're mad, all of you. It's pitiable to see such idiocy in a nation. There's the New York Times which I warned only in my last letter against such an act, and its consequences; and now I find the passage erased, and editorial assurances that war was *impossible* on such grounds. Egad, who knew best, Raymond or I? War is not only possible but inevitable on that ground; and *we* shall be forced to declare it. England can compel us to appear to act as the aggressors in future as now.

Thurlow Weed is here and hard at work on public opinion. He is excessively anxious about the meeting of Congress and thinks we shall be talked into a war. I have had some talk with him and like him very much. . . . The Government has not yet condescended to send us one single word as to the present question. I wonder what Seward supposes a Minister can do or is put here for, if he is n't to know what to do or to say. It makes papa's position here very embarrassing. . . .

CHARLES FRANCIS ADAMS, JR., TO HENRY ADAMS

Boston, December 17, 1861

I CLEARLY see that the little squall you refer to in yours of the 23d of November was a gentle zephyr in comparison with the gale that set in four days later. Your Manchester paper got here just too late. The Atlantic could not have printed it till January, and so, as you told me, I carried it to the Courier. It has been printed and I send it to you, but I doubt if any one has read it, or any notice will be taken of it; for you might as well expect the sailors on a sinking ship to pay attention to flourishes of a fiddle. It happened at exactly the wrong moment, and people were too much absorbed in the questions of the moment to pay attention to those of the day. I made a mistake, however, in sending it to the Courier, but I am under some obligation to them and this paid it off. I shall certainly have nothing to do in the future with that low toned and semi-treasonable sheet — that is, when I can use any other.

Is the present a case of war or of diplomacy? I cannot tell, but I do hope not war. The idea of two great countries setting to work to do each other all the injury in their power on a technical point of law, or error into which one fell in its desire not to offend the other. Still, if England will take that tone, so be it. We have our war paint and feathers on and we shall die hard. Do you remember how hard France was pressed just after the revolution and how she turned on her enemies? We can make a better fight now than we ever could before, and our two first measures would almost necessarily be those most troublesome to England — a decree of universal emancipation on the one hand, and a swoop on English commerce on the other. A true democracy is a pretty hard thing to whip and I cannot help thinking that, in a war forced upon us on this issue, England would find us as ugly a customer as she had often dealt with. Still it is a conclusion terrible to think of. As great a cause as ever men struggled for ruined forever by so needless a side issue! Yet for one I do not see how it can long be avoided and perhaps it would be as well to face it at once. . . .

I send you herewith a copy of a lecture by Boutwell of some interest just now. By the way, it is a hopeful sign to see that Seward on this question has Congress under the curb. I should n't wonder if the wily old bird changed his note now, as he did when the South kicked out, and you suddenly found him most suave and peaceable.

CHARLES FRANCIS ADAMS, JR., TO HENRY ADAMS

Boston, December 19, 1861

I RECEIVED yours of the 30th ultimo yesterday. You say "this nation means to make war." To this I have to reply that this nation does n't. England may force us into a war, but the feeling here is eminently pacific, and unless the Ministry has put themselves in an untenable position and driven us to the wall, no war will come out of this. Dana has sent a letter to the Governor by this mail, and if Lyons withdraws, the negotiation must be carried on in London. He wants me to add the peculiar injustice of the English talk of violence in seizing Slidell. The business was done in the most courteous manner in which it could be and the "sass" in the Trent was all English. Our men were abused and assaulted, called "pirates" and blackguarded, and answered not a word. And if England insists on war, it will be only because England is dissatisfied that we did n't insist on all our "belligerent" rights, and the curse be on her head. The facts in the case you will have before this and make the most of them.

My object in writing this is, however, to tell you that I have received my commission. I leave the State Tuesday next with my regiment for Annapolis. I am a 1st Lieutenant and to be Captain, so Colonel Williams says, and heard of it only an hour ago. This is all I hoped for and much more than I expected. . . .

CHARLES FRANCIS ADAMS TO HIS SON
London, December 20, 1861

. . . .

THE great event of the past week on this side is the death of the Prince Consort. From the time of my arrival I had formed a very favorable opinion of the man. Having a most difficult part to play he seemed to me to acquit himself most creditably. A feeble person would have fallen into contempt. A vicious one would have created discord. An intriguing one would have filled the Court with animosities and sharpened all the rivalries of parties. He was neither. His capacity and his acquirements commanded the respect of the most powerful subject. His moral character set at defiance all malevolence. And his prudence preserved his neutrality from the assaults of contending factions. Yet he can scarcely be said to have been popular in any class, and least of all among the nobility. He was reserved and shy, little versed in the arts which recommend a man to others. Few were disposed to give him much credit until they lost him. Now they are beginning to open their eyes to a sense of his value. They discover that much of their political quietude has been due to the judicious exercise of his influence over the Queen and the Court, and they do not conceal their uneasiness as to the future without him. The young Prince is just coming of age, with a character by no means formed. The younger children are coming forward with a strong curb removed. The Queen herself has no guide or adviser so well fitted to perform his part without danger of political complications to disturb her. There is no strength in any purely party organization that will keep the government steady. War with the United States seems imminent. It may spread itself all over Europe. Where is the master to direct this storm, if he cannot arrest it? Is it Lord Palmerston or Earl Russell? I trow not. Let any thing happen to Napoleon, and you will see. He is their buckler and their shield.

As to us I fancy you can understand the pleasantness of the position we are occupying in the mean time. The leading newspapers roll out as much fiery lava as Vesuvius is doing, daily. The clubs and the army and the navy and the people in the streets generally are raving for war. On the other side are the religious people and a large number of stock jobbers and traders, together with the radical following of Messrs. Cobden and Bright. The impression is general that Mr. Seward is resolved to insult England until she makes a war. He is the bête noir, that frightens them out of all their proprieties. It is of no use to deny it and appeal to facts. They quote what he said to the Duke of Newcastle about insulting England as the only sure passport to popular favor in America, and a part of a speech in which he talked of annexing Canada as an offset to the loss of the slave states. This is the evidence that Mr. Seward is an ogre fully resolved to eat all Englishmen raw. Pitiful as is all this nonsense, it is of no trifling consequence in its political effect. Even our friend Mr. Thurlow Weed with all his sagacity is baffled in every attempt to counteract it. And if war finally happens, it will trace to this source one of its most prominent causes.

Of course I feel most anxiously the position of my country, and of those who are enlisted in its cause. So far as I now see the field it is much less alarming than it looked some weeks ago. Many of the causes of apprehension are removed. The government has not authorised the act of Captain Wilkes, neither has it adopted it, as yet. So far, so good. But the British government will not rest satisfied with that position. The policy must be disavowed and the men replaced. Such is my understanding of the substance no matter how gently the sense may be conveyed. Shall we do either? For my part I think justice to our former professions demands it of us. I care not about quibbles concerning Sir William Scott's law, against which I was bred in a mortal aversion. He is no idol of mine, and I care not how soon both nations join to knock his image off its pedestal. But what my opinion may be is one thing. What the delusion of my countrymen is, is another and very different one. They may regard Messrs. Mason and Slidell as more precious than all their worldly possessions. May be so. For my part I would part with them at a cent apiece.

CHARLES FRANCIS ADAMS, JR., TO HIS FATHER

Boston, December 22, 1861

. . . .

You may imagine that we are waiting here anxiously to hear the news from England, but I think you overestimate it. People seem to have lost all apprehension of war, on the simple theory that it requires two to make a war, as it does to make a bargain, and we don't mean to fight — yet. By the way, why did you never tell me of the tone of Seward's despatches? Here they excite the greatest admiration. I must say, I don't think I ever read more admirable state papers, and I look with renewed admiration on the consummate genius which could produce them. They have gone far to reinstate Seward in the estimation of all cultivated minds. Sumner, I see, is riding the "nigger" hobby still. Why can't he leave it alone. Can't he see that it has passed beyond laws and proclamations, and that day by day we are working at that volcano. . . .

CHARLES FRANCIS ADAMS TO HIS SON

London, December 27, 1861

. . . .

WE watch the progress of events in America by the lurid glare of the passions that burn on this side of the ocean. The last news we have brings the Europa to Cape Race. The next will probably shew us your countenances on receiving the details. I have been so often deceived in my calculations of late that I do not pretend to foresee what the picture will be. You took the affair of the Nashville so amiably that perhaps you will laugh now. I have never before met with an instance so striking of provoking simplicity in a nation. You do not even resort to the most ordinary habit of judging of others by yourselves. Here is all Europe from end to end arrayed in opinion against you, and not a shade of suspicion that you may not be right yet rests upon your brows. Lord Stowell carries the day as if he were your legitimate ruler by the grace of God. It is unlucky for me that I was bred up in declared hostility to the arbitrary dogmas against neutral rights of that impersonation of Anglican egotism, so that I have never partaken of your security. A day or two will show whether the government will prove true to its ancient well-established principles, or whether under the paltry inducement of personal pique it will strike into a new path that will lead it neither to glory nor success. My own convictions still are that it will determine right. Thus far it has not shown a false color as I feared under the first popular impulse that it might. Yet I confess I dread the effect of the pressure to which it may be subjected. The result will soon be upon us. . . .

Apropos of this let me say a word about the notion you still seem to entertain that Mr. Seward means to bring on a war. Thus far I have always maintained that this was a mistake founded on a bad joke of his to the Duke of Newcastle at Governor Morgan's dinner to the Prince of Wales. The Duke has however succeeded in making everybody in authority here believe it. Lord Lyons and Mr. Sumner have helped on the delusion at home. Yet I have no hesitation in my opinion, neither do I find that Mr. Thurlow Weed, with whom I compare notes, entertains any other. Be it as it may, *now* will be his chance. He can have a war, if he wants one. He has but to do what the Duke says he told him he meant to do, i.e. *insult the British govern-*

ment in his answer, and he will have it to his heart's content. In my opinion he will do no such thing. But if I am right, I trust that from that time no more reliance will be placed upon a poor pleasantry uttered after a hospitable entertainment, to a mischief-making guest. . . .

The people of Great Britain are just beginning to think that the Queen's husband, though a German, was something of a person, after all. I am inclined to believe that they have not seen a royal personage equal to him since the days of William the Third. Had he lived the country would have felt more and more the influence of his presence. For parties are in process of disintegration, and personal qualities are growing more important. The old Whig dynasty will die out with Lord Palmerston, and the Tories will scarcely outlive Lord Derby. New issues will take the place of the old ones, just as they have done with us, but I hope for their sakes not to be attended with a similar convulsion. Yet just that is the thing they in their inmost hearts dread, and the poor people fancy they are going to avoid it by means of our calamities.

HENRY ADAMS TO CHARLES FRANCIS ADAMS, JR.

London, December 28, 1861

. . . .

THE difficulty of our position here consists first in the fact that the South are in London a nation, and in Washingon no nation; and second, that Seward will not submit to this fact as an evil of which the least said the better. No doubt you have read his state papers and see what I mean. They are admirable works; they show great ability; but they want tact. He shaves closer to the teeth of the lion than he ought. No one has a right to risk so much for a mere point of form.

It *is* a mere point of form. The Nashville business can have only one of two results: one, the recognition of the belligerent rights of the South by our Government; the other, a suspension of relations, either preceding or following measures of force, as threatened in the despatch I spoke of to you, now published.

Again, about the Trent affair. Our lawyers have shown a strange want of close logic. The seizure of the commissioners can only be justified in one of two ways. If Seward sticks to his rebel theory, he must claim a right to do that which is most repugnant to our whole history and sense of right. He must defend a violation of the right of asylum.

If he claims them as contraband, setting aside other legal objections, he acknowledges the South as belligerents, by the act. From every word he has written I am bound to believe that he will not do the latter. But if he adheres to his old view, I can see no means of preserving our relations with this Court in either the Nashville or the Trent difficulties.

For these reasons I think that our stay here is at an end. But I do not believe in war. I have written at some length on this in my letter to the Times this evening, and from that you can judge whether there will be war or no. Lord Lyons' departure will not make ours necessary unless Seward wishes it.

For my own part I am tired of this life. Every attempt I have made to be of use has failed more or less completely. I stand no stronger than the first day I arrived. I cannot find that I have effected a lodgment anywhere, in spite of many exertions. I am now at a loss again to what new point to turn, having been beaten back everywhere; and hope for an idea.

You are going into the army. I do not think it my duty to express any regrets at the act, or at the necessity for it. They are understood, and I do not mean to make the thing any harder for either you or myself, by mourning or maundering about it. About my own fortunes I am becoming more and more callous and indifferent; but about yours, I feel differently, and if it were not for the strange madness of the times, which has left no longer any chance of settled lives and Christian careers, I should be vehement against your throwing yourself away like this. As it is, I can only tell you to do what you think best, and I shall be always ready to stand by you with what aid I can give.

Inclosed is my quarterly draft on Raymond. With this and what money of mine you have now in your hands, there ought to be something more than two hundred dollars. I want you to use this on your outfit, to buy a horse, or equipments, or to fit out your company. It is my contribution to the war and to your start in pride, pomp and circumstance. . . .

Thurlow Weed is still here, very active indeed. I have tried to be of what use to him I could, but without much result. He's a large man; a very tall man indeed; and a good deal taller than I am. So I can only watch and admire at a distance.

1862

1862

CHARLES FRANCIS ADAMS, JR., TO HENRY ADAMS

New York, January 3, 1862

. . . .

HERE I am in barracks in New York and under orders for Port Royal, with the thermometer about zero and a small pandemonium all around me. I went out to camp about eight days ago in the dead of winter, and when the strong north wind blew. Sunday we struck our camp and moved for the South. It wasn't a pleasant day, for the Blue Hills looked cold and dreary and snow packed on the deserted camp ground; and while the earth was covered with ice the sky was grey and uncompromising and the wind rough and cold. It was dismal enough I assure you and I was glad enough when we were hurried into the cars. John was the only person to see me off, much to my relief, for I was in the cross and hungry rather than the sentimental mood.

Then came a chapter of accidents. Our Major got drunk before we left and has continued so ever since, and the battalion has taken care of itself. That officer has now disappeared, we hope forever, and at last we have got ourselves comfortably quartered. We are barracked in a German amusement building and grove on 64th street, and our horses are stabled in large sheds not far off, and the room in which I am writing is the parlor and sleeping room of the officers and the headquarters of the battalion. The weather is beastly cold and very windy, and the horses suffer though the men are comfortable. As for me I never was better in my life. The exposure has been pretty severe and the change of life great; but I am always well in the open air and jolly among a crowd of fellows, so no sympathy need be wasted on me. I like it and like it better than I expected. I fall into the life very easily and find my spring experience at the fort of inestimable service. Already I feel as much at home in charge of the guard or the company stables as I ever did in my office. I'm sure if I like it so far I shall continue to do so, for we've had a pretty rough time, and Caspar Crowninshield says the most disgusting he ever had. But I certainly like it so far and expect to continue to do so.

We are off soon — probably within ten days — for Port Royal. We like the idea fairly, though we would prefer to go to other places. For myself I should prefer to winter at Annapolis, and next to that to be sent to Texas, but as for being cooped up on Hilton Head all winter, I don't relish the idea much, though as regards climate it will be a pleasant change. As for active service, it's just impossible. You could n't get our horses within a mile of firearms, and the drilling task before us is something terrible to contemplate. We are all green, officers, men and horses, and long practice is absolutely necessary. But we can do, I imagine, picket and camp duty. My wants (?) will probably be found on board ship.

CHARLES FRANCIS ADAMS TO HIS SON
London, January 10, 1862

. . . .

CAPTAIN WILKES has not positively shipwrecked us, but he has come as near to it without succeeding as he could. Thus far the country has been at least saved the danger of setting up military idols. This reconciles me a little to the slowness of our operations. Another consideration is the crushing nature of our expenditure which must stop this war, if something effective does not follow soon. It is idle to talk of putting down the rebellion whilst our power is resisted successfully within a dozen miles of the capital. This idea prevails so much here that it will undoubtedly become the basis of a movement for recognition before long. . . .

The first effect of the surrender of Messrs. Mason and Slidell has been extraordinary. The current which ran against us with such extreme violence six weeks ago now seems to be going with equal fury in our favor. The reaction in the city was very great yesterday, and even the most violent of the presses, the Times and the Post, are for the moment a little tamed. Possibly, if nothing else should intervene to break its force, this favoring gale may carry us through the first half of the session of Parliament, in other words, until the first of May. If by that time we shall have made no decided progress towards a result, we may as well make up our minds to disbelieve in our power to do it at all. Foreign nations will come to that conclusion if we do not. . . .

HENRY ADAMS TO CHARLES FRANCIS ADAMS, JR.

London, January 10, 1862

. . . .

THE news of the surrender of the unhung arrived yesterday, and gave us much satisfaction. It was particularly grateful to me because the ground taken is that which the Chief recommended in an early despatch to the Government, in which he quoted Madison's words. The effect here is good and will help us, but I have little hope that we shall be able to maintain ourselves here much longer. I fear that the meeting of Parliament will be the signal for a grand battle, and March will see us *en route* for somewhere.

Still there is great activity among our friends here in preparing for the struggle, and Thurlow Weed is organising our forces effectively. We shall die hard I think, and England will have little to be proud of. The blockade is the place where the shoe pinches, and the blockade is now very perfect, I should judge. We shall see what they mean to do. . . .

Financially we are dished. There is but one resort, and that is severe direct taxation. It is in this way alone that the expenses of all modern wars in Europe have been borne, and we must come to it at last, or repudiate. The latter is out of the question, but the Lord knows.

The Legation is tolerably quiet just now, with little doing. Government has behaved well in the Nashville business, and that vessel is now under our guns and without increased armament. Meanwhile the

Sumter has turned up and is making trouble in Spain. I wish to God the Tuscarora could catch her and sink her.

Today I find myself in a scrape that is by no manner of means agreeable. The Courier in putting my name to my "Diary" has completely used me up. To my immense astonishment and dismay I found myself this morning sarsed through a whole column of the Times, and am laughed at by all England. You can imagine my sensations. Unless something occurs to make me forgotten, my bed is not likely to be one of roses for some time to come. There is nothing to be done but to grin and bear it. But for the present I shall cease my other writings as I am in agonies for fear they should be exposed. I wish I could get at Raymond, as I don't want to write myself, for fear my letter should get out. Could n't you write to him and explain, without mentioning names, why his London correspondent has stopped for a time. My connection with him must on no account be known. The Chief as yet bears this vexation very good-naturedly, but another would be my ruin for a long time. I don't want him ever to know about it. . . .

CHARLES FRANCIS ADAMS, JR., TO HENRY ADAMS

"*Empire City,*" *Off Port Royal*
Friday, January, 1862

WE are just making harbor on the fifth day out, after a decidedly rough and long passage. We ought to have got in yesterday, but missed the harbor and for the last twenty-four hours have been cruising up and down the coast, in a northeaster, between Tybee island and Charleston light, and will barely get in today. The voyage has been very severe on our horses which look most decidedly used up, and a fair average of men have been down and could fully describe the pleasures of seasickness — as also could most of the officers, including myself, who passed the second day out on my back, but since then have picked up sufficiently to be on my feed, drink, and smoke, and round while my bed is made. We have left the winter fairly behind us and now in a couple of days we shall settle down at Beaufort, but what to do, the Lord only knows. . . .

You set up for a philosopher. You write letters *à la* Horace Walpole; you talk of loafing round Europe; you pretend to have seen life. Such twaddle makes me feel like a giant Warrington talking to an infant Pendennis. *You* "tired of this life"! *You* more and more "callous and indifferent about your own fortunes!" Pray how old are you and what has been your career? You graduate and pass two years in Europe, and witness by good luck a revolution. You come home and fall upon great historic events and have better chances than any young man to witness and become acquainted with them. You go abroad while great questions are agitated in a position to know all about them. Fortune has done nothing but favor you and yet you are "tired of this life." You are beaten back everywhere before you are twenty-four, and finally writing philosophical letters you grumble at the strange madness of the times and have n't even faith in God and the spirit of your age. What do you mean by thinking, much less writing such stuff? "No longer any chance left of settled lives and Christian careers!" Do you suppose the world is coming to an end now? Had n't you better thank God that your lot is cast in great times? How am I throwing myself away? Is n't a century's work of my ancestors worth a struggle to preserve? Am I likely to do so much that it won't do for me to risk my precious life in this great struggle? Come — no more of this. Don't get into this vein again, or if you do, keep it to yourself.... We shall come out all right and if we don't, the world will. Excuse me if I have been rough, but it will do you good....

We are just taking a pilot on board off Hilton Head and in a few hours we shall sully the soil of Carolina. Ah, would n't I like to ride into Charleston! I don't know when you will hear from me again, but perhaps my letters will come as regularly as ever. We shall be very busy and hard at work for some time and may soon see service. I well know how eagerly the news from Port Royal will be wished for in the breakfast room of the Legation at London. Meanwhile I am very well and in very good spirits and look forward to having a very pleasant time, though very monotonous and so keep the parents easy....

We have just arrived at Hilton Head and come to anchor. We are going up to Beaufort tomorrow. Weather delicious and all well....

HENRY ADAMS TO CHARLES FRANCIS ADAMS, JR.

London, January 22, 1862

. . . .

For life here is by no means what it is cracked up to be. The Trent business coming first destroyed all our country visits, for people have given up inviting us, on the just supposition that we would n't care to go into society now. The small list of friends that we have are not always so American as one would like. So we generally dodge "exposure" as much as possible. But I am personally flabbergasted by the explosion of my Manchester bomb, or more properly, the return of the boomerang which has made me too notorious to be pleasant. The Times gently skinned me and the Examiner scalped me with considerable savageness. For myself I care about as much for the Times or the Examiner as I do for the Pekin Gazette; but, unfortunately, the American Minister in London is at this time an object of considerable prominence; an eyesore to an influential and somewhat unscrupulous portion of the community. Accordingly I form a convenient head to punch when people feel vicious and pugnacious. I have, therefore, to change the metaphor, found it necessary to take in every spare inch of canvas and to run (on a lee-shore) under double-close-reefed mizzen to' gallant skysails, before a tremendous gale. In other words I have made myself as little an object of attack as possible. This reduces my means of usefulness to almost nothing and I might just as well be anywhere as here, except that I can't leave the parent birds thus afloat on the raging tide.

We are sometimes anxious still and are likely to be more so. The truth is, we are now in a corner. There is but one way out of it and that is by a decisive victory. If there's not a great success, and a success *followed up*, within six weeks, we may better give up the game than blunder any more over it. These nations, France probably first, will raise the blockade.

Such is the fact of our position. I am ready for it anyway, but I do say now that McClellan must do something within six weeks or we are done. This war has lasted long enough, to my mind.

There is precious little to tell you about here. France has again renewed her proposal to raise the blockade and there has been a discussion, or a battle about it. Prince Albert was strongly for peace with us, and now that he is dead it is understood that the Queen continues to favor his policy. Besides her, the King of Belgium has come over and is pressing earnestly for peace. His great object always is to counteract French influence when it points to war. We have a majority (probably) in the Cabinet of neutrality men, nor do I know whom to call the leader of the war-party in the Ministry. You must not misunderstand Palmerston. He means disunion, but not war unless under special influences.

We gave a dinner last week to Bishop McIlvaine, and I went with mamma another day to breakfast with Mr. Senior. Met there the chief man of the Times, Lowe. He never speaks to any of us, and I certainly should n't care to seem to make up to him. . . .

CHARLES FRANCIS ADAMS TO HIS SON

London, January 24, 1862

. . . .

THE Trent case has not blown hard enough to carry me away from my post of duty here. But it is not quite calm for all that. The rebel emissaries and their sympathisers are continually at work puffing up grievances and straining out falsehoods, and they find multitudes of not unwilling ears. One day it is the barbarism of savage blockade by filling up harbors; the next, it is the wretched pretence of paper blockade, respected by nobody. All this shows the eagerness to clutch at some pretext for interference. The expedition to Mexico is taking extraordinary proportions just now, which may not be without its significance under possible contingencies. Political matters being a little dull on this side, it would seem as if people would like to take a hand in the quarrel in America. I do not wish harm to any body, but if the Austrians and the Italians should fall to belaboring each other a bit just at this moment, so as to turn the public attention from our continent, I do not know that I should regard it as wholly a misfortune. . . .

CHARLES FRANCIS ADAMS TO HIS SON

London, January 31, 1862

. . . .

THE disputed mock-heroes, who came so near creating a war between people vastly better than themselves, have arrived safe and sound in this city. But for the usual notice in the newspapers nobody would have known it. I doubt whether the presence of one person more or less will have any very serious effect upon the current of public events, which depends far more upon the results now taking place with you than upon any action here. . . . In the meanwhile the newspapers indulge their respective fancies as freely as ever. Their abuse is not very pleasant, but I am always consoled for it, when I reflect that Lord Lyons is likely to get about as much on his side. The balance of national invective being thus kept about even, I do not see why we cannot consider the one side as neutralising the other, and nothing left. . . . In any event I shall retain the conviction that the endeavor to excite enmity against us here has a purely political origin, and does not find its root deep in the heart of the community. It pleases an influential class to think that the demon of democracy may be laid at home, if it can be stripped of its American garb. Perhaps they are right, though I do not believe it. No more fatal mistake can be committed by them than that of taking up the cause of a slaveholding oligarchy to prove the fact. Every step in its progress would be a new argument against them. For it would more and more establish the fact of their want of sympathy with free institutions and the progress of the age. Hence the decline of their power over the public mind would be precipitated rather than retarded, and the end would come just as surely. . . .

HENRY ADAMS TO CHARLES FRANCIS ADAMS, JR.

London, January 31, 1862

. . . .

WE are going ahead just as usual and our position has not varied. The only fault I am disposed to find is the old and chronic one with our Chief, and for that matter, with me also, of not extending his relations enough. I want him to cultivate the diplomatic corps, which has been greatly neglected and from which many advantages may be drawn. About the English it does not so much matter. They are so extremely jealous of whatever looks like foreign influence that on the whole they are better left to themselves. We have now a tolerably good organization in our branch of the press, and Weed is extending this rapidly. He can do everything that we cannot do, and a single blunder on our side that would bring the Legation into discredit, would much more than compensate for any advantage we are likely to get from bold action. Since my exposure in the papers here, I have wholly changed my system, and having given up all direct communication with the public, am engaged in stretching my private correspondence as far as possible. This I hope to do to some purpose, and with luck I may make as much headway so, as I could in any other way.

The two unhung arrived after all. Evidently they are born for the gallows, as the sea casts them out. Their detention of two months was a great stroke of luck for us in my opinion. Their party here had made all their preparations for a war, and stopped their old game almost wholly. Peace was a great blow to them, and has disconcerted all their plans. For two months they ceased to send supplies to the South; they kept the Nashville in port; and they worked on a whole line of manœuvres which are now regularly knocked into a cocked hat. Slidell might have been dangerous in France, for the Emperor was very shaky, but Seward's course and Weed's dexterity just turned the corner and now Slidell's first reception is the announcement of Napoleon's continued neutrality. Up to the last moment the beggars were confident that directly the opposite course would be taken. Then, in expectation of a war, the Nashville was kept in port. The Tuscarora arrived just in time; and now Mason is received here with the news that the Nashville can no longer remain in port but that both she and the Tuscarora must proceed to sea.

And now the great battle is coming and we shall see lively times. Parliament meets on the 6th. The reprobates are as usual very sanguine that there will be intervention, and that the Ministry will be compelled to recognize or resign. A battle there will be, no doubt, but unless we are defeated at home, I think we shall yet maintain ourselves here. The opposition to intervention of any sort will be bitter in the extreme. They are well organised, I understand, but they are too vulnerable to stand a long contest, and we shall not give up with a short one. Still, much is yet in the dark as to our relative strength. Lord Russell distinctly stated the other day, in private conversation with the Duc D'Aumale, that he thought we should conquer the South in the end. If he thinks so he surely won't countenance interference. And if the Ministry are firm, we are safe.

Parliament will bring society, and this I dread. The son of the American Minister is likely to meet with precious little favorable criticism in London society in these days, and, after all, I'm very little of a society man. I do not mean to press myself on this quarter, but rather to avoid notice and be all the more active where no one sees me. I can't do much, but I think I can make myself of some use.

I was surprised to hear that you were to go to Port Royal. I can't conceive of your being placed there except for service, but I should guess that at least half your regiment would be more likely to break their own necks than to hurt an enemy in a battle. If you see the correspondent of the London Star there, a youth named Edge, pray make his acquaintance and tell him that Moran, Wilson and I are all particularly anxious to know whether *that* travelling suit is worn out yet, or the telescope used up. He is not a bad fellow, though rather long-winded, and his employers are warm allies of ours here with great influence. They like his letters, as we all do, but wish there were more of them and longer. At last accounts he was doing the fever and toping on quinine. I hope you will forswear that luxury, not uncommon, it appears, in that neighborhood.

We are dreading the next news. I hardly dare think of a battle and we all are tacitly agreed not to talk about it. I am sorry to say that our advices are not quite so satisfactory as we would like. But the darkest hour before the dawn. . . .

CHARLES FRANCIS ADAMS, JR., TO HIS MOTHER

Beaufort, S.C., February 2, 1862

. . . .

I WAS then in the delicious doubt of our first picket detail which I was to command. After all it did n't come to much and the only danger I had to face arose from the terror of my own horses at the sight of the sabres of my men and at the dulcet sounds of the band at guard mounting. Lord! what a time I had, and for an instant your son proved himself a trooper in profanity at least. But imagine the feelings of a young officer leading the first detail of his regiment ever seen at a public parade on seeing his men and horses go shooting over the field in all directions like squibs on the 4th of July. With stern decision I at once disgraced and sent home two horses and their riders and paraded the rest in style, marching them in review in a way which almost restored our honor. Then I escorted the officer of the day to his post and stationed my details and then visited the outposts.

We are all alone on an island here, and on its shores our pickets stand and gaze placidly at the pickets of the enemy on the shore opposite. About three times a week one party or the other try to cross in boats and get fired at, but no one ever seems to be hurt and so the danger is apparently not alarming. I visited our furthest pickets and found them on Barnwell's Island at the house of Mr. Trescot, the author of whom we have heard. It is n't a pleasant picture, this result of war. Here was a new house on a beautiful island and surrounded with magnificent cotton fields, built evidently by a gentleman of refinement and very recently, and there was the garden before it filled with rubbish, and within broken furniture, scraps of books and letters, and all the little tokens of a refined family. Scattered over the floors and piled in the corners were the remains of a fine library of books of many languages, and panels and glasses were broken wherever so doing was thought an easier course than to unlock or open. I wandered round and looked out at the view and wondered why this people had brought all this upon themselves; and yet I could n't but pity them. For I thought how I should feel to see such sights at Quincy. . . .

HENRY ADAMS TO CHARLES FRANCIS ADAMS, JR.

London, February 14, 1862

Good morrow, 't is St. Valentine's day
All in the morning betime.
And I a maid at your window
To be your Valentine.

HAIL, noble lieutenant! I have received your letter written on board ship, and I am with you. Now that you are at work, if you see or do anything or hear something that will make a good letter to be published, send it to me and I think I can promise that it shall see the light. Thus you can do double work, and if you write well, perhaps you can get double pay. I shall exercise my discretion as to omissions. . . .

You find fault with my desponding tone of mind. So do I. But the evil is one that probably lies where I can't get at it. I've disappointed myself, and experi-

JOHN BRIGHT

ence the curious sensation of discovering myself to be a humbug. How is this possible? Do you understand how, without a double personality, *I* can feel that *I* am a failure? One would think that the *I* which could feel that, must be a different *ego* from the *I* of which it is felt.

You are so fortunate as to be able to forget self-contemplation in action, I suppose; but with me, my most efficient channels of action are now cut off, and I am busy in creating new ones, which is a matter that demands much time and even then may not meet with success.

Politically there is no news here. We shall be allowed to fight our battle out, I think; at least for some time yet. Parliament has met and the speeches have been very favorable to neutrality. I think our work here is past its crisis. The insurgents will receive no aid from Europe, and so far are beaten. Our victory is won on this side the water. On your side I hope it will soon be so too. . . . John Bright is my favorite Englishman. He is very pleasant, cheerful and courageous and much more sanguine than I have usually been. . . .

CHARLES FRANCIS ADAMS TO HIS SON

London, February 21, 1862

. . . .

OF course if you remain on the island there can be little use for your arm of the service, so I presume you may be employed mainly in the labor of the manège. And even if on the mainland I cannot well conceive what business you can have in a region so sparsely settled with whites and with few elements of aptitude for military operations. Neither Savannah nor Charleston can be taken by cavalry, and apart from these ports what is there in that country important to the object of the war?

To be sure you may individually obtain much insight into the economy of that densely populated slave region, and thus reinforce your means of speculating on the cotton producing theory. If so, I should very well like to see the conclusions to which you may come. To me at this distance it looks very much as if the slave tenure must be irreparably damaged by the social convulsion through which the country is passing, but I confess myself puzzled to see what is likely to take its place. I learn that some letters reach here from Carolina planters declaring that they are utterly ruined. The end to them may then be emigration. And what then? Is it a community of negroes requiring to be taught the very rudiments of social and political economy? . . .

The Trent affair has proved thus far somewhat in the nature of a sharp thunderstorm which has burst without doing any harm, and the consequence has been a decided improvement of the state of the atmosphere. Our English friends are pleased with themselves and pleased with us for having given them the opportunity to be so. The natural effect is to reduce the apparent dimensions of all other causes of offense. The Manchester people are patient and uncomplaining. The distress is not yet of such a kind as to give rise to much uneasiness, and the blockade shuts up the expectation of cotton enough to stimulate the prospect of production in other quarters, so that England shall not be again subject to a similar catastrophe. In the meantime industry naturally seeks new channels, and emigration affords a steady outlet. So that I am now quite encouraged to think that the prospect of interference with us is growing more and more remote. All that I have ever sought for has been the opportunity of developing our policy of repression. At first I confess I had little confidence in its success. But of late I have been thinking better and better of it. And it seems to me that the same impression is growing all around me. . . . The struggle is a tremendous one, and must not be measured hastily. I pity the people of the southern states, but I have no mercy for their profligate leaders, who have wantonly brought them to such a catastrophe.

CHARLES FRANCIS ADAMS, JR., TO HIS FATHER

Beaufort, S.C., February 28, 1862

. . . .

MY life here is very charming and pleasant, but is growing monotonous. I dread the idea of being here much longer, though any change is almost certain to be for the worse and the sameness of stable-duty, drill and camp life is telling on all of us. A prettier place than Beaufort would be hard to find, and a finer climate I do not want to see; but nothing marks the days as they pass, and few know less of the progress of the war than we, in the heart of South Carolina and in sight of the enemy's pickets. How long this will last we can't tell, but I fear for a good while; for there are no signs of real activity here, and now we all feel a desire to soon leave this Capua for the free, changing life of Tennessee, Missouri or even Texas. Nothing, I fear, but foreign intervention will get us out of this, however, and I imagine our destiny is either to fight at home against England and France or to march into Charleston.

Meanwhile I am very well and very comfortable, save in some respects of position with which I will not trouble you and which will cure themselves. To us it is now more of a picnic than war, and I live in as much luxury almost in my tent as I ever did at home. We are all very well and as brown and dirty as nuts, and I have never enjoyed life more than in the army. In fact, my college days seem to have come back to me, but bereft of most of their cares. I have been doing a good deal of detailed duty and have pretty thoroughly explored this island and last week they made me Judge Advocate to a Court of Inquiry, and these give quite a variety to life and took me away effectually from certain annoyances of my camp life; but they've found me out now and I'm steadily kept here, while my pleasant rides and expectations have come to an end. Socially also things are extremely agreeable here. Colonel Sargent is in immediate command and recent experiences have made me feel as if walled in with friends. My tentmate, Davis, is the very man I need and it is generally supposed in camp that he is a sort of nurse and guardian for me and that without his fostering care I should be a tentless wanderer. In fact my family will be pleased to know that my announcement that at home I had always been considered rather an old Betty was received with shouts of derision, and in camp here, in all matters of comfort, I enjoy the reputation of being the most careless, shiftless and slipshod devil in the whole battalion. Still I get on well enough, but I do not grow here, or, rather, should not long. The life and experience will have its uses for me and they will be great, but it is not the life for me for a permanency. The mind is perfectly fallow. . . .

CHARLES FRANCIS ADAMS, JR., TO HIS FATHER

Beaufort, S.C., March 11, 1862

. . . .

WHAT I see here only confirms my previous impressions gathered mainly from Olmsted and developed in the articles I wrote for the Independent. We can do nothing for these people until the cotton monopoly is broken down and a new state of political economy forces the cotton producer here to employ a new and cheaper machinery. Edward Pierce arrived here on Sunday in command of forty missionaries. They had better have kept away; things are not ripe for them yet and they are trying to force the course of nature. Yet the problem is a difficult one. We have now some 7000 masterless slaves within our line and in less than two months we shall have nearer 70,000, and what are we to do with them? I have not thought sufficiently to express an opinion. My present impression is in favor of a semi-military system for the present. Dis-

trict the territory, oblige the young to go to school,
punish rigidly all thieving and violence, and then teach
them all the first great lesson, that they must work to
live; establish low wages and let the blacks support
themselves or starve. If they choose to live in their
own huts and cultivate their own land and so support
themselves I see no objection, if the young went to
school; but the first lesson must be work or starve.
These blacks will not starve. They are just such as the
white has made them and as we have heard them described.
They are intelligent enough, but their intelligence
too often takes the form of low cunning. They
lie and steal and are fearfully lazy; but they will work
for money and indeed are anxious to get work. They
are dreadful hypocrites and tomorrow would say to
their masters, as a rule, what today they say to us.
As a whole my conclusion is that the race might be
devoted, if man were what he should be; but he being
what he is, it will be destroyed the moment the world
realises what a field for white emigration the South
affords. The inferior will disappear — how no man can
tell — before the more vigorous race. The world has
seen this happen before many times and this, though
the newest, will not be the last instance. This war,
I think, begins the new era from which, while freedom
has much, the African has little to hope. . . .

Some things in your letters filled me with astonishment
and laughter. First and foremost among them
was the idea of your new intimacy with Thurlow
Weed — Thurlow of the unopened letter, Thurlow the
unforgiving and corrupt, coming at this very time

when the star of the injured Sumner — Sumner the philanthropist, the persecuted and the beaten — was no longer in the ascendant. Verily politics does give and take strange bed-fellows, and to find you working heart and hand with Weed, advising with him, confiding in him and believing in him, is something I did not dream to see. I am glad of it. The devil is not indeed so black as he is painted, and in this I think I see the last link needed in a political alliance — a Puritan and New York political confederacy — destined to be potent for good in the affairs of this Continent. Surely never did we need that all motives and all faculties should work together as we do now, and I hope lead and pestilence will spare me to do what I may as a member of the new league. . . .

HENRY ADAMS TO CHARLES FRANCIS ADAMS, JR.

London, March 15, 1862

TIMES have so decidedly changed since my last letter to you, which was, as I conceive, about three weeks or a month ago, that I hardly know what to write about. My main doubt is about your prospects. I see no reason why Davis and his whole army should n't be shut up and forced to capitulate in Virginia. If so, you will be spared a summer campaign. But if he is allowed to escape, I shall be disgusted, and God only knows what work may be before you.

Meanwhile it worries me all the time to be leading this thoroughly useless life abroad while you are acting such grand parts at home. You would be astonished at the change of opinion which has taken place here already. Even the Times only this morning says: "The very idea of such a war is American, multitudinous, vast, and as much an appeal to the imagination as the actual brunt of arms." And again in speaking of the tone of the Southern papers it says in a striking way: "Some of their expressions recall those in which the Roman historians of the later Empire spoke of the Northern tribes." The truth is, as our swarm of armies strike deeper and deeper into the South, the contest is beginning to take to Europeans proportions of grandeur and perfection like nothing of which they ever heard or read. They call us insane to attempt what, when achieved, they are almost afraid to appreciate. A few brilliant victories, a short campaign of ten days or a fortnight, rivalling in its vigor and results those of Napoleon, has positively startled this country into utter confusion. It reminds me of my old host in Dresden, who, when he heard of the battle of Magenta, rushed into my room, newspaper in hand, and began measuring on the map the distance from the Ticino to Vienna. The English on hearing of Fort Donnelson and the fall of Nashville, seem to think our dozen armies are already over the St. Lawrence and at the gates of Quebec. They don't conceal their apprehensions and if we go on in this way, they will be as humiliated as the South itself. The talk of intervention, only two months ago so loud as to take a semiofficial tone, is now out of the minds of everyone. I heard Gregory make his long-expected speech in the House of Commons, and it was listened to as you would listen to a funeral eulogy. His attacks on us, on

Seward and on our blockade were cheered with just enough energy to show the animus that existed in a large proportion of the members, but his motion, a simple and harmless request for papers, was tossed aside without a division. I saw our friend Mason on the opposite side of the House to where I was sitting with Thurlow Weed. He is unlucky. One of the Bishops who happened to have come in and was seated near the door, heard a "Hear! hear!" behind him, and looking round saw Mason. For a stranger to cheer is a breach of privilege, and the story went all over town creating quite a row. Mr. Mason now denies it, I am told, and says it was some one else who cheered. He maintains now that the South always expected to lose the border States and that now that they are retiring to the cotton region the war has just begun. He coolly talks this stuff to the English people as if they had n't always asserted that the border States were a vital point with them. We on the other hand, no longer descend to argue such stories, or to answer the new class of lies; but smile blandly and compassionately on those who swallow them and remark that so far as advised, the nation whom we have the honor to represent is satisfied with the progress thus far made, and sees no reason to doubt that the Union will be maintained in its fullest and most comprehensive meaning.

The blockade is now universally acknowledged to be unobjectionable. Recognition, intervention, is an old song. No one whispers it. But the navy that captured Port Royal, Roanoke and Fort Henry, and that is flying about with its big guns up all the rivers and creeks of the South, is talked of with respect. And the legion of armies that are winning victory after victory on every side, until we have begun to complain if a steamer arrives without announcing the defeat of some enemy, or the occupation of some city, or the capture of some stronghold, are a cause of study to the English such as they've not had since Napoleon entered Milan some seventy years ago. I feel like a King now. I assert my nationality with a quiet pugnacity that tells. No one treads on our coattails any longer, and I do not expect ever to see again the old days of anxiety and humiliation. . . .

CHARLES FRANCIS ADAMS TO HIS SON

London, March 21, 1862

. . . .

NOWHERE has the condition of the western campaign been productive of better effects than in this country. The change produced in the tone towards the United States is very striking. There will be no overt acts tending to recognition whilst there is a doubt of the issue. It is nevertheless equally true that whatever ability remains to continue the contest is materially aided by the supplies constantly and industriously furnished from here. Every effort to run the blockade is made under British protection. Every manifestation of sympathy with the rebel success springs from British sources. This feeling is not the popular feeling, but it is that of the governing classes. With many honorable exceptions the aristocracy entertain it as well as the commercial interest. So did they in 1774. So did they in 1812. So will they ever, when their narrow views of British interests predominate. . . .

CHARLES FRANCIS ADAMS TO HIS SON

London, April 4, 1862

. . . .

THE late military successes have given us a season of repose. People are changing their notions of the power of the country to meet such a trial, which is attended with quite favorable consequences to us in our position. Our diplomacy is almost in a state of profound calm. Even the favorite idea of a division into two states is less put forward than it was. Yet the interest with which the struggle is witnessed grows deeper and deeper. The battle between the Merrimack and our vessels has been the main talk of the town ever since the news came, in Parliament, in the clubs, in the city, among the military and naval people. The impression is that it dates the commencement of a new era in warfare, and that Great Britain must consent to begin over again. I think the effect is to diminish the confidence in the result of hostilities with us. In December we were told that we should be swept from the ocean in a moment, and all our ports would be taken. They do not talk so now. So far as this may have an effect to secure peace on both sides it is good. . . .

We are much encouraged now by the series of successes gained, and far more by the marked indications of exhaustion and discouragement in the south. They must be suffering in every way. Never did people pay such a penalty for their madness. And the worst is yet to come. For emancipation is on its way with slow but certain pace. Well for them if it do not take them unaware.

CHARLES FRANCIS ADAMS, JR., TO HENRY ADAMS

*Milne Plantation, Port Royal Island
Monday, April 6, 1862*

YOURS of the 14th of February reminds me of our long interrupted correspondence. My last to you, if I remember right, was from on shipboard nearly three months ago, and was of a savage tenor. This is from an old South Carolina plantation, the headquarters of our cavalry pickets, and is likely to be of an eminently pacific tone. Here I am surrounded by troopers, missionaries, contrabands, cotton fields and serpents, in a summer climate, riding immensely every day, dreadfully sick of the monotony of my present existence, disgusted with all things military and fighting off malaria with whiskey and tobacco. So far, the island of Port Royal is a small Paradise, and no men were ever so fortunate in the inception of a military career, barring the immense labor of organizing such a regiment as this and our peculiarly rigid discipline, than we have been. So far our privations have been next to nothing and our career has been more that of a winter picnic than anything else. The future I fear has less agreeable things in store for us. Still sweets cloy, and drilling in a South Carolina cotton field hour after hour daily for weeks in succession is one of those sweets which cloy early. Perpetual roll-calls too become tiresome, and the daily superintendence of the grooming of eighty-five horses is not a pleasant phase of existence. I make no objection however to my duties, though I do to my superiors. But all in the fullness of time, and when you next see me you probably won't know me.

Just now I am on picket and also specially detailed by General Stevens to build a road, which I had the rashness to recommend in a report the other day. So this morning I diversified my cavalry pursuits by driving a gang of niggers on my new road, which connects the sea board plantations. You would n't have known me. I had ten slaves and drove by example. My horse was tied to a tree and my pistols and coat lay near him, while I, in heavy boots and spurs and my shirt sleeves, handled a spade by the side of my sable brethren in the midst of a combination of rice-field and cotton swamp, while my sergeant, axe in hand, headed another gang in clearing away underbrush. I am happy to say such energy was not unrewarded, as I succeeded in connecting and repairing three miles of road in one day instead of two, as I calculated. I am happy to say the Africs worked well and spared me much prepared execration; but from personal experience I am qualified to assert, that an African has about as much idea of a shovel and its uses as a wild Irishman might have of a quadrant or a cotton-hoe. My work however was completed at two o'clock and I then indulged in a delicious sea bath, declared myself a half holiday and determined to devote it to you. . . .

You and his Excellency always ask for my impressions of things here and, though I have sent them to him in little, I will enlarge them to you here and you may do with them as you see fit, only don't publish unless my views are likely to enliven the English.

Here I am on the Milne Plantation in the heart of Port Royal Island. Cotton fields, pine barrens, contrabands, missionaries and soldiers are before me and all around me. A sick missionary is in the next room, a dozen soldiers are eating their suppers in the yard under my window and some twenty negroes of every age, lazy, submissive and as the white man has made them, are hanging about the plantation buildings just as though they were not the *teterrima causa* of this consuming *bella*. The island is now just passing into its last stage of spring. The nights are cool, but the days are hot enough to make the saddle no seat of comfort. The island, naturally one of the most delightful places in the world, is just now at its most delightful season. The brown unhappy wastes of cotton fields unplanted this year and with the ragged remnants of last years crop, still fluttering in the wind, do not add to its beauty, but nothing can destroy the charm of the long plantation avenues with the heavy grey moss drooping from branches fresh with young leaves, while the natural hedges for miles along are fragrant with wild flowers. As I canter along these never ending avenues I hear sounds and see sights enough to set the ornithologist and sportsman crazy. The mocking-bird is never silent, and the varieties of plumage are to the uninitiated infinite, while hares and grey squirrels seem to start up under your horse's feet; wild pigeons and quail from every field, and duck and plover from every swamp. Nor are less inviting forms of animal life wanting, for snakes cross your path more frequently than hares and, even now, the soldiers under my window are amusing themselves with a large turtle, a small alligator and a serpent of curious beauty and most indubitable venom, a portion of the results of their afternoon's investigations.

One can ride indefinitely over this island and never exhaust its infinite cross-roads and out-of-the-way plantations, but you cannot ride fifteen minutes in any direction, however new, without stumbling over the two great facts of the day, pickets and contrabands. The pickets are recruits in active service without models — excellent material for soldiers and learning the trade, but scarcely soldiers yet. The contrabands were slaves yesterday and may be again tomorrow, and what slaves are any man may know without himself seeing who will take the trouble to read Olmsted's books. No man seems to realize that here, in this little island, all around us, has begun the solution of this tremendous "nigger" question.

The war here seems to rest and, for the present, Port Royal is thrown into the shade, and yet I am much mistaken if at this minute Port Royal is not a point of greater interest than either Virginia or Kentucky. Here the contraband question has arisen in such proportions that it has got to be met and the Government is meeting it as best it may. Some ten thousand *quondam* slaves are thrown upon the hands of an unfortunate Government; they are the forerunners of hundreds of thousands more, if the plans of the Government succeed, and so the Government may as well now decide what it will do in case of the success of its war plans. While Government has sent agents down here, private philanthropy has sent missionaries, and while the first see that the contrabands earn their bread, the last teach them the alphabet. Between the two I predict divers results, among which are numerous jobs for agents and missionaries, small comfort to the negroes and heavy loss to the Government. Doubtless the world must have cotton and must pay for it, but it does not yet know what it is to pay for it if the future hath it in store that the poor world shall buy the next crop of Port Royal at prices remunerative to Government. The scheme, so far as I can see any, seems to be for the Government, recognizing and encouraging private philanthropy and leaving to it the task of educating the slaves to the standard of self-support, to hold itself a sort of guardian to the slave in his indefinite state of transition, exacting from him that amount of labor which he owes to the community and the cotton market. The plan may work well; if it does, it will be the first of the kind that ever has. Certainly I do not envy the slaves its operation. The position of the Government is certainly a most difficult one. Something must be done for these poor people and done at once. They are indolent, shiftless, unable to take care of themselves and plundered by every comer — in short, they are slaves. For the present they must be provided for. It is easy to find fault with the present plan. Can any one suggest a better? For me, I must confess that I cannot. I think it bad, very bad, and that it must end in failure, but I can see no other more likely to succeed.

That this is the solution of the negro question I take it no one but the missionaries and agents will contend. That is yet to come, and here as elsewhere we are looking for it, and trying to influence it. My own impression is that the solution is coming — may already in some degree be shadowed out; but that it is a solution hurried on by this war, based on simple and immutable principles of economy and one finally over which the efforts of Government and individuals can exercise no control.

This war is killing slavery. Not by any legal quibble of contrabands or doubtful theory of confiscation, but by stimulating free trade. Let any man ride as I do over this island. Let him look at the cotton fields and the laborers. Let him handle their tools and examine their implements, and if he comes from any wheat-growing country, he will think himself amid the institutions and implements of the middle ages — and so he would be. The whole system of cotton growing — all its machinery from the slave to the hoe in his hand — is awkward, cumbrous, expensive and behind the age. That the cultivation of cotton is so behind that of all the other great staples is the natural result of monopoly, but it is none the less disgraceful to the world, and to give it an impulse seems to have been the mission of this war. The thorough and effectual breaking up of its so much prized monopoly will be the greatest blessing which could happen to the South, and it seems to be the one probable result of this war. Competition involves improvement in ruin, and herein lies the solution of this slavery question. Northern men with Northern ideas of economy, agriculture and improvement, are swarming down onto the South. They see how much behind the times the country is and they see that here is money to be made. If fair competition in the growth of cotton be once established a new system of economy and agriculture must inevitably be introduced here in which the slave and his hoe will make room for the free laborer and the plough, and the change will not be one of election but a sole resource against utter ruin. The men to introduce this change or any other are here and are daily swarming down in the armies of the Government, soon to become armies of occupation. A new tide of emigration has set in before which slavery has small chance.

But how is it for the African? Slavery may perish and no one regret it, but what is to become of the unfortunate African? When we have got thus far we have just arrived at the real point of interest in the "nigger" question. The slaves of whom I see so much here may be taken as fair specimens of their race as at present existing in this country. They have many good qualities. They are good tempered, patient, docile, willing to learn and easily directed; but they are slavish and all that the word slavish implies. They will lie and cheat and steal; they are hypocritical and cunning; they are not brave, and they are not fierce — these qualities the white man took out of them generations ago, and in taking them deprived the African of the capacity for freedom. My views of the future of those I see about me here are not therefore encouraging. That they will be free and free soon by the operation of economic laws over which Government has no control, I thoroughly believe; but their freedom will be the freedom of antiquated and unprofitable machines, the freedom of the hoes they use which will be swept aside to make way for better implements. The slave, however, cannot be swept aside and herein lies the difficulty and the problem. My impression from what I see is that Emancipation as a Government measure would be a terrible calamity to the blacks as a race; that rapid emancipation as the result of an economic revolution destroying their value as agricultural machines would be a calamity, though less severe; and finally, that the only transition to freedom absolutely beneficial to them as a race would be one proportioned in length to the length of their captivity, such a one in fact as destroyed villeinage in the wreck of the feudal system. Were men and governments what they should be instead of what they are, the case would be different and all would combine in the Christian and tedious effort to patiently undo the wrongs they had done, and to restore to the African his attributes. Then the work could be done well and quickly; but at present, seeing what men are, and how remorselessly they throw aside what has ceased to be useful, I cannot but regard as a doubtful benefit to the African anything which by diminishing his value increases his chances of freedom.

A revolution in cotton production springing from competition may work differently by gradually changing the *status* of the African from one of forced to one of free labor, but I do not regard this as probable. The census already shows not only that cotton can everywhere be cultivated by free labor, but also that the best cotton now is so cultivated, and the most probable result of a permanent reduction in the price of cotton would seem to me to be a sudden influx of free white emigration into the cotton fields of the South. Such a result would produce untold advantages to the South, to America and to the white race; but how about the blacks? Will they be educated and encouraged and cared for; or will they be challenged to compete in the race, or go to the wall, and finally be swept away as a useless rubbish? Who can answer those queries? I for one cannot; but one thing I daily see and that is that no spirit exists among the contrabands here which would enable them to care for themselves in a race of vigorous competition. The blacks must be cared for or they will perish, and who is to care for them when they cease to be of value? I do not pretend to solve these questions or do more than raise them, and their solution will come, I suppose, all in good time with the emergency which raises them. But no man who dreams at all of the future can wander over Port Royal Island at present and mark the character and condition of its inhabitants, without having all these questions and many more force themselves upon his mind. I am a thorough believer in this war. I believe it to have been necessary and just. I believe that from it will flow great blessings to America and the Caucasian race. I believe the area of freedom will by it be immensely expanded in this country, and that from it true principles of trade and economy will receive a prodigious impetus throughout the world; but for the African I do not see the same bright future. He is the foot-ball of passion and accident, and the gift of freedom may prove his destruction. Still the experiment should and must be tried and the sooner it is tried the better. . . .

HENRY ADAMS TO CHARLES FRANCIS ADAMS, JR.

London, April 11, 1862

. . . .

MODEST and unassuming as I am, you know, society is not the place for pleasure to me. Even at the Club I talk distantly with Counts and Barons and numberless untitled but high-placed characters, but have never arrived at intimacy with any of them. I am a little sorry for this because there are several very nice fellows among them, and all are polite and seem sufficiently social. Then, too, my unfortunate notoriety, which, I told you of, in a letter that I trust and pray may not be lost, some three months ago, tells against me, though it certainly has brought me into notice. I have no doubt that if I were to stay here another year, I should become extremely fond of the place and the life. There is, too, a certain grim satisfaction in the idea that this people who have worn and irritated and exasperated us for months, and among whom we have lived nearly a year of what was, till lately, a slow torture, should now be innocently dancing and smiling on the volcano, utterly unconscious of the extent of hatred and the greediness for revenge that they've raised. When the storm does finally burst on them, they will have one of their panics and be as astonished as if they'd never heard of anything but brotherly love and affection between the two nations. Of course it would be out of the question for me to hint at the state of things to them. I have only to smile and tell gross lies, for which God forgive me, about my feelings towards this country, and the kindness I have received here, which, between ourselves, so far as the pure English go, has been brilliantly conspicuous for its almost total absence. Only a fortnight ago they discovered that their whole wooden navy was useless; rather a weakness than a strength. Yesterday it was formally announced and acknowledged by Government, people and press, that the Warrior and their other new iron ships, are no better than wood, nor can any shot-proof sea-going vessel be made. In order to prove this, they've proved their Armstrong guns a failure, for he has given up the breech-loading system and been compelled to return to the old smooth-bore, muzzle-loader. So within three weeks, they find their wooden navy, their iron navy, and their costly guns, all utterly antiquated and useless.

To me, they seem to be bewildered by all this. I don't think as yet they have dared to look their position in the face. People begin to talk vaguely about the end of war and eternal peace, just as though human nature was changed by the fact that Great Britain's sea-power is knocked in the head. But for my private part, I think I see a thing or two. And one of these things is that the military power of France is nearly doubled by having the seas free; and that our good country the United States is left to a career that is positively unlimited except by the powers of the imagination. And for England there is still greatness and safety, if she will draw her colonies around her, and turn her hegemony into a Confederation of British nations.

You may think all this nonsense, but I tell you these are great times. Man has mounted science, and is now run away with. I firmly believe that before many centuries more, science will be the master of man. The engines he will have invented will be beyond his strength to control. Some day science may have the existence of mankind in its power, and the human race commit suicide by blowing up the world. Not only shall we be able to cruize in space, but I see no reason why some future generation should n't walk off like a beetle with the world on its back, or give it another rotary motion so that every zone should receive in turn its due portion of heat and light. . . .

We are putting on the diplomatic screws. A few more victories and it will be all straight. We understand that the Nashville has been taken or destroyed, and it is today telegraphed privately to us that the crew of the Sumter are to be paid off, and her captain is coming to London. Bankrupt. The long purse, the big guns, and the men carry the day. . . .

The Chief saw and conversed with a number of French celebrities. They are surprisingly well-disposed towards us now that we are looking up in the world. Here in London we are as comfortable as possible. The newspapers are dumb except for an occasional sneer, or assertion, which is invariably acknowledged to be false the next day. I tell you it's not a bad thing to have seven hundred thousand fighting men behind one, to back one's words up. I am more and more convinced every day that we are very much feared. Indeed you can imagine what the change must be when we all here know on the very highest authority that in May last it was supposed that the revolution was complete, and the recognition was a matter of course. Men who have made such a political blunder as that are apt to open their eyes wide when they find it out.

As for home affairs and your position, we are so ignorant that I shall not discourse on the subject. Of course we know all that the newspapers tell us and are waiting with a sort of feeling that is now chronic for the flash and the thunder that is soon to come from the cloud over Richmond and New Orleans. I despise a mail that does not tell of a victory, and indeed for some time past we have been pampered. But every time that the telegram comes and its yellow envelope is torn open, I feel much like taking a little brandy to strengthen me up to it. There is a nervous tremor about it that is hard to master. The 24th did well at Newbern. I wish to God I had been with it, or were with the Richmond army now. I feel ashamed and humiliated at leading this miserable life here, and since having been blown up by my own petard in my first effort to do good, I have n't even the hope of being of more use here than I should be in the army. But I can't get away till you come over. . . .

CHARLES FRANCIS ADAMS TO HIS SON

London, April 17, 1862

. . . .

THE successes, which I was so earnestly praying for in my letter to you, have come and have had all the effect I anticipated. There is just now nobody who professes to think well of the South. Neither will there be any more until the war varies. Of course, our position here becomes comparatively easy and comfortable. The quantity of official work has sensibly declined, and I can look round to interest myself in the scenes that are more immediately before me.

But just as the public work diminishes, as men cease to offer themselves as soldiers, or to propose all sorts of contracts for ships, cannon, rifles, and every imaginable death dealing invention, my correspondence has taken a wholly new direction. Good Mr. Peabody, having made more money than he can hold, takes it into his head to give to the poor of the city of London an endowment of a hundred and fifty thousand pounds. To carry out his idea he conveys the sum to five gentlemen, the minister of the United States being ex officio one of them. No sooner did my name appear in the papers than all the poor women of the city begin to pelt me with applications for aid, and all the useful societies present their claims for consideration. The consequence is that I bid fair to become the most widely known American envoy that ever came here, and furthermore that all the army of beggars in this great Babylon feel as if they had a special right to importune me. Such is fame! In the meantime the great question how the most beneficially to apply this enormous sum is about to be imposed upon us, and I am to bear one-fifth of the responsibility of a decision. Whichever way it is made the cry of the disappointed majority which expect a dividend of a sovereign apiece will be loud and long. I know not that I should take this view so coolly, if I did not feel that it cannot be long before I bid my friends here farewell, and devolve all cares as well as honors upon a successor. That successor will devolve all the odium of the action taken upon his predecessor, so that both will be safe; and again I shall exclaim, such is fame! . . .[1]

HENRY ADAMS TO CHARLES FRANCIS ADAMS, JR.

London, May 8, 1862

ONE always begins to doubt at the wrong time and to hesitate when one should strike hardest. Knowing this my infirmity, I have made it my habit here abroad to frown it down with energy and to persuade myself, when seeing most cause for anxiety, that the moment of suspense was nearest to its end. It needs to be here, among a people who read everything backwards that regards us, and surround us with a chaos of croaking worse than their own rookeries, to understand how hard it is always to retain one's confidence and faith. The late indecisive military events in America are looked upon here as the sign of ultimate Southern success. I preach a very different doctrine and

[1] Removed in April from 5 Mansfield Street to 5 Upper Portland Place, the house of Russell Sturgis.

NO. 5 UPPER PORTLAND PLACE, LONDON, OCCUPIED BY THE AMERICAN MINISTER

firmly believe that the war in its old phase is near its end. I do not see how anything but great awkwardness on our part can prevent the main southern army from being dispersed or captured in Virginia. But there is no doubt that the idea here is as strong as ever that we must ultimately fail, and unless a very few weeks show some great military result, we shall have our hands full again in this quarter. There is no fear of armed intervention, or even, I think, of immediate recognition; but a moral intervention is not impossible, or rather, it is inevitable without our triumph before July. By moral intervention I mean some combined representation on the part of the European powers, in friendly language, urging our two parties to come to an understanding. If this catches us still in Virginia, it will play mischief. The worst of it is that the Governments here are forced to it. The suffering among the people in Lancashire and in France is already very great and is increasing enormously every day without any prospect of relief for months to come. This drives them into action, and has at least the one good side that if we do gain decisive advantages so as to make the Southern chances indefinitely small, we shall have Europe at our control and can dictate terms.

On the other hand, if it is right to suppose that we shall soon end the war, I am afraid we have got to face a political struggle that will be the very deuce and all. The emancipation question has got to be settled somehow, and our accounts say that at Washington the contest is getting very bitter. The men who lead the extreme Abolitionists are a rancorous set. They have done their worst this winter to over-ride the Administration rough-shod, and it has needed all Seward's skill to head them off. If we are completely victorious in the field, we shall see the slave-question come up again worse than ever, and Sumner and Chandler and Trumbull and the rest are just the men to force a new explosion. Gradual measures don't suit them, and yet without their support it will be hard to carry gradual measures. I have immense confidence in Seward however, and there is said to be the most perfect confidence between him and the President, so that we shall go into the struggle with a good chance of carrying it through.

As for this country, the simple fact is that it is unanimously against us and becomes more firmly set every day. From hesitation and neutrality, people here are now fairly decided. It is acknowledged that our army is magnificent and that we have been successful and may be still more so, but the feeling is universal against us. If we succeed, it will still be the same. It is a sort of dogged, English prejudice, and there is no dealing with it.

Socially, however, we do not feel it to any unpleasant degree. People are very polite, and we seem to be in a good set and likely to get on well. The season has begun and we have engagements in plenty. I hope, with time, to get well into society, though just now I am hovering on the outskirts of it. My greatest achievement in this career came off the other night when we were invited to the old Dowager Duchess of Somerset's, who is decidedly original, and to my unutterable horror, I found myself performing for the first time in my life, a double-shuffle in the shape of a Scotch reel, with the daughter of an unbelieving Turk for a partner. For twenty minutes I improvised a dance that would have done honor to Taglioni. When I got through, in a state of helpless exhaustion and agony of mind, I was complimented by the company on my success.

Last night who should I meet at a little reception, but our friend Russell, the Special Correspondent of the London Times. Some one offered to introduce me to him and I consented with pleasure. He was a little embarrassed, I thought, but very good natured. I said I was sorry he had returned, whereat he laughed and remarked that personally he was glad, but he regretted having lost the chance of showing his goodwill to us by describing our successes. I only was with him a moment, and he closed the conversation by saying that if I thought it would be agreeable to my father, he would like to call upon him. I assented to this the more willingly because I am told that Russell declares on all sides that he is wholly a Northerner and always has been, and that between his private opinions and his opinions as suited to the doctrines of the Times, there is a decided difference.

I think it is about time for us now to begin to expect another breeze here in London and the usual panic and expectation of departure. If you were at home I should write particulars, but as I've never yet had one of my letters to you acknowledged or answered since you've been at Port Royal, and as I've written pretty regularly every fortnight, there's no great encouragement to trust secrets to paper. So much, however, is pretty well known. Since we made our great step from Kentucky into Alabama, our Government has been pressing the European Governments energetically to withdraw themselves from their belligerent position. But anyone who knows English sentiment and politics now, knows that there is not the remotest chance of any such step. The sympathy of the Administration, of the Lords, of the Commons and of the people throughout the country may be dormant perhaps; I hope it is, though I believe it's not; but beyond a doubt it is not with our Union. I have no fear that there will be any hostile acts on the part of this country, but before Parliament closes, which may be in June, you may be sure that the Ministry will do nothing that is likely to provoke attack; least of all anything so unpopular as the throwing over of the South would be. Meanwhile the contest between the two gentlemen here is getting to be flavored with as copious dashes of vinegar as you would wish to see. About once a week the wary Chieftain sharpens a stick down to a very sharp point, and then digs it into the excellent Russell's ribs. The first two or three times the joke was borne with well-bred politeness and calm indifference; but the truth is, the stick's becoming so sharp that now things are being thrown round with considerable energy, and our friend Russell is not in entirely a good temper. The prospect at this moment is that the breeze will soon change into settled rough weather and perhaps we shall have a regular storm. For if we conquer in Virginia, I hope and trust that Seward will give this

Government the option of eating their words, or being kicked. And I don't know whether I should derive a keener satisfaction from seeing them forced to overthrow their whole political fabric as regards the South, at our demand, or from seeing our Minister here take his leave of the country until they are able at last to bring their stomachs down to that point without further prompting. . . .

CHARLES FRANCIS ADAMS TO HIS SON

London, May 16, 1862

. . . .

PEOPLE here were quite struck aback at Sunday's news of the capture of New Orleans. It took them three days to make up their minds to believe it. The division of the United States had become an idea so fixed in their heads that they had shut out all the avenues to the reception of any other. As a consequence they are now all adrift. The American problem completely baffles their comprehension. The only wish I have is that they would let it alone. But strange to say, that is the very last thing to which they are inclined. Some future historian of ours may have an amusing task in extracting from the Times of the last year its daily varying prognostications on this subject. A friend of ours, Sir Charles Lyell, was sitting with your mother on Sunday when I came in, and remarking how frequently he had found the American news of the next day flatly contradicting the Times's affirmations at a given moment. "Now," said he, "last week they proved conclusively that the United

States could not control the Mississippi and seize New Orleans. I should not wonder if tomorrow's steamer were to show the contrary." And thereupon I showed him a telegram just received from Mr. Seward, by the steamer Canada, announcing the capture of that city. "There now," said he, "is it not just as I said?" Even the Americans here get soon impregnated with the spirit of doubt. It was not without difficulty that I could get some of them to credit that the Government of the United States was transmitting trustworthy information.

The Exhibition does not as yet draw such great crowds as were expected. Things are a little out of joint. The Queen secludes herself and does not get over her grief. The Prince of Wales is sent on his travels to get him out of the way. The ministry have no power in Parliament, and yet the opposition are afraid to take their places. Napoleon does not know what to do with the Pope. The King of Prussia does not know what to do with his subjects. Everything seems a little mal à propos and yet goes on somehow. Cotton goes, but does not come. The operatives are getting poorer and poorer, and yet there is so much capital in the city that interest is at two and one-half per cent. The country really seems to be rolling in wealth, and yet there are miserable beggars in rags assailing you at every corner. Such is a summary of European life so far as London is concerned. . . .

HENRY ADAMS TO CHARLES FRANCIS ADAMS, JR.

London, May 16, 1862

. . . .

BEFORE this reaches you I suppose you will be in motion, and I hope that the war will be at an end. It would be a mere piece of unjustifiable wantonness for the Southern generals to defend Charleston, if they are defeated in Virginia. So, although I would like to see you covered with glory, I would be extremely well satisfied to hear that you had ended the campaign and ridden into Charleston without firing a shot or drawing a sabre.

Last Sunday afternoon, the day after my letter to you had gone, telling how hard it was to sustain one's own convictions against the scepticism of a nation, I returned from taking a walk on Rotten Row with my very estimable friend Baron Brinken, and on reaching home, I was considerably astounded at perceiving the Chief in an excited manner dance across the entry and ejaculate, "We've got New Orleans." Philosopher as I am and constant in a just and tenacious virtue, I confess that even I was considerably interested for the moment. So leaving Sir Charles Lyell regarding my abrupt departure through one eye-glass with some apparent astonishment, I took a cab and drove down to Mr. Weed. Meeting him in the street near his hotel, I leaped out of the cab, and each of us simultaneously drew out a telegram which we exchanged. His was Mr. Peabody's private business telegram; mine was an official one from Seward. We then proceeded together to the telegraph office and sent a despatch to Mr. Dayton at Paris, and finally I went round to the Diplomatic Club and had the pleasure of enunciating my sentiments. Here my own agency ended, but Mr. Weed drank his cup of victory to the dregs. He spread the news in every direction, and finally sat down to dinner at the Reform Club with two sceptical old English friends of our side and had the pleasure of hearing the news-boys outside shout "Rumored capture of New Orleans" in an evening extra, while the news was posted at Brookes's, and the whole town was in immense excitement as though it were an English defeat.

Indeed the effect of the news here has been greater than anything yet. It has acted like a violent blow in the face on a drunken man. The next morning the Times came out and gave fairly in that it had been mistaken; it had believed Southern accounts and was deceived by them. This morning it has an article still more remarkable and intimates for the first time that it sees little more chance for the South. There is, we think, a preparation for withdrawing their belligerent declaration and acknowledging again the authority of the Federal Government over all the national territory, to be absolute and undisputed. One more victory will bring us up to this, I am confident. That done, I shall consider, not only that the nation has come through a struggle such as no other nation ever heard of, but in a smaller and personal point of view I shall feel much relieved and pleased at the successful career of the Chief.

You can judge of the probable effect of this last victory at New Orleans from the fact that friend Russell of the Times (who has not yet called) gravely warned the English nation yesterday of the magnificent army that had better be carefully watched by the English people, since it hated them like the devil and would want to have something to do. And last night I met Mr. John Bright at an evening reception, who seemed to feel somewhat in the same way. "Now," said he, "if you Americans succeed in getting over this affair, you must n't go and get stuffy to England. Because if you do, I don't know what's to become of us who stood up for you here." I did n't say we would n't, but I did tell him that *he* need n't be alarmed, for all he would have to do would be to come over to America and we would send him to Congress at once. He laughed and said he thought he had had about enough of that sort of thing in England. By the way, there is a story that he thinks of leaving Parliament.

This last week has been socially a quiet one and I have seen very little of the world, as I have no time to frequent the Club. I don't get ahead very fast in English society, because as yet I can't succeed in finding any one to introduce me among people of my own age. It's the same way with all the foreigners here, and a young Englishman, with whom I talked on the subject, comforted me by acknowledging the fact and saying that as a general thing young Englishmen were seldom intimate with any one unless they had known him three or four years. He gave a practical illustration of the principle by never recognizing me since, although we sat next each other three hours at a dinner and talked all the time, besides drinking various bottles of claret. With the foreigners I do much better, but they are generally worse off than I am in society. Except for a sort of conscientious feeling, I should care little for not knowing people at balls, especially as all accounts, especially English, declare young society to be a frantic bore. . . .

Now as to your letter and its contents on the negro question. I've not published it for two reasons. The first is that the tendency here now is pro-slavery and the sympathy with the South is so great as to seek justification in everything. Your view of the case, however anti-slavery, is not encouraging nor does it tend to strengthen our case. If published, especially if by any accident known to be by you, it might be used to annoy us with effect.

My second reason, though this alone would not have decided me, is that it seems to me you are a little needlessly dark in your anticipations. One thing is certain; labor in America is dear and will remain so; American cotton will always command a premium over any other yet known; and can be most easily produced. Emancipation cannot be instantaneous. We must rather found free colonies in the south such as you are now engaged in building up at Port Royal; the nucleus of which must be military and naval stations garrisoned by *corps d'armée*, and grouped around them must be the *emeriti*, the old soldiers with their grants of lands, their families, their schools, churches and Northern energy, forming common cause with the negroes in gradually sapping the strength of the slave-holders, and thus year after year carrying new industry and free institutions until their borders meet from the Atlantic, the Gulf, the Mississippi and the Tennessee in a common center, and the old crime shall be expiated and the whole social system of the South reconstructed. Such was the system of the old Romans with their conquered countries and it was always successful. It is the only means by which we can insure our hold on the South and plant colonies that are certain of success. It must be a military system of colonies, governed by the Executive and without any dependence upon or relation to the States in which they happen to be placed. With such a system I would allow fifty years for the South to become ten times as great and powerful and loyal as she ever was, besides being free.

Such are my ideas and as the negroes would be extremely valuable and even necessary to the development of these colonies, or the Southern resources at I trust they will manage to have a career yet.

CHARLES FRANCIS ADAMS TO HIS SON

London, May 20, 1862

. . . .

IT has rained every day at some time in the day for eight or ten days. People begin to look dismal and croak about the crops. To Great Britain every day of sunshine lost is equal to an expense of just so many thousand pounds. The islands never produce breadstuffs sufficient for the consumption of the people annually. They must beg some millions of quarters of wheat at any rate. In bad years they buy just so much more. Hence it is that at this season every bad day sensibly affects the price of stocks. No country ever had a more sensitive thermometer of the weather. But if this be true in ordinary times, how much more so in this season. The supply of cotton is rapidly and steadily declining. And the poor operatives of Lancashire are coming nearer and nearer to the time of starvation for want of work. If upon the top of this there should come a dearth of bread, it is not difficult to understand the extent of the social distress that may ensue. So there are miseries quite as acute as those of war which now afflict us.

In the meanwhile things are looking better rather than worse with us. The game of secession looks as if it might be nearly played out. The country is just putting forth its power whilst the rebel armies are gasping for breath. I have been here now more than a year, during which time I have gone through nearly every variety of emotion in connection with this war. The time is approaching, I trust, when this anxiety will disappear, and with it the uncertainty of my own situation. Doubtless others may succeed, of an equally serious nature. We shall have upon us the dangerous and critical task of restoration of the civil and a diminution of the military power. All this is very likely. But at any rate that condition presents a different face to external nations. It does not materially impair the entireness of the national position. I shall therefore accept the transition with cheerfulness and accommodate myself to the new state with more cheerfulness than to the old. . . .

HENRY ADAMS TO CHARLES FRANCIS ADAMS, JR.

London, May 22, 1862

WE are still in great anxiety to know the results of the Yorktown business, having as yet arrived only as far as Williamsburg and West Point. On McClellan's success in dispersing the Southern army and capturing all the means for carrying on a war will depend more than I like to think of. If we can disperse them, too, we can immediately reduce our army one-half, and all our expenses on the same scale. I dread the continuance of this war and its demoralizing effects more than anything else, and happy would be the day when we could see the first sign of returning peace. It's likely to be hard enough work to keep our people educated and honest anyway, and the accounts that reach us of the wholesale demoralization in the army of the west from camp-life, and of their dirt, and whiskey and general repulsiveness, are not encouraging to one who wants to see them taught to give up that blackguard habit of drinking liquor in bar-rooms, to brush their teeth and hands and wear clean clothes, and to believe that they have a duty in life besides that of getting ahead, and a responsibility for other people's acts as well as their own. The little weaknesses I speak of are faults of youth; but what will they become if America in its youth takes a permanent course towards every kind of idleness, vice and ignorance?

As for our position here, it is all that could be wished. Everyone congratulates us on the success of our arms and there is no longer any hint at even a remonstrance, though there are questions between the Governments which in our bitter state of feeling may bring difficulty. I am very anxious to avoid anything of this sort. We must have peace for many years if we are to heal our wounds and put the country on the right track. We must bring back or create a respect for law and order and the Constitution and the civil and judicial authorities. The nation has been dragged by this infernal cotton that had better have been burning in Hell, far away from its true course, and its worst passions and tastes have been developed by a forced and bloated growth. It will depend on the generation to which you and I belong, whether the country is to be brought back to its true course and the New England element is to carry the victory, or whether we are to be carried on from war to war and debt to debt and one military leader to another, till we lose all our landmarks and go ahead like France with a mere blind necessity to get on, without a reason or a principle. No more wars. Let's have peace, for the love of God.

England will truckle to us low enough when we regain our power, and we can easily revenge ourselves on the classes of English who have been most venemous, without fighting them all. It is but to shut out their trade and encourage our own development. I am now a protectionist of the most rabid description. I want to see us developing our mines, manufactures and communications, with the most success possible. There is England's vulnerable point; but we shall have committed a blunder of the worst sort if we allow our personal prejudices to affect our national policy to the extent of a war. . . .

The last week we have had that whited sepulchre General Cameron here, and as we were to have our first large dinner on Wednesday, he was invited to it. Then last night I took him to Monckton Milnes, where he was the object of considerable interest. I can't say that I was proud of my charge, nor that I like his style. Thurlow Weed is quite as American, and un-English, but is very popular and altogether infinitely preferable. We all like Mr. Weed very much, and are sorry that he is going home this week. As for Cameron, I hope he will vanish into the steppes of Russia and wander there for eternity. He is of all my countrymen one of the class that I most conspicuously and sincerely despise and detest. . . .

HENRY ADAMS TO CHARLES FRANCIS ADAMS, JR.

London, June 6, 1862

. . . .

THE evening before the Derby, the Chief and I were down at the House of Commons from five o'clock P.M. till one A.M., listening to the great debate of the season. This is one of the sights that I enjoy most. With us debate has gone out, and set speeches and personalities have taken its place. But here, though they no longer speak as they used in the old days of Pitt and Fox, with rhetorical effort and energy, there is still admirable debating. That night we heard Palmerston, Disraeli, Horsman and Cobden. Palmerston is a poor speaker, wants fluency and power, and talks the most miserable sophistry, but he does it so amusingly and plausibly and has such prestige that even Disraeli's keenness puts no quencher on him. Gladstone is the best speaker in the house, but next to him I should place Disraeli. He looks precisely like the pictures in Punch, and speaks with a power of making hits that is infinitely amusing. He kept me in a roar three quarters of an hour, and the House cheered him steadily. Cobden was very good too. He damaged Horsman dreadfully. But the most striking part of the debate was that not a word as to America or interference was said in it. This was peculiar because the debate was on the subject of retrenchment, and retrenchment was necessary because of the American war. Six months ago such a debate would not have taken place, but in its place we should have had war speeches with no end.

Our position here now, putting aside a few diplomatic questions, is much as it might be at home. The Speaker calls the Chief "The Conqueror," and it is only now and then, when our armies stop a moment to take breath, and they think here that we are in trouble, that the opposition raises its head a little and barks. Indeed the position we have here is one of a great deal of weight, and of course so long as our armies march forward, so long our hands are elevated higher and higher until we bump the stars. I hear very little about our friend Mason. He is said to be very anxious and to fear a rebellion within the rebellion. He has little or no attention paid him except as a matter of curiosity, though occasionally we are told of his being at dinner somewhere or other. A Southern newspaper called the Index lately started here, contains numbers of southern letters, all of which are so excruciatingly "never conquer" in their tone, that one is forced to the belief that they think themselves very near that last ditch. . . .

CHARLES FRANCIS ADAMS, JR., TO HIS FATHER

John's Island, S.C., June 18, 1862

YOURS of May 23d reached me here last night, keeping up the series of your weekly despatches. Whatever may happen to me in this war I assure you there has been no item in it which has touched me so much as this series of letters coming so regularly in spite of all you had to occupy your mind. They have not been answered as they should have been, but do not suppose that I have failed to appreciate them, or the great thoughtfulness which dictated them. This one found me well and in good spirits, and with two bulletins already sent to John and Louisa informing them of these facts, I had left it for them to notify you and given up the idea of writing myself, for writing here is no small effort; but as General Williams orders all of us to sit up all night, I am going to devote my two hours of dawn to you.

You have probably heard, through Southern sources and with their usual degree of truth, of the action yesterday and you may have been anxious for my safety, though I hope you were sufficiently ignorant of all the facts not to be apprehensive for me personally. The amount of the whole story is that we had a severe action and were repulsed with very heavy loss. This much you know; and for myself, General Williams' brigade was in the advance of one of the attacking columns, was under fire about four hours, during the whole of which time the danger of his men was fully shared by the General and his staff. I would not have missed it for anything. I had never been really under fire before and the sensation was glorious. There we were, mounted officers, either standing right before the enemy's works, while the shells went shrieking and hurtling just over our heads and sometimes broke close to us, or else carrying orders to all parts of the line, feeling that you carried life and death in your hands. I was frightened of course — every one is, except a few who don't know what danger is; but my fear was not what I had imagined it might be. My face was a little fixed I imagine. I knew that my nerves were a little braced, but my mind was never clearer or more easily made up on points of doubt, and altogether the machine worked with a vigor and power which, under the circumstances, I had never hoped it possessed. To all his staff, collectively and individually, General Williams has expressed the highest satisfaction, saying that he was perfectly satisfied and that a difficult and dangerous work could not have been better executed; and if you knew General Bob, and had seen how recklessly he exposed himself, and were aware how he does snub and how he does n't praise, you would allow that this was something. In a word I don't care if I'm never in action again, and I would rather not run its risk, though I should like once to join in the shouts of victory; but I would not for anything have lost the experience of yesterday and, without affectation, it was one of the most enjoyable days I ever passed.

GENERAL ROBERT WILLIAMS

I don't pretend to give you a history of the engagement. You will get that from the lying prints, and a very false one it will be; but being on the staff I saw all the Generals and all the movements. There was Benham, an old hen, cackling round, insulted by messages from angry Brigadiers sent through boyish aids, and he himself mainly anxious for cover, indecisive, and, many thought, frightened. There was Wright, a little excited at times but growing genial and kindly as the fire grew hot. There was your friend, Stevens, dirty and excited, but clear headed and full of fight, with a dirty straw hat on his head and his trousers above his knees from the friction of riding. And finally, there was handsome Bob Williams astride of his big horse, defiantly planted in front of the battery in open field, full of all sorts of humors — the long sabre hanging from the saddle-bow and his eyes beaming, sparkling and snapping according to the turn of the fight. In the hottest fire he grew genial and took the occasion of a shell splashing us with mud to tell me an old and not very good story. Then the retreat was ordered and he grew savage, though not to us; and finally I thought old Benham would have to put him under arrest, he treated him with such undisguised contempt. My rides round the battle field too were curious. Here was a long line of wounded men toiling to the rear, and the different ways in which they bore their wounds, from the coward limping off untouched to the plucky fellow with his leg hanging by the skin making faces that he might not yell. There were knots of men behind hedges and in the ditches, stragglers and cowards, men who could not be shamed to the front. To talk of the horrors of a battle field is a misnomer. The hospital is horrid and so are the stretchers and ambulances running blood; but in the heat of battle a corpse becomes a bundle of old clothes and you pass the most fearful wounds with a mere glance and without a thought.

There was nothing disgraceful in our repulse, and our retreat was a model of good order and regularity. The regiments when overcome retired in column in common step and with their colors flying and formed exactly where their officers ordered. There was no running, no panic, and I felt proud of New England as I saw the 3d N.H. coolly hold their position between two murderous fires. We should have whipped them dreadfully had they followed us. . . .

CHARLES FRANCIS ADAMS TO HIS SON

London, June 27, 1862

· · · · · · · · ·

BUT the main thing is now the issue at Richmond. At the latest dates things were getting uncomfortably close. McClellan was making his movements steadily and slowly until the choice only remained to attack at disadvantage or to move. In this case my impression is strong that the rebels will move. They did so at Manassas, and at Yorktown, at Williamsburg and at Corinth. Why not do so again? The only question is to know where to go to. Money is scarce, and confederate promises have lost what little credit they had. The means to feed and support great bodies of men are not so easily to be had from a country already pretty heavily drawn upon. My conclusion is that before long the attempt to keep a large army in the field must be abandoned, and that from that time hostilities will be continued by small bands who will sustain themselves by levies on the country. Such is the policy sketched out by Mr. Yancey in a letter to somebody here of which I have heard. The effect of this will doubtless be to complete the devastation and ruin which seems to be the fate of the slaveholding region. I scarcely see the good it will do to anybody. If cotton be not grown here, it will come from Surat and Bombay. In the meanwhile what are the slaves to do?

The cotton problem in England is becoming more and more serious. The stock has got down to about two hundred and fifty thousand bales, and there is a demand for export which is reducing it faster than was anticipated. At present it is calculated that by November there will be none left. Provided always that the slaveholders should be so foolish as to persevere in destroying it and themselves. It has seemed to me all along that they were mere suicides, and I believe it more firmly every day.

CHARLES FRANCIS ADAMS, JR., TO HIS FATHER

James Island, S.C., June 28, 1862

I RECEIVED yours of May 30th last week and it found me still here. Since then, however, the news of the engagement of the 16th has been carried home and today we receive the return blast from Washington. They tell us we are to see Charleston, but not now to enter it; that we are to go back to Hilton-head and generally to confess ourselves as out-generaled, while Benham is to be made the scape-goat for all our misfortunes — and the last is the only item of news which gives us any satisfaction. The army is a great place to learn philosophy, I find, and in it you not only get careless of danger, but indifferent as to what disposition is made of you. The enemy have again begun to shell us and yet I find I do not even any longer go to the door of my tent to see where and how their shells burst. And today, though under every circumstance I have looked on riding into Charleston as a sure and ample reward for all I might be called on to undergo, I hear that the chances are immense against *my* ever receiving that reward with an indifference which surprises me. I am ordered and I can't help it; though it seems strange to me that we must turn our backs on these fellows for lack of ten poor regiments out of the grand army of the republic. I do so know we could whip these men if we had two chances out of five, and we would so like to do it; and now to go back with nothing but failure — oh! for one hour of generalship!! Everything here but honor has been sacrificed to the fussy incompetence of Benham, the unmilitary amiability of Hunter, and the misplaced philanthropy of Edward L. Pierce. . . . Philanthropy is a nuisance in time of war and I sympathised somewhat with Governor Stanley. There are 3000 men at Beaufort in the service of philanthropy and tomorrow we turn our backs on Charleston because they are not here. What good is Beaufort to us? A gun-boat can take it any day. I respect the missionaries for their objects and perseverance, but they have no business here. Their time is not yet and they make us fight in fetters. . . .

General Williams has seen fit in a special order to his brigade to make honorable mention, among others, of each member of his staff by name. He also yesterday requested me in my next letter to you to mention *from him* his extreme satisfaction with my conduct in the action. . . .

CHARLES FRANCIS ADAMS TO HIS SON

London, July 4, 1862

. . . .

THIS detestable war is not of our own choosing, and out of it must grow consequences important to the welfare of coming generations, not likely to issue from a continuance of peace. All this is true, and yet here in this lonely position of prominence among a people selfish, jealous, and at heart hostile, it needs a good deal of fortitude to conjoin private solicitude with the unavoidable responsibilities of a critical public station. I had hoped that the progress of General McClellan would have spared us much of this trouble. But it is plain that he has much of the Fabian policy in his composition which threatens to draw the war into greater length. Of course we must be content to take a great deal on trust. Thus far the results have been all that we had a reasonable right to expect. Let us hope that the delay is not without its great purposes. My belief is unshaken that the end of this conflict is to topple down the edifice of slavery. Perhaps we are not yet ready to come up to that work, and the madness of the resistance is the instrument in the hands of Divine Providence to drive us to it. It may be so. I must hold my soul in patience, and pray for courage and resignation.

This is the 4th of July. Eighty-six years ago our ancestors staked themselves in a contest of a far more dangerous and desperate character. The only fault they committed was in omitting to make it more general and complete. Had they then consented to follow Thomas Jefferson to the full extent of his first draught of the Declaration, they would have added little to the seven years severity of their struggle and would have entirely saved the present trials from their children. I trust we shall not fall into any similar mistake, and if we are tempted to do so, I trust the follies of our enemy will avert from us the consequences of our weakness. This is the consideration which makes me most tolerant of the continuance of the war. I am not a friend of the violent policy of the ultras who seem to me to have no guide but their own theories. This great movement must be left in a degree to develope itself, and human power must be applied solely to shape the consequences so far as possible to the best uses. . . .

HENRY ADAMS TO CHARLES FRANCIS ADAMS, JR.

London, July 4, 1862

IT is some time since I last wrote. I have hardly had the courage to do so in the face of what is now going on at home, and today we hear news of a battle near

Charleston on the 16th which has done little to encourage me. Your last letter speaking of your illness and general position troubled our camp much. I had to pooh-pooh it more than I liked in order to stop the noise. Hard as your life is and threatens to become, I would like well to share it with you in order to escape in the consciousness of action a little of the struggle against fancied evils that we feel here.

The truth is we are suffering now under one of those periodical returns of anxiety and despondency that I have often written of. The last was succeeded by that brilliant series of successes which gave us New Orleans, Yorktown, Norfolk and Memphis, and perhaps this may end as well; but meanwhile we are haunted by stories about McClellan and by the strange want of life that seems justly or not to characterize our military and naval motions. You at Charleston seem to be an exception to the rule of stagnation which leaves us everywhere on the defensive even when attacking. A little dash does so much to raise one's spirits, and now our poor men only sicken in marshes. I think of it all as little as I can.

Our own position here is now so uninteresting as to give us nothing to think of. After some pretty sharp fighting and curious experiences that I dare n't trust to paper, we are again quiet and undisturbed, waiting the event of the struggle at Richmond. Things are not over-inspiriting with us, but I don't know that they look much brighter with the English or French. The suffering among the operatives in Lancashire is very great and is increasing in a scale that makes people very uncomfortable though as yet they keep quiet about it. Cotton is going up to extraordinary prices; in a few days only it advanced three cents a pound and is still rising. Prices for cotton goods are merely nominal and vary according to the opinions of the holders, so that the whole trade is now pure speculation. Mills are closing in every direction. Add to this that the season has been bad and a short crop is now considered a certainty, and you can comprehend how anxious people must be to know how they are to weather next winter. No doubt this state of things will soon produce fresh agitation for mediation or intervention before long if no progress is made by our armies, but as yet we enjoy quiet. . . .

If it were not for home matters it would be all well enough, but they have a good deal of influence here, which is felt rather than seen. We have entertained a good deal — evening receptions once a week for Americans, and several state dinners for English. . . .

CHARLES FRANCIS ADAMS, JR., TO HIS FATHER

Hilton Head, S.C., July 16, 1862

. . . .

MCCLELLAN'S reverses fell on us with sufficient weight here and 10,000 of our troops are being hurried to the north, destroying all chance of operations here and leaving only artillery to hold these points. For artillery and cavalry they say they do not need, so our poor regiment seems likely to go into garrison duty in the midst of active war, and that too when all the operations of the war in Virginia indicate the vital necessity of good cavalry and this regiment is here considered the best in our volunteer service. However personal considerations don't amount to much and I want to discuss the news and its effects. How do you look at this terrible fighting in Virginia? Not, I mean, in a military or even immediate point of view, but in its remote bearing on our country's future? For myself I must confess I begin to be frightened. The questions of the future seem to me too great for us to grapple with successfully and I have really begun to fear anarchy and disorganisation for years to come. If we succeed in our attempt at subjugation, I see only an immense territory and a savage and ignorant populace to be held down by force, the enigma of slavery to be settled by us somehow, right or wrong, and, most dangerous of all, a spirit of blind, revengeful fanaticism in the North, of which Sumner has come in my mind to be typical, which, utterly deficient in practical wisdom, will, if it can, force our country into any position — be it bankrupt, despotic, anarchical, or what not — in its blind efforts to destroy slavery and the South. These men, and they will always in troublous times obtain temporary supreme control, will bankrupt the nation, jeopard all liberty by immense standing armies, debauch the morality of the nation by war, and undermine all our republican foundations to effect the immediate destruction of the one institution of slavery. Do you not think that this is so? . . .

CHARLES FRANCIS ADAMS TO HIS SON

London, July 18, 1862

. . . .

You can have very little notion of the effect the Richmond news is having here. It has set all the elements of hostility to us in agitation, and they are working to carry the House of Commons off their feet in its debate tonight. To that end a story has been manufactured of an alleged capitulation of General McClellan on the third coming out by the Glasgow that sailed on the fifth, in the face of a later telegram dated the seventh, which reported his address to his army pledging himself to continue the war. Yet the people here are fully ready to credit anything that is not favorable. I have no doubt that the matter is bad enough, but it is not quite to that extent. Yet the consequences are likely to be as unfavorable as if it was. . . .

HENRY ADAMS TO CHARLES FRANCIS ADAMS, JR.

[*London,*] *Saturday, July* 19, 1862

KNOWING that you would probably be anxious to hear from us what effect the bad news of June 26–30 might have on our position here, I take the last moment to write in order to tell you what I think we are to expect. Certainly it was a violent blow. We suffered several days of very great anxiety, knowing that the current here was rising every hour and running harder against us than at any time since the Trent affair. This reverse called out at once all the latent hostility here, and there was nothing to do but to give way. I shut myself up, went to no more parties and avoided contact with everyone except friends. . . . The only bright spot in the week was the reception of your letter. As we had all relied on your being safe in the hospital, or if not there, with your regiment which we knew was not engaged, your letter was quite welcome, as it told us first both of your going in and your coming out. I congratulate you, and apropos to that, I congratulate your General Hunter on his negro-army letter. We *all* here sustain him and I assure you that the strongest means of holding Europe back is the sight of an effective black army.

Nevertheless our trouble here was extreme. As the week passed it was not diminished. Nor is it now, I fear, permanently so. It arrived however at its culminating point last night. It so happened that last night was the occasion of an expected debate in the Commons on a motion in favor of mediation. We had been busy in preparing for it and had assurances that all was right. But lo and behold, at two o'clock yesterday afternoon in rushes a member of the Commons, and half a dozen alarmists in his rear, with an evening paper whose telegraphic column was headed in big letters, "Capitulation of McClellan's Army. Flight of McClellan on a steamer. Later from America." This astounding news for a moment made me almost give way. But a single glance at dates showed us that it was an utter swindle, and that we had bulletins from McClellan of two days later than the day of the reported surrender. The next reflexion led us to see that it was intended for the debate of the same evening, and we, who know the seal, recognized the stamp of our old friends the Southern liars, who juggled Georgia out of the Union by telegraph. But the consternation among our friends was incredible and even when they knew it must be false, they still shook and shuddered with terror. Every Englishman believed it, or doubted in a tone that showed he wanted to believe it. As for me, I have come to consider it my whole duty here to keep up the spirits of the community and so did the best I could to laugh the lie off. Luckily its effect on the Commons was very good, for it disposed them to postpone action and tended to quiet them. Palmerston made a good speech, and the motion was not pressed to a division. This morning the Arabia's news has arrived, three days later, which relieves us again for a time of our anxiety, and induces us to believe that the enemy were as much crippled by their victory as we by our defeat.

Thus the pinch has again passed by for the moment and we breathe more freely. But I think I wrote to you some time ago that if July found us still in Virginia, we could no longer escape interference. I think now that it is inevitable. The only delay thus far has been caused by the difficulty in inducing the five great powers to unite, and Russia and Austria to act with England in any sense favorable to the South. That unity cannot much longer fail to be obtainable. England alone or with France will not move, but their idea is that if all the great powers were to unite in offering mediation, they could by their moral influence alone force some result. If the North defied them, a simple recognition of the South by them would, they think, secure her independence. And this belief is probably correct.

It must now be the effort of the North to cast upon the South the responsibility of standing against a settlement. Here will be three means of hampering European attempts: the slavery question, the boundary question, and the Mississippi; and it is the slavery question from which we can derive the greatest strength in this running battle. You see we are stripping and squaring off, to say nothing of sponging, for the next round. If our armies sustain us, we shall win. If not, we shall soon see the limit of our hopes.

CHARLES FRANCIS ADAMS, JR., TO HIS FATHER

Hilton Head, S.C., July 28, 1862

. . . .

I READ your 4th of July reflections with much interest and on part of them my last letter to you had bearing. Our ultra-friends, including General Hunter, seem to have gone crazy and they are doing the blacks all the harm they can. On this issue things are very bad. General Hunter is so carried away by his idea of negro regiments as, not only to write flippant letters about his one to Secretary Stanton, but even to order *their exemption* from *all* fatigue duty; so that while our Northern soldiers work ten hours a day in loading and unloading ships, the blacks never leave their camp, but confine their attention to drill. There may be reasons for this, but it creates intense feeling here and even I cannot see the justice of it. The course of Sumner, Wade, Stanton, etc., have ruined us, I fear, in the war, by making success subservient to their preconceived plans of negro good, instead of allowing the movement to develope itself. I no longer see anything but our ruin on our success, and no escape from it save in our defeat as to the ends of the war. Still I do not lose faith, but go into the future as cheerfully, if, in my own opinion, a little more blindly than heretofore. I liked the innuendoes in Hawthorne's article in the July Atlantic.

CHARLES FRANCIS ADAMS, JR., TO HENRY ADAMS

Hilton Head, S.C.
July 28, 1862

. . . .

THIS place is not at all the pestilential spot you all seem to suppose, and if you will convince yourself of that, you will all save yourselves a great deal of anxiety. The deaths here of all descriptions, arising from disease, wounds and accidents, are not more than six a week out of some 5000 men, which is about six per cent a year and that in the very heart of the summer. From this you will see that the station, however disagreeable, and General Williams says it's the most so he ever saw, certainly cannot be considered unhealthy. . . .

We get nothing new here. Col. Williams' nomination as Brigadier was among the unfinished business of Congress and so falls to the ground; but I shall act on his staff, though I expect very soon to return to the regiment, though not to my old company. . . . Ben Crowninshield is at home on furlough and at Sharon. . . . Lawrence Motley is really down sick, as also is Rand. Greely Curtis has also been on his back — all of them four times as sick as ——. Henry Higginson is acting in command of the regiment and more than a third of the officers are away sick or on detached duty. By way of variety our horses have the glanders and we have lost some forty and not yet succeeded in wholly getting rid of it. So we feel the necessity of some change, somehow.

General Hunter is very unpopular — arbitrary and wholly taken up with his negro question. His one regiment is a failure, and becoming more so, and I have no faith in the experiment anyhow. I smiled audibly at your idea of my taking a commission in one of them; after all my assertion of principles to become a "nigger driver" in my old age, for that is what it amounts to, seeing that they don't run away, or shirk work or fatigue duty. No! Hunter and you are all wrong, and, for once, the War Department was right. The negroes should be organized and officered as soldiers; they should have arms put in their hands and be drilled simply with a view to their moral elevation and the effect on their self-respect, and for the rest they should be *used* as fatigue parties and on all fatigue duty. As to being made soldiers, they are more harm than good. It will be years before they can be made to stand before their old masters, unless (and the exception means a great deal) some leader of their own, some Toussaint rises, who is one of them and inspires them with confidence. Under our system and with such white officers as we give them, we might make a soldiery equal to the native Hindoo regiments in about five years. It won't pay and the idea of arming the blacks *as soldiers* must be abandoned.

To my mind the ultras are doing all the harm they can and it is yet a question whether they will not save slavery out of this war, rather than let Providence work its destruction in ways other than those preconceived by them. I sincerely hope Sumner will be defeated in the fall election. As to the army, so far as I see it, it is completely demoralized on this question by the conduct of these men, and it makes me sick to hear New England men talk on the subject of the negroes here and all who would aid them. Such prejudice and narrow bigotry I never met in Southerners. There is no abolitionism or, I fear, even emancipation in the army here. The ultras in their eagerness have spoilt all. It is all right, you know, and for the best; but is n't it enough to make an equine laugh to see a man like Sumner, so convinced that he alone sees the clear way, so absolute in his opinions and wholly devoid of charity to others, withal such an utterly blind instrument in the hand of Providence. The plot thickens and I hope this war will spare me, as I don't want to die, until I see how all this turmoil, confusion and disaster, is, on pure philosophical principles, to result, as we know it will, in the advancement of the human kind. How much and how long must you and I suffer that that advancement may be worked out.

CHARLES FRANCIS ADAMS TO HIS SON

London, August 1, 1862

. . . .

WE have been much prejudiced here by the unfortunate turn things took at Richmond. It is impossible for a non-military man to form any judgment of the events of the campaign, but one thing seems to be certain, that General McClellan must have made some egregious miscalculation of the strength of his right wing. Otherwise the attack of Stuart could not have been successful. As to the future I dare not count upon anything. From this point I should hardly suppose that we had any forces left anywhere. The only accounts we get are of the multitudes on the other side. Our newspapers and quidnuncs delight in counting them with additions of many ciphers, until I am bound to infer that the census of 1860 is all a northern forgery, and that the slave states have had the fertility of the northern hordes that overran the Romans in the days of the lower Empire. So far as foreign countries are concerned I am very much of opinion that our press does more harm than good to our cause. It discloses all our own position, whilst it exaggerates that of the rebels of which it knows really nothing. As a consequence evil minded people here take every advantage of both practices, to our harm. . . .

If you are still with General Williams I beg you to express to him my thanks for his remembrance of me in the commendation he was disposed to give you. Nothing could have been more grateful to my feelings. Much as I deplore this unfortunate war, brought on by the infatuation of men who are only sealing their own fate in persevering in it, I see and admit the necessity which forces you to take your share in it. And such being the fact, it is consoling to me to reflect that you are doing your duty with credit and with honor. Should the time arrive when you are released in safety and with propriety I shall hail it with joy. Redeunt saturnia regna. In the meantime I look to the emancipation of the slaves as the veritable solution of the problem. After that is accomplished I care comparatively little what may be the determination of the southern states, or of their people. . . .

CHARLES FRANCIS ADAMS, JR., TO HIS FATHER

Hilton Head, S.C., August 10, 1862

. . . .

AFFAIRS here are as dull as dull can be. We have had a little excitement about your old friend the Fingal, which has turned up in Savannah harbor as an ironclad of much force, but that seems to be dying out now, though I can't help thinking that we shall some day hear from her when we least expect or desire to.

General Hunter's negro regiment was disbanded yesterday and now they have all dispersed to their old homes. Its breaking up was hailed here with great joy, for our troops have become more anti-negro than I could have imagined. But, for myself, I could not help feeling a strong regret at seeing the red-legged darkies march off; for, though I have long known that the experiment was a failure, yet it was the failure of another effort at the education of these poor people and it was the acknowledgment of another of those blunders which have distinguished all and every our experiments on slavery throughout this war. When did an educated people ever bungle so in the management of a great issue! I feel sick and almost discouraged at what I see and hear. What God made plain we have mixed up into inextricable confusion. We have had declarations of emancipation ingeniously framed so as not to free a slave and yet to thoroughly concentrate and inflame our enemy. We have wrangled over arming the slaves before the slaves showed any disposition to use the arms, and when we have never had in our lives 5000 of them who could bear arms. Why could not fanatics be silent and let Providence work for awhile. The slaves would have moved when the day came and could have been made useful in a thousand ways. As it is, we are Hamlet's ape, who broke his neck to try conclusions. . . .

CHARLES FRANCIS ADAMS, JR., TO HIS FATHER

At Sea, Steam Transport McClellan
August 22, 1862

HERE I am at sea once more and heading north, but not as I had hoped I might be going north about this time, leaving this conflict literally settled behind me, but only on my way to the dark and bloody ground in Virginia. Our regiment most unexpectedly received orders for the north one day last week at about the same time that I received my orders to report to General Pope. Accordingly I go north with them. As to my future, this unexpected change has set it all afloat. The war is evidently going to continue some time longer and my regiment is now going into active service. Is it wise for me now to separate myself from a Massachusetts regiment, and shall I not be more useful where I am than on an ornamental staff? These reflections puzzle me much and I do not know what will become of me. I shall try to decide for the best and I do know that we now seem to be going into the thick of the conflict. . . .

We left the shores of South Carolina on Wednesday last, just seven months to a day from the time when I first set foot on them. I don't think any of us felt much regret at leaving the State and certainly none of us at leaving Hilton Head. Of all the places it has ever been my fate to set foot on Hilton Head is by many degrees the meanest. Of Beaufort and Port Royal island I retain many pleasant memories, particularly of the last, than which I have never seen a more delightful island. But Hilton Head — dust, sand, government warehouses and fleas, constitute all its attractions. Thus ends my first campaign, and has n't it been a failure! — a failure personally and publicly, nothing in itself and leading to nothing. Here I am just where I was when I started. I have seen nothing but the distant spires of Charleston and have not been promoted. I have had a bitter contest with my Captain and seen little active service. . . .

CHARLES FRANCIS ADAMS, JR., TO HIS FATHER

Willard's Hotel, Washington
August 27, 1862

HERE I am once more in the city of Washington. Since I last wrote the first detachment of our regiment has arrived at Fortress Monroe, and is now in camp at Acquia Creek, while I have come up here to see about this business of Pope's staff. I find the old city much as usual, but still not the same. It was indeed pleasant for me to get here and at least to see something familiar once more, and I looked at all the public buildings and even at Willard's as at old friends. Once more I have really slept in a bed and I really never enjoyed anything in my life, in its kind, more than the delicious little supper which Gautier got up for me. You don't know how much eight months of coarse fare improve one's faculties for gastronomic enjoyment, and last evening I experienced a new sensation.

Here I am though, and what next? Shall I go onto Pope's staff? I think not. This is a very different place from Hilton Head and here I am learning many strange things which make me open my eyes very wide, which make me sorrow over our past and do not encourage me for the future. Here I have access to certain means of information and I think I can give you a little more light than you now have. Do you know that just before leaving the Peninsula McClellan offered to march into Richmond on his own responsibility? Do you know that in the opinion of our leading military men Washington is in more danger than it ever yet has been? Do you know that but for McDowell's jealousy we should have triumphantly marched into Richmond? Do you know that Pope is a humbug and known to be so by those who put him in his present place? Do you know that today he is so completely outgeneraled as to be cut off from Washington? Yet these are not rumors, but facts, doled out to me by members of McClellan's and Halleck's staffs.

Our rulers seem to me to be crazy. The air of this city

seems thick with treachery; our army seems in danger of utter demoralization and I have not since the war begun felt such a tug on my nerves as today in Washington. Everything is ripe for a terrible panic, the end of which I cannot see or even imagine. I always mean to be one of the hopeful, but just now I cast about in vain for something on which to hang my hopes. I still believe in McClellan, but I *know* that the nearest advisers of the President — among them Mr. Holt — distrust his earnestness in this war. Stanton is jealous of him and he and Pope are in bitter enmity. All pin their hope on Halleck and we must do as the rest do; but it is hinted to me that Stanton is likely to be a block in Halleck's way, and the jealousies of our generals are more than a new man can manage. We need a head and we must have it; a man who can keep these jealousies under subordination; and we must have him or go to the wall. Is Halleck going to supply our need? I hope he is, but while the question is in doubt we may lose Washington. You will think that I am in a panic and the most frightened man in Washington. I assure you it is not so. I do consider the outside condition of affairs very critical, but it is my glimpse behind the scenes, the conviction that small men with selfish motives control the war without any central power to keep them in bounds, which terrifies and discourages me.

Take the history of the Peninsular campaign. My authorities are one aid of McClellan's and Halleck's Assistant Adjutant General, but the facts speak for themselves, and the inferences any man may draw.

Stanton, contrary to the first principle of strategy and for motives not hard to comprehend, divides Virginia into four independent departments. McClellan takes charge of one and a column is taken from him to form another under charge of McDowell. It is solemnly promised McClellan that McDowell shall join him before Richmond, and meanwhile he is retained where he is to protect Washington. Mark the result. McClellan fights the battle of Hanover Court House, with all its loss of life and time, simply to open the road for McDowell to join him and he does open it. McDowell's advance guard hears his cannon on that day, but McDowell does not stir, and McClellan, still looking for him, forms that fatal Chickahominy front of twenty miles. Doubtless McDowell was kept back by orders, but in how far was he instrumental in procuring these orders to suit himself? McClellan's staff do not hesitate to say that he dictated them on pretence of danger to Washington, in reality because his advance would have absorbed his command in that of McClellan. Take the pretence. Jackson makes his raid in the valley of the Shenandoah, and again McDowell's advance hears the sound of his guns. Washington is in danger now. As before he does not move and Jackson escapes and returns to attack McClellan. Had McDowell done his duty either for McClellan or against Jackson, we should now have Richmond and McClellan would now be the conquering hero. He did neither and is now in disgrace, as subordinated to Pope; but McClellan is not the conquering hero. Not half an hour ago Halleck's nephew and private secretary told me that I could not imagine the trouble these jealousies gave his uncle. Said he, "McDowell and Sigel will not fight under Pope. McClellan and Pope are not in sympathy"; and he added an intimation that McClellan was most restive under Halleck.

Under these circumstances what can we expect? What can we hope for? Sigel stands well, but all our army officers are bitter and jealous against him. In Burnside there is indeed hope. He has been true and generous and, what is much, successful. He did not hesitate to award to McClellan the credit of planning his Carolina campaign, and, unlike McDowell, when told to send to McClellan all the troops he could spare, he at once sent him twenty-eight regiments and six batteries, leaving himself and the Major General under him some 3000 men in all. We have some grim old fighters who do their work and do not scheme. Such they tell me are Sumner and Heintzelman; but even of these the last is outspoken against McClellan because he will not fight with more energy. The simple truth is the man has not come and now we mean to supply his place with vast numbers of undrilled recruits. Shall we succeed? You can judge as well as I.

Thus the war is gloomily enough approaching its last and bloodiest stage. Unless Halleck is the man of iron who can rule, it will be discordant numbers against compact strategy. We must face the music, though we do not like the tune....

CHARLES FRANCIS ADAMS, JR., TO JOHN QUINCY
ADAMS

Willard's Hotel
Washington, August 28, 1862

. . . .

THINGS here look badly enough and amid this atmosphere of treason, jealousy and dissension, it requires good courage not to despair of the republic. As I said, I am going back to my regiment instead of onto Pope's staff, and you must take it out in cursing my instability. My reasons are manifold. The regiment and Colonel think I ought to come back or resign; we are about to see active cavalry service; and finally, between ourselves, I am ashamed at what I hear of Pope. All army officers say that he is a humbug and is sure to come to grief; "as big a liar as John Pope" is an old army expression; he has already played himself out in the army of Virginia and he has got himself into such a position that he will be crushed and Washington lost, unless McClellan saves him. He may come out with colors flying, for he a lucky man; but if he does, he is a dangerous one, and I am advised not to connect my fortunes with his. . . .

HENRY ADAMS TO CHARLES FRANCIS ADAMS, JR.

London, September 5, 1862

. . . .

YOUR appointment reached us some time ago and I was rejoiced at it, because I think such a place as this gives more room for expansion than that of a regimental officer. I doubt whether the atmosphere of Lieutenants is healthy, or of Captains or Majors. I think you have grown rusty at Hilton Head and I want to hear more vigorous talk. As to your speculations about the end of the war and a peace, I won't say that I would n't consent to argue about it some day, but you know perfectly well that until we've driven the South into their cotton fields we have no chance even to offer those terms. Perhaps on the broad national question I look at the matter differently from you. Apart from other causes, I am here in Europe and of course am influenced by European opinion. Firmly convinced as I am that there can be no peace on our continent so long as the Southern people exist, I don't much care whether they are destroyed by emancipation, or in other words a vigorous system of guerilla war carried on by negroes on our side, or by the slower and more doubtful measures of choaking them with their own cotton. Perhaps before long we shall have to use both weapons as vigorously as we are now using the last. But one thing is clear to my mind, which is that we must not let them as an independent state get the monopoly of cotton again, unless we want to find a powerful and bitterly hostile nation on our border, supported by all the moral and social influence of Great Britain in peace; certain in war to drag us into all the European complications; sure to be in perpetual anarchy within, but always ready to disturb anything and everything without; to compel us to support a standing army no less large than if we conquer them and hold them so, and with infinite means of wounding and scattering dissension among us. We must ruin them before we let them go or it will all have to be done over again. And we must exterminate them in the end, be it long or be it short, for it is a battle between us and slavery.

I see that your regiment is ordered to Virginia which shows a gleam of reason in the War Department. What it was ever sent to Port Royal for, the Lord he knows. At any rate, however, it has spared you some hard fighting, and with the prospect you have now before you, I think you need n't be sorry for that. For my own part I confess that I value human life at a pretty low price, and God knows I set no higher value on my own than on others. I always was a good deal of a sceptic and speculator in theories and think precious small potatoes of man in general and myself in particular. But I confess to feeling very badly when the news comes of our disasters and losses. Poor Stephen Perkins. I have a kind of an idea that Stephen thought much as I do about life. He always seemed to me to take rather a contemptuous view of the world in general, and I rather like to imagine him, after the shock and the pain was over, congratulating himself that at last he was through with all the *misères* of an existence that had bored him and that offered him little that he cared for; and now he could turn his mind to the exploring of a new life, with new duties and a new career, after having done all that man can do to discharge his debt to his God and his fellow-men in the old. There are men enough in Europe who hold these ideas with more or less variation, but Stephen and perhaps Arthur Dexter are the only ones among us whom I should call bitten with them — with Stephen, his eyes excused them. With Arthur, his digestion.

Our life here is quiet but very busy. No more is heard of intervention. Six hundred thousand men have put an end to that, and the English think besides that the South need no help. Of late the troubles in Italy have drawn people's minds away from us and as their harvest is very poor, our grain is too necessary to joke about. . . .

CHARLES FRANCIS ADAMS TO HIS SON

London, September 19, 1862

. . . .

ENGLAND is at peace, and in spite of the drawback occasioned by the failure of the cotton crop is prosperous. During the last twenty years the great development of the manufacturing policy has poured vast sums into her lap, whilst the outlets furnished to her poor populations in the colonies and in America have prevented the growth of any discontent at the unequal distribution of that wealth. In all my different journeys through the interior I find every evidence of substantial thrift. No dilapidated houses, or neglected lands or broken windows or ruinous barns. Even the oldest dwellings seem cared for and elaborately put in order. The question naturally arises are there no very poor people? It must be answered, not in the agricultural districts, but you must look for them in the populous towns. Go through many parts of London and you will be at no loss to understand where they are.

And so it will be in the great manufacturing centres in Lancashire and Yorkshire. Thus it appears as if England showed two distinct faces — one of happiness and one of misery, the first owing to the last. For however great may be the prosperity of the manufacturer, it appears to be resting only upon the extent to which the share in it of his operative can be reduced to a minimum. Were it not for the resource of emigration I doubt whether this condition of things could last long. As it is, I see no prospect of any change. The rich are growing richer, and conservatism gains rather than loses in its struggles for power. . . .

CHARLES FRANCIS ADAMS, JR., TO HIS MOTHER

Sharpsburg, Md.
September 25, 1862

. . . .

NEXT morning my only good horse was fairly done up and in the name of humanity I had to leave her at Frederick to take my chance of ever seeing her again, and with her, as I could not burden my other horse, I had to leave all my baggage and left everything including my last towel, my tooth-brush, my soap and every shirt and this, alas! was a fortnight ago! As soon as I left her I followed the regiment and had hardly left the town when the sound of artillery in the front admonished me that now we were practically in the advance. I pressed forward and rejoined the column some three miles from the town at a halt and with sharp artillery practice in front. Here we stood three hours resting by the side of the road and waiting for it to be opened for us. Now and then the shot and shell fluttered by us, reminding me of James Island. Some of them came disagreeably near and at last some infantry came up and for a moment sat down to rest with us. I told a Captain near me that the enemy had a perfect range of the road and he'd better be careful how he drew their fire and just as I uttered the words, r-r-r-h went a round shot through the bushes over my head, slid across Forbes and Caspar as they lay on the ground some thirty yards further on and took off the legs of three infantry men next to them. After that it did n't take long for the infantry to deploy into the field and leave us in undisturbed possession of the road. Still the infantry did it and the enemy soon limbered up and were off, having delayed our pursuit some three hours.

Then we followed and pushed over the hills wondering at the strength of the enemies' position. As we got to the top we pushed on faster and faster until we went down the further side at a gallop. The enemy were close in front and now was the time. Soon we took to the fields and then, on the slope of a hill, with the enemy's artillery beyond it, formed in column. More shelling, more artillery, and the bullets sung over our heads in lively style, and then "forward" as fast as we could go, over the hill, pulling down fences, floundering through ditches, struggling to outflank them. But the fences were too much for us and we had to return to the road, all losing our tempers and I all my writing materials, the one thing I had clung to. We made the road, however, in time to witness some of the humbug of the war. As we clattered into the town the Illinois cavalry, commanded by Colonel Farnsworth, not unknown to my father, were in front of us and, having hurried into the town were cracking away with their carbines and giving to me, at least, the idea of a sharp engagement in process. We followed them and got our arms all ready, but, as I rode through the single street of the pretty little town, a little excited and pistol in hand, I was somewhat surprised at the number of women who were waving their handkerchiefs, hailing us with delight as liberators and passing out water to our soldiers. For now we were in the truly loyal part of Maryland and everywhere were greeted with delight. It certainly did n't look to me much like a battle, and yet there were those carbines snapping away like crackers on the 4th of July. In vain I looked for rebels, nary one could I see and at last it dawned on my mind that I was in the midst of a newspaper battle — "a cavalry charge," "a sharp skirmish," lots of glory, but n'ary reb.

Here we paused, while I thought we should have pressed forward, and our artillery battered away from the hill to see if any one was there. Meanwhile the rebels burned the bridge before us and made off for the range of hills on the other side of the valley. Presently we followed, forded the stream and followed them up the road, through the most beautiful valley I ever saw, all circled on three sides with lofty wooded ranges surrounding a beautiful rolling valley highly cultivated and blooming like a garden. A blazing bridge and barn in the middle of it suggested something unusual. We hurried through the valley and up the hills on the other side and there we made a pause, brought to a dead stand. It did n't look like much, but we did n't like to meddle with it. It was only a single man on horseback in the middle of the road some few hundred yards before us, but it stopped us like a brick wall. We stood on the brow of one hill, with a straight road running through the valley below and disappearing in a high wooded range on the other side. We did n't know it then, but we were looking on what next day became the battle field of South Mountain. In the road below us were a few rebel videttes and on the hill beyond were posted, hardly to be distinguishable even with our glasses, a battery of artillery. We stood and looked and debated and at last our leaders concluded that it was n't healthy to go forward, and so we went back. We went into camp on a hill-top and passed a tedious night. It was very cold, and we were hungry, but still we slept well and in the morning feasted on an ox we killed the night before.

At seven o'clock we moved forward to our position of the day before, struggling along to the front through a dense advancing army corps. We got there and took up our position in support of a battery and soon our artillery opened and after about an hour the enemy began to answer. Presently we were moved far to the front and of course a blunder was made, and we found ourselves drawn up in a cornfield in front of our most advanced battery and between it and the enemy, with the shells hurtling over us like mad, and now and then falling around us, but fortunately doing us no harm save ruffling our nerves. Here we sat on our horses for two hours, doing no good and unpleasantly exposed. At last we were moved from there and sent round to our left to support some infantry and there we passed the afternoon, listening to the crackle of musketry and the roar of artillery till night, when it ceased and the men lay down in ranks and slept, holding the bridles of the horses. This was all we saw of the battle of South Mountain, which at the time we supposed to be a heavy skirmish. . . .

Here we lay all that day and I think the next, with a continual spattering of shells around, some of which injured other commands adjoining but all spared ours, and, at last, one day we were ordered early to the rear and we knew there was to be a big fight. Then came the battle of Antietam Creek and we saw about as much of it as of that at South Mountain. We were soon brought hurriedly to the extreme front and posted in support of a battery amid the heaviest shelling and cannonade I ever heard. It was a terrific artillery duel, which lasted where we were all day and injured almost no one. At first, as we took up position, we lost a horse or two, and the storm of artillery, the crashing of shells and the deep reverberations from the hills were confusing and terrifying, and yet, so well were we posted and so accustomed to it did we become, that ten minutes after the imminent danger was over and we were ordered to dismount, I fell sound asleep on the grass and my horse got away from me.

In fact this whole subject of battle is misunderstood at home. We hear of the night before battle. I have seen three of them and have thought I saw half a dozen when the battle did n't come off, and I have never yet seen one when every officer whom I saw did not seem, not only undisturbed, but wholly to fail to realise that any thing unusual was about to occur. In battle men are always frightened on coming under fire, but they soon get accustomed to it, if it does little execution, however heavy it may be. If the execution is heavy they're not nearly so apt to go to sleep, and I can't say I have ever yet fallen in with that lust for danger of which I have read. . . .

CHARLES FRANCIS ADAMS TO HIS SON

London, September 26, 1862

. . . .

LATTERLY indeed we have felt a painful anxiety for the safety of Washington itself. For it is very plain that the expedition of the rebels must have been long meditated, and that it embraced a plan of raising the standard of revolt in Maryland as well as Pennsylvania. It has been intimated to me that their emissaries here have given out significant hints of a design to bring in both those states to their combination, which was to be executed about the month of September. That such a scheme was imaginable I should have supposed, until the occurrence of General Pope's campaign and the effects of it as described in your letter of the 29th ulto. . . .

Thus far it has happened a little fortunately for our comfort here that most of our reverses have been reported during the most dead season of the year, when Parliament was not in session, the Queen and Court and ministry are all away indulging in their customary interval of vacation, and London is said to be wholly empty — the two millions and a half of souls who show themselves counting for nothing in comparison with the hundred thousand magnates that disappear. It is however a fact that the latter make opinion which emanates mainly from the clubhouses. Here the London Times is the great oracle, and through this channel its unworthy and degrading counsels towards America gain their general currency. I am sorry for the manliness of Great Britain when I observe the influence to which it has submitted itself. But there is no help for it now. The die is cast, and whether we gain or we lose our point, alienation for half a century is the inevitable effect between the two countries. The pressure of this conviction always becomes greatest in our moments of adversity. It is therefore lucky that it does not come when the force of the social combination is commonly the greatest also. We have thus been in a great degree free from the necessity of witnessing it in society in any perceptible form. Events are travelling at such a pace that it is scarcely conceivable to suppose some termination or other of this suspense is not approaching. The South cannot uphold its slave system much longer against the gradual and certain undermining of its slaveholding population. Its power of endurance thus far has been beyond all expectation, but there is a term for all things finite, and the evidences of suffering and of exhaustion thicken. The war now swallows up the children and the elders. And when they are drawn away, what becomes of the authority over the servants? It may last a little while from the force of habit, but in the end it cannot fail to be obliterated. . . .

CHARLES FRANCIS ADAMS TO HIS SON

London, October 17, 1862

. . . .

GENERAL MCCLELLAN'S work during the week ending the 18th has done a good deal to restore our drooping credit here. Most of the knowing ones had already discounted the capture of Washington and the capitulation of the Free States. Some had gone so far as to presume the establishment of Jefferson Davis as the President instead of Lincoln. The last number of the Edinburgh Review has a wise prediction that this is to be effected by the joint labors of the "*mob*" and of "*the merchants*" of the city of New York. This is the guide of English intelligence of the nature of our struggle. Of course it follows that no sensible effect is produced excepting from hard blows. If General McClellan will only go on and plant a few more of the same kind in his opponent's eyes, I shall be his very humble servant, for it will raise us much in the estimation of all our friends. Mr. Gladstone will cease to express so much admiration of Jefferson Davis, and all other things will begin to flow smoothly again.

We are all very quietly at home. Last week I made a flying trip into the north to pay a visit to a good friend of America in Yorkshire.[1] It gave me an opportunity to see a very pretty region of country, and

[1] William E. Forster.

the ruins of Bolton Abbey and Barden Towers in the picturesque valley of the river Wharfe. If they only had a little more sunlight, it would be very exquisite. But the excessive profusion of verdure unrelieved by golden rays, and only covered with a leaden sky, gives an aspect of sadness to quiet scenery which I scarcely relish. On the whole I prefer the brilliancy of America, even though it be at the cost of a browner surface.

My friend is a Colonel of a volunteer regiment, after the fashion of almost everybody here. For the fear of Napoleon has made the whole world turn soldier. Whilst I was with him he had some exercise at target practice with two sections of his riflemen. I went up to witness it, and thought it on the whole very good. The distances were three, four and five hundred yards. The best hits were nineteen in twenty. Three tied at eighteen, and then all the way down to eleven, which was the poorest. It seemed to me excellent practice, but I do not profess to be a judge. I suppose our people in the army by this time are able to do full as well if not better. . . .

CHARLES FRANCIS ADAMS TO HIS SON

London, October 24, 1862

. . . .

YOUR account of the campaign in Maryland was exceedingly interesting to us all. It contrasted admirably with those of the newspaper writers in telling only what you saw; whereas they, with far less of opportunity, undertake to say they see many things which did not happen. I have lost all confidence in any accounts which do not come with responsible names attached to them. I am not sure since General Pope's time that I always credit official statements. His mistakes have however had one good effect in reducing the tone and style of our other generals. They now do not overstate their success, nor boast of gains they have not made. Still the war drags on. I scarcely know what to think of the prospect. . . .

CHARLES FRANCIS ADAMS, JR., TO HENRY ADAMS

Washington, D.C., November 19, 1862

I AM certainly very well and in very good spirits, though the downfall of McClellan was a heavy blow to all below the rank of a General. The army believed in McClellan, but the Generals are jealous and ambitious and little, and want to get a step themselves, so they are willing to see him pulled down. We believed in him, not as a brilliant commander, but as a prudent one and one who was gradually learning how to handle our immense army, and now a new man must learn and he must learn by his own mistakes and in the blood of the army. It is all for the best and the Lord will in his own good time bear witness for us; but oh! the blunders and humbug of this war, the folly, treachery, incompetence and lying!!! They tell me here that Halleck is a very strong man, and that his touch is already felt in the West and soon will be in the East, and that the winter will restore our fortunes. I hope it may prove so, but my theory is that there will be much more fighting this year in Virginia, but that while we are

GEORGE BRINTON McCLELLAN

to hold the enemy here, the war is to rage on the Mississippi and the sea-board. But who knows — not I. Keep up your heart.

HENRY ADAMS TO CHARLES FRANCIS ADAMS, JR.

London, November 21, 1862

. . . .

MY work is now limited to a careful observation of events here and assistance in the manual labor of the place, and to a study of history and politics which seem to me most necessary to our country for the next century. The future is a blank to me as I suppose it is also to you. I have no plans nor can have any, so long as my course is tied to that of the Chief. Should you at the end of the war, wish to take my place, in case the services of one of us were still required, I should return to Boston and Horace Gray, and I really do not know whether I should regret the change. The truth is, the experience of four years has done little towards giving me confidence in myself. The more I see, the more I am convinced that a man whose mind is balanced like mine, in such a way that what is evil never seems unmixed with good, and what is good always streaked with evil; an object seems never important enough to call out strong energies till they are exhausted, nor necessary enough not to allow of its failure being possible to retrieve; in short, a mind which is not strongly positive and absolute, cannot be steadily successful in action, which requires quietness and perseverance. I have steadily lost faith in myself ever since I left college, and my aim is now so indefinite that all my time may prove to have been wasted, and then nothing left but a truncated life.

I should care the less for all this if I could see your path any clearer, but while my time *may* prove to have been wasted, I don't see but what yours *must* prove so. At least God forbid that you should remain an officer longer than is necessary. And what then? The West is possible; indeed, I have thought of that myself. But what we want is a *school*. We want a national set of young men like ourselves or better, to start new influences not only in politics, but in literature, in law, in society, and throughout the whole social organism of the country — a national school of our own generation. And that is what America has no power to create. In England the Universities centralize ability and London gives a field. So in France, Paris encourages and combines these influences. But with us, we should need at least six perfect geniuses placed, or rather, spotted over the country and all working together; whereas our generation as yet has not produced one nor the promise of one. It's all random, insulated work, for special and temporary and personal purposes, and we have no means, power or hope of combined action for any unselfish end.

One man who has real ability may do a great deal, but we ought to have a more concentrated power of influence than any that now exists.

For the present war I have nothing to say. We received cheerful letters from you and John today, and now we have the news of McClellan's removal. As I do not believe in Burnside's genius, I do not feel encouraged by this, especially as it shakes our whole structure to its centre. I have given up the war and only pray for its end. The South has vindicated its position and we cannot help it, so, as we can find no one to lead us and no one to hold us together, I don't see the use of our shedding more blood. Still all this makes able men a necessity for the future, and if you're an able man, there's your career. I have projects enough and not unpromising ones for some day, but like most of my combinations, I suppose they'll all end in dust and ashes.

We are very comfortable here in London fog. Some sharp diplomatic practice, but, I hope, not very serious. People don't overwhelm us with attentions, but that is excusable.

CHARLES FRANCIS ADAMS, JR., TO JOHN QUINCY ADAMS

Potomac Bridge, Virginia
November 28, 1862

HERE we are back with the Brigade at last. I hope you yesterday remembered us at home in your cups, for not a drop to drink, save water, had we, and our eating was of the toughest and slimmest. Here we are though, through mud and mire and rain, up with the army at last. A winter campaign here, by the way, is just impossible, no more and no less, and you who sit so snugly at home by the fire and round the hearth, and discuss our laziness in not pressing on, may as well dry up. We will allow everything to please you, waste of life, loss of labor, extreme exposure without tents, existence in a foodless country and all you will, and yet any movement is just simply impossible on account of mud. Horses can't walk, artillery can't be hauled, and ammunition can't be carried through this country after this season. Of course, we don't expect to get any forage, rations or tents through, but it is simply impossible to go ahead and carry the arms and ammunition to enable us to fight, though we should consent to starve and freeze cheerfully. So I look on it after the experience of a few days' march. I may be wrong and hope I am. But Lord! how it vexes and amuses me to think how easy it is, after a full dinner, to sip your wine in the gas light, and look severely into a fine fire across the table, and criticise and find fault with us poor devils, at that very time preparing to lie down before our fires, mud to the middle, wet through, after a fine meal of hard bread and water, and with nothing between us and the sky but November clouds. I don't complain of these little incidents of our life myself, and only I do wish they found less fault at home. . . .

CHARLES FRANCIS ADAMS, JR., TO HIS FATHER

Potomac Bridge, near Falmouth, Va.
November 30, 1862

. . . .

HERE we are once more with the army, but not on the move. We passed six days in Washington and it stormed the whole time, varying from a heavy Scotch mist to a drenching rain. Our camp was deep in mud, at times a brook was running through my tent, and altogether we were most unfortunate as regarded weather. Still we succeeded in completing our equipment and I started out on our new campaign tolerably prepared to be comfortable in future. Nor did I, I am glad to say, waste my time while there, but I fed on the fat of the land, feasting daily, without regard to expense, at Buhler's. I no longer wonder at sailors' runs on shore. Months of abstinence and coarse fare, cooked anyhow and eaten anywhere off anything, certainly lead to an acute appreciation of the luxuries of city life. It seems to me now as if I could n't enjoy them enough. While here I saw Aunt Mary repeatedly and she seems much the same as ever. She was very kind and hospitable. I also saw Governor Seward for an instant. He invited me to dinner and was very cordial; but he looks pale, old and careworn, and it distressed me to see him.

Here we remained till Friday evening, on which day the two Majors and myself succeeded in getting paid off, after immense exertion and many refusals, when we had our last dinner at Buhler's and on Saturday, when we saw the sun for the first time for a week, we struck camp and moved over to Alexandria, on our way to join the brigade. We got into Alexandria by two o'clock and went into camp on a cold, windy hill-side. We were under orders to join our brigade at Manassas, but when we got to Alexandria we found Manassas in the possession of the enemy and we did not care to report to them. Accordingly we sent back for orders and passed Sunday in camp, a cold, blustering, raw November day, overcast and disagreeable. The damp and wet, combined with the high living at Washington, had started my previous health, and now I not only was n't well, but was decidedly sick and lived on opium and brandy. In fact I am hardly well yet and my disorder followed me all through our coming march.

Sunday afternoon we got our orders to press on and join the brigade at the earliest possible moment near Falmouth, so Monday morning we again struck camp and set forth for Falmouth. It was a very fine day indeed, but the weather is not what it was and the country through which we passed is sadly war-smitten. The sun was bright, but the long rains had reduced the roads almost to a mire and a sharp cold wind all day made overcoats pleasant and reminded us how near we were to winter. Our road lay along in sight of Mt. Vernon and was a picture of desolation — the inhabitants few, primitive and ignorant, houses deserted and going to ruin, fences down, plantations overgrown, and everything indicating a decaying country finally ruined by war. On our second day's march we passed through Dumfries, once a flourishing town and port of entry, now the most God-forsaken village I ever saw. There were large houses with tumbled down stairways, public buildings completely in ruins, more than half the houses deserted and tumbling to pieces, not one in repair and even the inhabitants, as dirty, lazy and rough they stared at us with a sort of apathetic hate, seemed relapsing into barbarism. It may be the season, or it may be the war; but for some reason this part of Virginia impresses me with a sense of hopeless decadence, a spiritless decay both of land and people, such as I never experienced before. The very dogs are curs and the women and children, with their long, blousy, uncombed hair, seem the proper inmates of the delapidated log cabins which they hold in common with the long-nosed, lank Virginia swine.

To go back to our march however. Our wagons toiled wearily along and sunset found us only sixteen miles from Alexandria, and there we camped. During the latter part of the day I was all alone riding to and fro between the baggage train and the column. I felt by no means well and cross with opium. It was a cold, clear, November evening, with a cold, red, western sky and, chilled through, with a prospect of only a supperless bivouac, a stronger home feeling came over me than I have often felt before, and I did sadly dwell in my imagination on the intense comfort there is in a thoroughly warm, well-lighted room and well-spread table after a long cold ride. However I got into camp before it was dark and here things were not so bad. The wind was all down, the fires were blazing and we had the elements of comfort. The soup Lou sent me supplied me with a hot supper — in fact I don't know what I should have done if it had not been for that, through this dreary march; and after that I spread my blankets on a bed of fir-branches close to the fire and slept as serenely as man could desire to sleep.

The next morning the weather changed and it gradually grew warmer and more cloudy all day. Our road lay through Dumfries and became worse and worse as we pushed along, until after making only eight miles, we despaired of our train getting along and turned into an orchard in front of a deserted plantation house and there camped. Our wagons in fact did get stuck and passed the night two miles back on the road, while we built our fires and made haste to stretch our blankets against the rain. It rained hard all night, but we had firewood and straw in plenty, and again I slept as well as I wish to. Next day the wagons did not get up until noon and it was two o'clock before we started. Then we pushed forward until nearly dark. An hour before sunset we came up with the flank of the army resting on Acquia Creek. We floundered along through the deep red-mud roads till nearly dark and then, having made some five miles, turned into a beautiful camping ground, where we once more bivouacked. One thing surprises me very much and that is the very slight hardship and exposure of the bivouac. Except in rains tents are wholly unnecessary — articles of luxury. Here, the night before Thanksgiving and cold at that, I slept as soundly and warmly before our fire as I could have done in bed at home. The reason is plain. In a tent one, more or less, tries to undress; in the bivouac one rolls himself, boots, overcoat and all, with the cape thrown over his head, in his blankets with his feet to the fire, which keeps them warm and dry, and then the rest will not trouble him. A tent is usually equally cold and also very damp.

The next day was Thanksgiving Day — 27th November. It was a fine clear day, with a sharp chill in the little wind which was stirring. I left the column and rode forward to General Hooker's Head Quarters through the worst roads I ever saw, in which our empty wagons could hardly make two miles an hour. I saw

General Hooker and learnt the situation of our brigade, and here too we came up with our other battalion. We passed them however and came over here to our present camp, where we have pitched our tents and made ourselves as comfortable as we can while we await the course of events.

As to the future, you can judge better than I. I have no idea that a winter campaign is possible in Virginia. The mud is measured already by feet, and the rains have hardly begun. The country is thoroughly exhausted and while horses can scarcely get along alone, they can hardly succeed in drawing the immense supply and ammunition trains necessary for so large an army, to say nothing of the artillery which will be stuck fast. The country may demand activity on our part, but mud is more obdurate than popular opinion, and active operations here I cannot but consider as closed for the season. As to the army, I see little of my part of it but my own regiment. I think myself it is tired of motion and wants to go to sleep until the spring. The autumn is depressing and winter hardships are severe enough in the most comfortable of camps. Winter campaigns may be possible in Europe, a thickly peopled country of fine roads, but in this region of mud, desolation and immense distances, it is another matter.

CHARLES FRANCIS ADAMS, JR., TO HIS MOTHER

Potomac Run, near Falmouth, Va.
December 9, 1862

. . . .

AFTER a day or night of duty, it is strange what a sense of home and home comfort one attaches to the bivouac fire. You come in cold, hungry and tired and I assure you all the luxuries of home scarcely seem desirable beside its bright blaze, as you polish off a hot supper. And such suppers! You've no idea how well we live, now we've added experience to hunger. This evening, I remember, I had army-bread fried in pork — and some day I'll let you know what can be made of that dish — hot coffee, delicate young roast pig, beefsteak and an arrangement of cabbage, from the tenement of a neighboring mud-sill. This, with a pipe of tobacco, a bunk of fir branches well lined with blankets and a crackling fire before it left little to be desired. There is a wild luxury about it, very fascinating to me, though I never realise the presence of danger and that excitement which some men derive from that; to me camp always seems perfectly secure and my horses kick and champ on the other side of my fire, and my arms hang on the ridge of my bunk, practically as little thought of by me as though the one were in the stable at Quincy, and the other hanging over my mantelpiece in Boston. My enjoyment springs from the open air sense of freedom and strength. It's a lawless sort of feeling, making me feel as if I depended only on nature and myself for enjoyment.

This is all very well when the weather is fine, even in December; but next morning a change came o'er me, for early in the morning it began to rain and snow and, by the time we were relieved, at noon it snowed most heartily, so that I sincerely pitied the miserable creatures who relieved us. Home we rode, wet and cold, and as I walked sulkily along, I tried to think of one crumb of comfort awaiting me when I got back into camp. I could n't think of one, unless indeed the commissary might have procured some whiskey. Wrong again! I got into camp and found Colonel Sargent there with three companies from Hooker's head-quarters and things looked lively enough, though far from cheerful, and as luck would have it Henry Davis was there, established in the midst of discomfort in his usual comfort. So I passed the evening with him, cursing Colonel —— (in which chorus we all unanimously concur), smoking the best of tobacco, drinking hot whiskey punch and eating plum-cake fresh from Washington. . . .

The next time Henry passes a bookstore let him stop and buy for her [Mary] a little volume called "Ten Years of Soldiers' Life in India." It contains the life of Major Hodson taken from his own letters and is one of the most touching and charming books of these later days, to say nothing of the character of Hodson himself — my ideal of a Christian gentleman and soldier. I wonder none of you ever heard of him.

CHARLES FRANCIS ADAMS, JR., TO HIS FATHER

In the woods, near Falmouth, Va.
December 15, 1862

MY DEAR MOTHER:

Potomac Run, Va.
December 21, 1862

MY DEAR FATHER:

I LEAVE the above heading to my letter for two reasons. In the first place to show you that I did n't forget you while we were at the front; and in the second because this is my last sheet of paper and when this is gone I must borrow or be silent.

My last was written on Tuesday the 9th and while we were under orders for the front. The orders however did not come until Thursday and on Wednesday we had nothing to contend with but our new Colonel. He, however, was a host in himself and worried us very thoroughly. You've no idea what a nuisance such an ass as —— is at the head of a regiment. Ignorant to the last degree of his supposed profession, his ignorance is only surpassed by his conceit and vanity and his love of display. He has two and only two of the qualities of an officer of cavalry: he is a good and daring horseman and a man of great personal courage. At the same time he is the most cruel man on horses I ever saw in my life, and his courage, combined with his plenteous lack of judgment, only endangers the lives of those under his command. He prides himself on being a disciplinarian, knowing nothing of discipline, and so wears out his officers and men by an inordinate attention to useless trifles. He considers himself a tactician and yet he could not drill a corporal's guard without making ludicrous blunders. His mistakes on the drill ground, his theories of war and his absurdities in camp are, as John will tell you, the laughing stock of the regiment. He is universally disliked as well as ridiculed. He has already cost us the best officers in our regiment, and we all fear that he will ultimately ruin it. We of course can do nothing, but I assure you we keep up a devil of a thinking. This particular day certain horses were to be condemned and he nearly drove the commanders of companies wild. Their horses were led out and then led back again, and then led out and kept standing. Then some blanks were made out and then some more horses were ordered out, and then some were inspected and ordered to be shot or turned over to the Quarter Master, and then some messages were sent round and then we were ordered to pick out our worst horses to hand over to another regiment, and the Majors laughed and cursed, and the Captains cursed and swore, and the men grumbled and looked sullen, and he strutted round, overwhelmed with a sense of his own importance and utterly unaware with what a hearty contempt the general camp, pioneers and all, were cursing him and laughing at him. We see how ridiculous he makes us in the army and what a tool he becomes in the hands of others; and yet, discuss it as we will among ourselves, to the world we must put our tongues between our teeth and bear it as best we may. As for me, I have no great trouble with him. I am in command of my company and go near him only when I can't help doing so. My company is a very good one and so I'm not often drawn into scrapes. . . .

Early Thursday morning, clear and cold, the brigade got into line and began to advance to the front. While we were at the stable call a heavy cannonade had opened towards Fredericksburg and it was clear that work was before some one. Our column was not formed until nine o'clock and then we began to move towards the front, but very slowly. It was at first very cold, and our fingers and feet felt it sharply; but as the sun rose this passed away and the weather moderated.

Then the battery in front of us got stuck and delayed us an hour, during which we listened to the firing and discussed the prospects. For, instead of going out to operate on the right flank as we had expected, it was now clear that we were going straight towards Fredericksburg. Finally we passed the battery by a path through the woods, leaving it fairly mired and then pushed rapidly forward. Presently we came to a large field, about I should say a mile and a half from the point of cannonading, and there the brigade drew up, dismounted and began to wait. Around us were deserted infantry camps. On our left, on a rising ground, was an infantry line of battle, beyond and above them was a cloud of white smoke, and this was all I saw of Thursday's fighting.

For ourselves, we waited. The warm sun had started the frost and converted our field into a fine mire, and in that we stood from eleven o'clock to sunset. As long as I could I stood by my horse and eat hard-bread and smoked. When that was played out, I found the driest place I could, spread the cape of my overcoat on the mud, laid down on it and went to sleep. So the day passed tediously and disagreeably away. Rumors of doings at the front reached us from time to time; our pontoons were knocked to pieces and the engineers killed and we were not getting ahead very fast. Finally it became clear that we were to do nothing that day, so we watered our horses and presently the column started for a camp. It was dark before we reached it, but finally we found ourselves packed away in a pine wood, full of camp fires and pine smoke. I have ceased to be a believer in any necessity for discomfort under any circumstances. On this occasion Davis and I at eight o'clock, with the horses groomed and fed, had had a very comfortable supper ourselves and then with blankets unrolled were lying before our fire and smoking the pipe of great content. The weather too had moderated and though it froze stiff during the night, in the woods we rolled ourselves in our blankets and were as comfortable as need be.

Friday the 12th, instead of moving as was expected, we lay all the morning in the camp, listening to the artillery firing which still continued, but we noticed no musketry. The day was warm and bright and we found picnicing in the woods in December not so bad. To be sure the Colonel worried the officers all he could — among other trifles in one morning threatening the Lieutenant Colonel, Major and Adjutant with arrest; but I was fortunately at the extreme further end of the camp and took good care not to lessen my distance. As it was I began to enjoy myself very much. I am growing more and more attached to out of door life, so that it is pleasant even in December. We found that our camp was most prettily situated in a little strip of pine wood surrounding a little hollow in which the 4th Pennsylvania was encamped. The weather was delightful and we had nothing to do but to while away the time watching our neighbors and listening to the cannonade. The Pennsylvanians were a source of endless delight to Davis and myself — they were so ragged, so independent, and so very peculiar. No officers troubled their repose, and stable calls worried them not.

They were grave and elderly men and very, very old campaigners. They were curiously clad in defiance of all rule whether military or civil, and we pondered long as to where they could have got their clothes, until Davis happily suggested that, having all started as civilians, they had been picking up old soldier clothes ever since, until they had arrived at their present degree of uniformity. They had strange ways of leaving camp whenever they saw fit and returning ladened with well filled haversacks; whereat the faces of their comrades would light up with grim satisfaction. Water they had not now and soap they had evidently never known; but they were old soldiers, for they cooked strange messes and when boots and saddles sounded, undisturbed by the cannonade they would saddle their horses carefully, slowly and meditatively, evidently with respect for the beast if not in the fear of God. They compared so curiously with our own men so comparatively young, clean and well dressed, full of intelligence and yet subject to such rigid and never ending discipline. Then as the afternoon crept on the most beautiful lights and shadows I ever saw crept over the little hollow in which our friends were encamped, the smoke of the camp fires rising among the pines, while the sunlight played round the horses and riders among them gave effects which in pictures we should declare unnatural. At two o'clock orders came for us to saddle. We did so and got all ready to start and then, anxious and waiting for orders, we killed away the time until dusk, when again we watered and unsaddled, and again Davis and I after a comfortable supper lay before our fire enjoying the charms of tobacco and December moonlight.

Saturday the 13th, we did not change our position at all, but, as before, our horses were kept saddled the greater part of the day; but learning by experience I made myself comfortable, reading Holmes and observing the preparation of our dinner. Still, at best, this comfort was a very relative term that day, for all day long, from before day-break to long after dark, the heavy cannonade was broken only by long and terrific vollies of musketry, now before us, now on the right, now far away to the left. Evidently a terrible battle was going on, but with what result we could only guess, for we could only hear, and during all these days did not see an enemy or hear the whir-r-r of a single shot. There we lay, cold, idle and anxious, aware only of the severity of the contest, expecting soon to take part in it and knowing nothing of the result. The day passed slowly away, ending in the heaviest musketry fire by all odds that I ever heard, and again we passed a moonlight evening over our camp-fires. . . .

An order has just come for me to go out with two days' rations and twenty pounds of forage on some unknown job. If we meet an enemy God save us, for I understand Colonel —— is to command.

Wednesday, 24th. We got back from our scout yesterday at about noon, having accomplished nothing and now, as Colonel Sargent has kindly put me under arrest, I hope to be able to quietly finish my letter. Where did I leave off? I had accounted for Saturday I believe. Sunday the 14th found us still in the woods and still the weather continued clear and warm. At daybreak the usual firing began and at times there seemed to be explosions of musketry and cannon, but it was not at all the fire of yesterday. Our horses were still kept saddled and all our traps packed, but I had ceased to believe that we should move, and lay peaceably before my fire, enjoying the soft air and the strange lively scene and reading Browning's poems.

Towards evening rumors of some great success were rife and made us all very cheerful, and we again hoped soon to be in the saddle and following the enemy briskly up on the road to Richmond. I put less faith in the rumors than most and accordingly next day my disappointment was less. For next day our hopes most suddenly collapsed. There was a desultory firing going on all day, but not amounting to a great deal as compared with what had been going on. We lay in the woods as usual and I started this letter, but was suddenly cut short by an order to shift all the picket ropes, which, while it increased my comfort, took up the rest of the day and cut off your letter.

Tuesday the 16th, they actually took us out to drill, to exercise the horses and occupy the time. We skirmished round a hilly field opposite the camp for a couple of hours, and then the Colonel blundered us into camp. It began to grow clear that we should not immediately be wanted. When I got in I was informed that I was to be officer of the day and was to go out and post some pickets to protect the rear of the camp. I should just as soon have thought of posting pickets in State Street, as we were all surrounded by the camps of our friends;

but I did as I was told and posted at least half a dozen miserable men in positions in which they seemed least likely to be ridiculous and returned to camp to be worried by my Colonel. That night it rained smartly and, as usual, the drops pattering on my face reminded me that we were in bivouac. Like a knowing campaigner I called to my servant to throw my rubber poncho over me, pulled my boots under the blankets and my cape over my head and chuckled myself to sleep, as the rain came down harder and harder, to think how comfortable I was and how very much I had got ahead of the elements this time. The next morning it cleared away at about the time when decent people get up. I suppose, of course, that you bear in mind that eight o'clock P.M. is our bed time and that the regular hour of réveillé is half past six — one hour before sunrise — which we vary on special occasions by having it at three o'clock and so down. I assure you I have seen all the sun-rises I ever want to see and I thoroughly believe in lying abed until the earth is dry.

Hardly was the sun out when the announcement seemed to run at once all through the camps that our whole army had recrossed, that the bridges were all up and the campaign was a terrible failure — in a word, all our cake was dough. Even Colonel Sargent concluded that his regiment would not advance for a few days and left camp. Hardly was he gone when "The General" sounded and it was announced that we were to go back whence we came. It was a muddy, sullen, discouraging march home. The sky was cloudy and threatening and the mud deep, liquid, and slippery. It was rapidly growing cold and the wind was rough and chilling. We had been to the front and had not been under fire or seen an enemy, and we were going back with a campaign ruined and winter quarters before us. For myself I did hope that now we should put through this winter campaign and not sit down under this blow. I never had any confidence in this advance, but we had tried it and now I, and I think all, felt that it would not do to give it up so, and we did earnestly hope that we might be called upon to face and be able to surmount all the exposures, dangers and obstacles of a winter campaign. At any rate we felt willing to try and I do so now, but I understand this feeling does not extend to the body of the army which crossed the Rappahannock. We got into camp by three o'clock, finding it dirty, unprepared, bleak and cold, and there finished as quietly disheartening a day as I care to pass, with a miserable and insufficient dinner and a night passed wretchedly cold in a wet overcoat and frozen blankets. I had n't got ahead of the elements the night before as I had calculated.

A change of weather had taken place and we had got back to our tents just in time to meet it. It was cold, very cold, ice an inch and a half thick and now and then men frozen to death — only stragglers and serve them right; but then you know "a soldier's life is always gay." As for us, again we went shivering round camp, frozen out of our tents and miserably grouping round first one fire and then another. Our camp is the coldest, bleakest, most exposed place in the whole surrounding country, and we wanted to move into the woods; but our Colonel, fully impressed with the idea each day that tomorrow we are going to advance in triumph to Richmond, did n't think it worth while to make us comfortable just for a day, and, as he has a large tent with a fireplace in it, he is n't frozen out as we poor devils are. Anyhow, the next three days until Sunday passed uncomfortably enough, clear and bitter cold, the water in our blankets freezing even at noon. They drilled us Friday and Saturday, and that was a bore; but on Friday my patience gave out and I resolved to be comfortable if only for a day. So I set men to work and had a fireplace built behind my tent, of rough stone. The seam in the rear of the tent was then opened and closed around its mouth, and lo! in one corner of my tent was a mean, ugly little open fireplace. Then I had a shelf put up on one side, on which I am now writing, and a bed of fir-tree branches on the other side on which I spread my blankets. Thus I become more comfortable than I had ever been before and, though the wind sweeps and the rain drips through my tent, and Davis in abject despair calls it a "dirty kennel," in it I can be comfortable and I can write in the coldest weather, and there I am writing now, and tomorrow in it Davis and I will have our Christmas dinner, if we can raise one, which seems doubtful; but your dinner in London and John's in Boston will not taste better than ours, though we do eat tough beef and drink commissary whiskey out of battered and campaign worn old tin plates and cups. And even if it does, I am very sure that my health will be drunk and I shall be remembered in Newport and Boston and London and that if it lay in the power of my family, I should eat and drink of the fat of the land.

However, to go back to my letter. I left off, I believe, just where I began this letter — at Sunday noon. We got our orders — 250 men from the command, with two days rations and twenty pounds of forage, and were to report in an hour. It struck hard, for though the weather had moderated it was cloudy and threatened rain and it was still rough and we were just comfortable. However, out it was and my fifty-six men were in line at the time the fifty-six horses having had two quarts of oats and no hay, thanks to the shortcomings of the brigade Quarter Master, that day. We got out and joined other details from the brigade, making 1000 cavalry all told, and somewhat after dark took up our line of march for Hartwood Church. We reached our advanced pickets at about nine o'clock and then encamped in the woods, lighting fires and feeding our horses and before eleven we were all asleep. At three o'clock Monday morning an orderly came round and woke us up, though why we did n't exactly see, as our horses were neither fed nor cleaned, and all we had to do was to get our breakfasts. I fed my horse and got myself up a fine breakfast of four hard-breads and was ready for a start, but the start did n't come until daybreak, and the sun rose, weak and cloudy, while we were still within our pickets, but yet on the road. Then came a long killing march, ending in nothing. We rapidly pushed directly forward, at times at a gallop, until after noon, when we pushed forward through some fields and woods as fast as our horses could go, using many up and finishing a man or two by tumbles and accidental shots. Here we drove in pickets, but I saw no signs of any force of the enemy having been in that vicinity. We then turned to the South and towards the river and ended by meeting Sigel's corps and marching home to our camp of the night before, having made a dashing reconnaissance with no results. ... We got into camp about five o'clock having covered I should say not less than thirty-five miles. We cleaned and fed the horses, cooked some supper and then went to sleep. Yesterday (Tuesday, 23d) at daybreak we were roused and got ready to come home. To show you how government kills horses, I will say that my fifty-six from twelve o'clock Saturday night to twelve o'clock Tuesday noon — sixty hours — travelled nearly sixty miles and had no hay and just thirteen quarts of oats apiece. I am glad to say only one gave out, and that one has since been brought in. We came leisurely in on a pleasant, warm, winter morning, and here befel my most lamentable arrest by my Colonel. He thinks himself a disciplinarian and is great on "marching orders," and leaving the column on a march. Now we were within sight of our camp and the brigade had stopped to water at a stream, and watering a thousand horses is a matter of time. As we were waiting I happened to hear that Colonel Buchanan was quartered just a hundred yards or so on our right in plain sight. I wanted to see him and said so to Major Higginson, with whom I was riding. He replied: "Why don't you go now? I would." I said I would come over again, there was n't time, etc.; but he still advised me to go until at last I said I thought I would and cantered over there. I found the Colonel in front of his tent and had a pleasant talk of about ten minutes with him. I then started to rejoin my column and found it had gone forward. I followed and came up just after my company had watered and found Colonel Sargent just finishing some unknown manœuvre through which he discovered my absence. As I calmly took my place, he summoned me before him and inquired where I had been. I pleasantly informed him, in that airy manner which makes me a universal favorite, and he immediately put me under arrest. Upon which, winking pleasantly at his orderlies, I retired to the rear of my company. I believe now he is debating in his own mind as to whether he will have me dismissed the service without a hearing or court martialed and cashiered. He is too ignorant to know that my having had the consent of my immediate superior to what I did covers me completely. So now I look upon this as a little vacation and to my release from the weary monotony of company duties you owe this letter. . . .

CHARLES FRANCIS ADAMS TO HIS SON

London, December 19, 1862

. . . .

To change the subject let me tell you of a pleasant little experience which diverted my thoughts from home last evening. The Queen's Advocate, Sir Robert Phillimore, learning that I had accepted an invitation of the Westminster School to attend their annual performance

SURGEON LUCIUS MANLIUS SARGENT

of a Latin play, asked me to join him at his own house to dinner, and proceed from there. I accepted very thankfully. The company I met was small but choice. It consisted of the Lord Chancellor (Lord Westbury), the Brazilian Minister, Lord Harris, now attached to the new household of the Prince of Wales, and a brother of the host. We had a lively dinner, as the Chancellor is a very ready talker, and has great resources, and soon after proceeded to Westminster School which is in close proximity to the famous old abbey. It dates from the time of Elizabeth and has produced many eminent men from Ben Jonson downward to Gibbon and Southey. The stage is set up in what is called the dormitory, a large hall, the bare walls of which are marked with the names in large letters of those who have been scholars with the date attached, apparently done by themselves without any order or method. The popularity of the school has declined of late years, whilst that of Eton has developed beyond all legitimate bounds. Nevertheless those who are attached to it cling with pride to its usages, and of these the most notable and peculiar is the performance about Christmas time every year of some old Latin play.

This year it happened to be the Andria of Terence. The scene was well got up. It represented Athens in the distance, as it may be presumed to have looked in its sunny days. The costumes were rigidly Grecian according to the best authority. The only modern things were the prologue and epilogue, and these were likewise in Latin.

I had seen the same thing done at Ealing in my boyhood. But now that I could understand it better I wanted to see it again. Not having read the piece for twenty years I had bought a copy of Terence previously and refreshed my memory with a careful perusal. The result was that I enjoyed it exceedingly. The boys articulated well and acted with spirit, one or two with power, so that I could form a very fair notion of the secret of the charm of old Menander. The audience, composed mostly of old Westminster scholars familiar with the play, was quiet and sympathetic, so that it really gave a good illusion. On the whole I must say that this is the pleasantest evening I have yet passed in England. The Queen's Advocate, Sir Robert Phillimore's son was what is called the Captain of the school, and played the part of Pamphilus very well. . . .

CHARLES FRANCIS ADAMS TO HIS SON

Mount Felix, Walton on Thames [1]
December 25, 1862

. . . .

PUBLIC matters remain yet in a profound state of repose, and probably will continue so for another month. The publication made by the Secretary of State of large portions of my Despatches for the past year has rather stirred a hornet's nest in the press, but I fancy it will prove only a nine days' wonder. I have said merely what everybody knows. The great body of the aristocracy and the wealthy commercial classes are anxious to see the United States go to pieces. On the other hand the middle and lower class sympathise

[1] Russell Sturgis' place.

with us, more and more as they better comprehend the true nature of the struggle. A good deal of dust was thrown into their eyes at first by the impudent pretense that the tariff was the cause of the war. All that is now over. Even the Times has no longer the assurance to repeat that fable. The true division now begins to make itself perceptible here as elsewhere in Europe — the party of the old and of the new, of vested rights and of well regulated freedom. All equally see in the convulsion in America an era in the history of the world, out of which must come in the end a general recognition of the right of mankind to the produce of their labor and the pursuit of happiness. Across all these considerations come occasionally individual and national interests which pervert the judgment for a time, but the world moves onward taking little note of temporary perturbations, and whatever may betide to us of this generation, the end is sure. . . .

HENRY ADAMS TO CHARLES FRANCIS ADAMS, JR.

London, December 26, 1862

. . . THE telegrams announce a battle on the 13th and from the scanty items I infer that it was another Antietam, only worse. In short I am prepared for a complete check and am screwing my courage up to face the list of killed and wounded. . . .

We have our hands full and things are in a very lively state. The notes are becoming savage, but we have a clear case and are making headway. I find myself, I think, of use, and am well content to be here. My former restlessness was caused by the Pope campaign which upset us all. On the whole I would infinitely prefer to be here to going into the army, and it is only when there really seems to be a superior call to the army that I feel disposed to move.

Anxiety has become our normal condition and I find a fellow can dance in time on a tight rope as easily as on a floor. It is harder to keep one's temper, but even that I now contrive to do in very trying cases. A steady pressure tells better here than anything else, and if our people will be cool, I think we can set England straight. . . .

I have been staying several days at Monckton Milnes' place in Yorkshire where we had a very jolly little bachelor party. . . .

Even the stoic steadiness of nerve that I am trying to cultivate, shakes under the apprehension of the next news.

1863

1863

CHARLES FRANCIS ADAMS, JR., TO HIS MOTHER

*Potomac Run, Va.
January 2, 1863*

. . . .

DURING the day [29th] two details of one hundred men each were ordered from our regiment, to join other details from other regiments in the brigade at eight o'clock the next morning. One of these details was to consist of picked men and horses, carefully armed, with three days' rations and twenty pounds of forage, and of these Colonel Curtis had command and Channing Clapp went with him as Major. I had command of the other detail, which was provided with ten pounds of forage and three days' rations. Both details got off at eight o'clock the morning of the 30th, Colonel Curtis reporting to General Averell in person and I to Major White of the 3d Pennsylvania. Evidently something was on foot. General Averell's force could not have been less than a couple of thousand picked men and horses under chosen officers and it was evident that work was cut out for them. Our force was about 325, far inferior men and horses, and I imagined we were merely to act as a reserve or to support a battery. It took us a long time to get off and it was while waiting in the saddle, on a chilly, cloudy December morning, that I received all your letters of November 21st, informing me of Sallie Hampton's death among other facts.

About ten o'clock we began to move, our detachment following General Averell's and taking the road towards our advanced pickets at the Hartwood Church. We got there at about noon and after a few minutes' rest Major White received his orders. We again mounted, passed Averell's force and took the westerly road. Here Major White sent me back word that he wished to see me, and I went forward and joined him and he proceeded to develop to me the plan of our scout, as it appeared I was next in command to himself. We were to march with the utmost despatch and caution to Warrenton Junction, there rest and feed, and start at the proper time to arrive at Warrenton at daylight, "where," the orders went on, "you will find two companies of rebel cavalry. You will capture these and return at once, reporting in person to Major General Hooker." White winked at me and I winked at White, and immediately I went to the rear, changed my mare for my heavy old working brute, and sent her, my servant and all my possessions back within the picket and then rejoined White and we went on our way rejoicing in the cold, heavy, rainy December afternoon. For once I really believed we were going to do something and my spirits rose accordingly.

We pushed briskly along, stopping only once for a few moments until nine o'clock, when we found ourselves close to Warrenton Junction and then turned into the woods to wait, for the next six hours. It had been raining, but not heavily, and now the air was very heavy and cold — damp. It was a sort of cold drizzle. Of course fires were not safe, so we fed our horses and then, after sharing Major White's supper, I smoked for a while and then lay down at the foot of a tree and slept as *un*comfortably as I care to, waking up chilled through and very disconsolate. At three o'clock we again got on the road and pushed on well enough, except that our guides once or twice lost the road, until we came to the Junction. There, the moon having gone down, it suddenly became intensely dark, our guides lost the road, we got wandering through the woods and morasses, and, for a time, things looked black enough. I never saw such darkness. I could not see a man and horse three feet before me, but blindly followed the jingling of the column, relying on my horse not to fall and to keep the road. We lost our advance guard, a message came up that the rear squadron had not been seen for a long time, and we lost our rear-guard and did n't find it until next day. We had finally to retrace our steps to the Junction and there, at least, we found our missing squadron, got back our advance guard and re-discovered the road and then pressed on once more.

Then came one of those disgusting night marches; cold and disgusted, one's only desire is to be in bed; so sleepy that to keep one's eyes open is impossible. You sleep and doze in wretched discomfort while your horse presses on. Good Lord! how for two hours I did wish myself comfortably back under arrest. Day broke at last and I woke up. We were late and pressing on fast, but it was eight o'clock before we entered Warrenton. White was to drive in the pickets and charge through the town with one squadron and I was to follow in the rear and support him with mine, while the third was to be left as reserve. As we approached the town I began to smell a rat. In vain I listened for the first shots telling that we were on their pickets. It did n't come, and I began to feel that we were sold. Still it had to be done. On a bright, cool morning in December, feeling like a fool, I charged through the quiet town of Warrenton at the head of my squadron, with their carbines advanced, making a devil of a racket, barked at by curs and astonishing and delighting peaceful citizens. They flocked out and looked at us, not exactly with admiration, but much as if it had been the great American Circus or Van Amburg's Menagerie, or any other show got up for their edification. They were very civil and certainly exhibited no signs of distrust or fear, and we justified their confidence; for, as soon as we had rushed through the town and sent our men up all manner of streets, satisfying ourselves that there was no organized body of rebels in that town, we turned round and left the town according to our orders on our way home. We felt, as I have said, like fools.

I have told you what was, now for what might have been. As we marched away we heard bells ringing and wondered what it was. It was a little signal. Two hours after we left, Stuart entered the town on his way back from Dumfries and was there joined by Lee and a few hours after he left Averell entered it in pursuit and thus Warrenton saw plenty of cavalry that day. On the one hand we just missed defeat and captivity, death or flight, and on the other, brilliant success. Had Stuart been there when we arrived we would savagely have assaulted his whole force, under the impression that they were the two companies we were after and now, the probabilities are, I should not have been writing this letter. Had Averell gone with us, instead of taking the road he did, Stuart would have been caught at last. . . .

CHARLES FRANCIS ADAMS, JR., TO HIS MOTHER

*Camp of 1st Mass. Cav'y
Potomac Run, Va., January 8, 1863*

. . . .

IT was clear that we were not going to the bridge, as Chamberlain of our regiment had charge of that party. I had the rear of the column and a ripping head-ache, otherwise I should have enjoyed the thing immensely, for it was a clear, cold, moonlight night and we went floundering through the marshes at a tremendous gait. All I could see was dissolving views of the rear of the column as we pelted through woods and across broad white marshes, intersected by creeks which we had to ford. Presently Ben [Crowninshield] came down the column and informed me that we were going up the railroad to destroy some smaller bridges and, if it took us long, we were to let the column go and find our own way home. Of course we lost the way and after riding up the road two miles and finding no bridge, we rode down two miles and a half, cutting down the telegraph poles as we went along, and then there was a halt and I heard the sound of the axes. "Ah," thought I, "here is the bridge," and my head-ache felt better.

So I rode up and looked at a miserable little culvert,

about three yards long, on which some twenty destroyers were at work. This was, then, the greatest humbug of all. We had come with artillery and cavalry and infantry, through rain and snow and ice, without shelter or forage, all the way up here to cut up a miserable little culvert which ten men could rebuild in five hours. It would have been very amusing had I felt well. There we were a hundred of us, some eighty in line and ready to fire into any unsuspecting train which might come along, and the other twenty, without direction, or system or tools, tugging away at a remarkably well-built railroad which resisted their utmost efforts. Ye Gods! how the mismanagement did stick out!! Our tools were six axes and the ground was hard frozen. Every one directed and every one worked on his own hook. My second Lieutenant, a son of Judge Parsons, was ordered to do the work and he bellowed and swore, and the men laughed and minded him or not as they chose. White, quite nervous and anxious to get through, complained that too many orders were given and did nothing to remedy it. Ben Crowninshield, very anxious to get the job done while yet there was time, seeing that the men had worked an hour without getting up a single rail, encouraged them by dancing round in high excitement, exhorting them somewhat generally to "do *something* to turn the whole thing over at once, *somehow*," and I sat on my horse in amused despair.

At length with immense effort we got up one rail and threw it into the creek, and White at once declared the bridge used up and we started back along the railroad.

It was eleven o'clock now and the last half hour we had heard a spattering fire of carbines and musquetry towards the river, indicating that Chamberlain was at work, but no artillery, which seemed to indicate that it was n't much of a job after all. As for us we went rapidly along the track and the first thing we knew we came to a bridge, as was a bridge. It was clear at once we had been at work on the wrong bridge hitherto, so we went to work again. It was the same old story, only a little better, for this time we made cleaner work, pulling up the track, cutting through the uprights and main beams and finally setting the middle pier on fire; having done which we mounted and went off better pleased.

Through the whole thing I must confess I felt like a fool. It was a small job and badly done; slight resistance would have turned us back and I have n't as yet gotten over an old prejudice against going round destroying property which no one tries to protect. Anyhow it was done and the fire of the burning bridge threw a bright light across the marsh as we rode away. We rejoined the main body and waited for Chamberlain, who had been at work on the main bridge and had, after some slight resistance, resulting in nothing, destroyed about one hundred and twenty feet of it. The whole party was in by three o'clock, and we at once started back and, as I rode along in the clear, cold moonlight, I very soon made up my mind as to the whole affair.

I don't know, but I imagine a newspaper success — "dashing raid" and all that — will be manufactured out of this. If it is I can only say it is a clap-trap and a humbug and was intended as such. It is, I fear, pure Joe Hookerism and wire pulling. The bridge was of no real value to the rebels or to us and was not protected. Even if it had been, Ned Flint, who is an engineer, said he would contract to repair with forty men all the damage done in four days. Anyhow, value or no value, two hundred cavalry could have done it twice as surely and effectually and in just half the time, and so Chamberlain had previously reported. But no! that would n't answer for political effect, and so the sledge is brought out to crush the fly, and infantry, artillery and cavalry are paraded out in the depth of winter to burn a bridge which no one used or means to use, and I expect to see an immense pow-wow over it. If there is, rest assured it's all a humbug. The thing amounted to nothing, was very badly done after no end of blunders and mismanagement, and was and is intended solely for political effect and has about as much bearing on the ends of the war as would the burning of Neponset Bridge or our barn at Quincy. . . .

At last, at half past one, we marched into camp and were dismissed. This was Saturday afternoon. I had been on continuous duty for thirty-four hours and in the saddle twenty-eight; my horse had not eaten for thirty hours. I had last washed my face and hands on Wednesday morning, and in this week, the first in January and by far the most severe of the winter, I had passed two nights in my tent and five in bivouac. I got something to eat and washed my face and hands and then went out to see that the horses were cared for, but that night my blankets felt like a bed of down and I slept like an infant.

I have been specific about this trip as I regard it as finishing my education. I had tried most kinds before, dry and wet, hot and cold. We have steadily been at it for months and I have thought that terrible discomfort was yet to come. This combined cold and wet and hunger and sleeplessness and fatigue and all that men regard as hard to bear. We had slept in melting snow and rain, had passed days in the saddle with soaking feet and freezing clothes, had waited hours in a pelting rain, and yet I had enjoyed it all, and not for an instant had wished myself away. I do not now believe in outdoor hardships. None of us are sick, we have no colds and no diseases, we are all far better than we were at home, and yet there is but one greater hardship than we have felt. A long continued, disastrous winter retreat would be worse and in the line of exposure this alone I now fear. . . .

HENRY ADAMS TO CHARLES FRANCIS ADAMS, JR.

London, January 9, 1863

. . . .

I AM deep in international law and political economy, dodging from the one to the other; and as I see nothing of the world and am much happier when I see nothing of it, I have no news to tell you. In point of fact I am better satisfied with my position now than ever before, and think I am of use.

At this moment public affairs are becalmed, but Parliament is soon to meet and then we shall all be put on the gridiron again. Luckily one's skin gets callous in time. We are pretty strong, however, and *very* active; that is, our party here is; and I hope we can check any hostile plots on this side. Of course we expect to come in personally for a good share of abuse and social annoyance, but I suppose we can stand that. Some day *et haec meminisse juvabit*. I'll make you laugh with our little passages at arms. As a general thing, however, we are simply avoided. By the way, if you can get Fred. Seward to send you down the volume of Diplomatic Documents just published, I think it will amuse you. It has made a great sensation here, and our opponents have paraded it about as though it were a collection of choice blasphemy, or a compilation of bawdy stories. You would think that the unpardonable sin was in that volume. Unfortunately it is seriously open to ridicule, but apart from that there is really nothing to cry out at and much to praise and admire.

I congratulate you on your Captaincy, if it is a cause of congratulation. You know I look on the service merely as a necessary duty, and my highest ambition would be reached by seeing you honorably and safely out of it. When that event arrives, I will resign you my place and retire to private life. . . .

CHARLES FRANCIS ADAMS, JR., TO HIS MOTHER

Potomac Run, Va.
January 20, 1863

. . . .

I SEE a great deal of Buchanan now and find him extremely pleasant and most unexpectedly kind and disposed to assist me. Did n't we formerly consider

Buchanan a little pompous? And were not we a little disposed to laugh at him? If we did a most surprising change has come over him, for he certainly is in his own quarters and in his intercourse with younger men by all odds the most genial and pleasant officer of rank I have ever met. You know he has been very badly used and bears it like a man. General Sumner alone of all the Army officers in this Department ranked him when the war began and now Lieutenants and Captains of his regiment are Brigadiers and Major Generals and he is still a Lieutenant Colonel commanding the 1st Brigade of Regulars. Yet he is universally respected as one of our best officers and most reliable men; as a soldier none stand higher and scarcely one would be trusted in a tight place as soon as he. He has been recommended for promotion over and over again and no man in the army doubts his loyalty. But Wilson does and he has not yet succeeded in working his way through the Military Committee of the Senate. Now he is coming up and will soon get what he most desires, the office of Inspector General. At any rate he is a good friend of mine, and I count his rise as in a good degree my own. I contrive to get over and see him very frequently and he advises me to leave this regiment and go into a staff. . . .

CHARLES FRANCIS ADAMS TO HIS SON

London, January 23, 1863

. . . .

OUR customary midweek intelligence has not arrived, owing I suppose to the violence of the storms delaying the steamers, so that we are now fifteen days back. In the meantime the President's proclamation is doing much for us on this side. That is put in contrast to the paper of Jefferson Davis, much to the advantage of the former. The middle classes generally see and comprehend the existence of a moral question apart from all political disquisitions. The effect is to bring out an expression in popular meetings which is doing something to neutralise the opposite tendency of the governing people. Mr. Seward has printed so largely from my Despatches of last year, that there is now no misunderstanding here of what I think on this matter. I fear that I have forfeited the favor of my aristocratic friends by performing my duty of disclosing their tendencies, but as I have had not unsimilar experiences heretofore at home, perhaps I take it with less uneasiness. There are always great exceptions to be made. And after all, the position of a foreign minister must necessarily be one to inspire caution in making intimacies. My acquaintance is already quite as extensive as I can keep up with.

The profound quiet of the months which intervene during the absence of Parliament is almost at an end. On the 5th of February the respective forces in the political campaign will be marshalled, and the war of ins and outs will begin. Although they are nearly equal in numbers I do not find much expectation of an overthrow of the ministry. Lord Palmerston is very popular, and he means to hold on to power as long as he can. If the opposition throw him in the House, he will only appeal to the people, and the chances are that he may sustain himself. For though the special vacancies have been filled rather favorably to the opposition, it is singular that the successful candidates generally pledge themselves to support Lord Palmerston. Thus is shown the singular spectacle of a leader who mounts two parties at the same time and yet having the entire confidence of neither. Such a state of things will not survive his Lordship. And he is nearly eighty years old! So it is not unreasonable to presume that a change cannot be far distant. The question what might be the effect on American affairs is that which gives us an interest in the result. I trust that before it happens we may be so far on our way to a result at home as to save all risk of trouble. . . .

CHARLES FRANCIS ADAMS, JR., TO HENRY ADAMS

Potomac River, Va.
January 23, 1863

. . . .

I DO wish you took a little more healthy view of life. You say "whether my present course of life is profitable or not I am very sure yours is not." Now, my dear fellow, speak for yourself. Your life may be unprofitable to you, and if it is, I shall have my own ideas as to why it is so; but I shall not believe it is until I see it from my own observation. As to me my present conviction is that my life is a good one for me to live, and I think your judgment will jump with mine when next we meet. I can't tell how you feel about yourself, but I can how I feel about myself, and I assure you I have the instinct of growth since I entered the army. I feel within myself that I am more of a man and a better man than I ever was before, and I see in the behavior of those around me and in the faces of my friends, that I am a better fellow. I am nearer other men than I ever was before, and the contact makes me more human. I am on better terms with my brother men and they with me. You may say that my mind is lying fallow all this time. Perhaps, but after all the body has other functions than to carry round the head, and a few years' quiet will hardly injure a mind warped, as I sometimes suspect mine was, in time past by the too constant and close inspection of print. I never should have suspected it in time past, but to my surprise I find this rough, hard life, a life to me good in itself. After being a regular, quiet respectable stay-at-home body in my youth, lo! at twenty-seven I have discovered that I never knew myself and that nature meant me for a Bohemian—a vagabond. I am growing and developing here daily, but in such strange directions. Let not my father try to tempt me back into my office and the routine of business, which now seems to sit like a terrible incubus on my past. No! he must make up his mind to that. I hope my late letters have paved the way to this conviction with him. If not, you may as well break it to him gently; but the truth is that going back to Boston and its old tread-mill is one of the aspects of the future from which my mind fairly revolts. With the war the occupation of this Othello's gone, and I must hit on a new one. I don't trouble myself much about the future, for I fear the war will not be over for years to come. Of course I don't mean *this* war, in its present form: *that* we all see is fast drawing to a close; but indications all around point out to me a troubled future in which the army will play an important part for good or evil, and needs to be influenced accordingly. I shall cast my fate in with the army and the moment reorganization takes place on the return of peace and the disbandment of volunteers I shall do all I can to procure the highest grade in the new army for which I can entertain any hope. I now lament extremely my early education and life. I would I had been sent to boarding school and made to go into the world and mix with men more than my nature then inclined me to. I would I had been a venturous, restive, pugnacious little black-guard, causing my pa-r-i-ents much mental anxiety. In that case I should now be an officer not at all such as I am. But after all it is n't too late to mend and enough active service may supply my deficiencies of education still. Meanwhile here I am, and here I am contented to remain. The furlough fever has broken out in our regiment, and the officers, right and left, are figuring up how they can get home for a time. Three only of us are untouched and declare that we would n't go home if we could, and the three are Greely Curtis, Henry Higginson and myself. Our tents and the regimental lines have become our homes. . . .

I've all along told you, you ought to remain in London, and I say so still; for that is your post and, pleasant or unpleasant there you should remain. I have told you all along, however, that I did n't like the tone of your letters. Your mind has become morbid and is in a bad way — for yourself — both for the *mens sana* and *corpus sanum*. A year of this life would be most advantageous. Your mind might rest and your body would harden. My advice to you is to wait until you can honorably leave your post and then make a bolt into the wilderness, go to sea before the mast, volunteer for a campaign in Italy, or do anything singularly foolish and exposing you to uncalled for hardship. You may think my advice absurd and never return to it again. I tell you I know you and I have tried the experiment on myself, and I here suggest what you most need, and what you will never be a man without. If you joined an expedition to the North pole you might not discover that *terra incognita*, but you would discover many facts about yourself which would amply repay you the trouble you had had. All a man's life is not meant for books, or for travel in Europe. Turn round and give a year to something new, such as I have suggested, and if you are thought singular you will find yourself wise.

Tuesday, 26th

I suppose you in London think it strange that I do not oftener refer to the war in my letters and discuss movements. The truth is that you probably know far more of what is going on than I do, who rarely see papers, still more rarely go beyond the regimental lines and almost never meet any one possessed of any reliable information. As a rule, so far as my knowledge goes, the letters of correspondents of the press are very delusive. They get their information from newspaper generals and their staffs and rarely tell what they see. Now and then, very rarely, I see a plain, true, outspoken letter of an evident eye-witness. The small means of observation I have are enough, however, to convince me that the army of the Potomac is thoroughly demoralized. They will fight yet, but they fight for defeat, just as a brave, bad rider will face a fence, but yet rides for a fall. There is a great deal of croaking, no confidence, plenty of sickness, and desertion is the order of the day. This arises from various causes; partly from the defeat at Fredericksburg and the failure, but mostly from the change of commanders of late. You or others may wonder or agree, as you choose, but it is a fact that McClellan alone has the confidence of this army. They would rally and fight under him tomorrow and under him only. Burnside has lost, and Hooker never had their confidence.

Under these circumstances my mind recurs more and more to the plan of the war which I suggested to you in my last letters from Hilton Head, after the seven days' fight. This army I now think should be broken up and the bulk of it at once transferred to the South West, where it could seize and hold against everything the territory west of the Mississippi. This would give us that river and its tributaries, including the States of Tennessee and Kentucky; it would circumscribe and ultimately destroy the Southern confederacy, and would settle forever the slavery question in the young South West. One measure alone would decide all this: let the army know that they are to have the territory they occupy and Congress pass liberal laws encouraging the army to settle where they have fought. I think that at least 100,000 fighting men would become *coloni*, would send for their families or marry and there settle; and this would at once insure to that immense country inhabitants, defenders and free labor. This would be now, as it was then, my plan of the war, and I would abandon at once the moral effect of the capture of Richmond in favor of the great material fact of an open Mississippi. That this will be the future plan of the war there are already indications, but I hardly hope that we shall throw our whole strength into it, as we should to insure success. I have given up philosophising and do not often, except in very muddy weather indulge in lamentation. I think indeed you in London will all bear witness that my letters, under tolerably adverse circumstances, have been reasonably cheerful, and I hope they will remain so, even if the days become blacker than these blackest days I ever saw. We all feel that we are right and that being right, there is for us good in this plan of Providence, if our philosophy could but find it out. Do you remember the first lines of the last chorus in Samson Agonistes? They begin, "Though we oft doubt," and I have often tried to recall them lately, but cannot get them all. I hope to live to see the philosophy of this struggle, and see the day when the Lord "will to his faithful servant in his place, bear witness gloriously." Meanwhile, if it is your place to wield the pen, to my no small astonishment I find the sword becoming my weapon and, each in his place, we are working off our shares of the coil. Let us try to do it in our several ways to the best of our ability and uncomplainingly receive whatever fate betides us.

HENRY ADAMS TO CHARLES FRANCIS ADAMS, JR.

London, January 23, 1863

. . . .

THE Emancipation Proclamation has done more for us here than all our former victories and all our diplomacy. It is creating an almost convulsive reaction in our favor all over this country. The London Times furious and scolds like a drunken drab. Certain it is is, however, that public opinion is very deeply stirred here and finds expression in meetings, addresses to President Lincoln, deputations to us, standing committees to agitate the subject and to affect opinion, and all the other symptoms of a great popular movement peculiarly unpleasant to the upper classes here because it rests altogether on the spontaneous action of the laboring classes and has a pestilent squint at sympathy with republicanism. But the Times is on its last legs and has lost its temper. They say it always does lose its temper when it finds such a feeling too strong for it, and its next step will be to come round and try to guide it. We are much encouraged and in high spirits. If only you at home don't have disasters, we will give such a checkmate to the foreign hopes of the rebels as they never yet have had. . . .

HENRY ADAMS TO CHARLES FRANCIS ADAMS, JR.

London, January 27, 1863

. . . .

SPRING has come again and the leaves are appearing for the third time and we are still here, nor does there seem any immediate probability of our moving. In fact we are now one of the known and acknowledged units of the London and English world, and though politics still place more or less barriers in our path, the majority of people receive us much as they would Englishmen, and seem to consider us as such. I have been much struck by the way in which they affect to distinguish here between us and "foreigners"; that is, persons who don't speak English. The great difficulty is in the making acquaintances, for London acquaintances are nothing.

After a fortnight's violent pulling, pushing, threatening, shaking, cursing and coaxing, almost entirely done through private channels, we have at least succeeded in screwing the Government up to what promises to be a respectable position. How steady it will be, I don't know, nor how far they will declare themselves, do I know. But between our Government at home and our active and energetic allies here, we seem to have made progress. I went last night to a meeting of which I shall send you a report; a democratic and socialist meeting, most threatening and dangerous to the established state of things; and assuming a tone and proportions that are quite novel and alarming in this capital. And they met to notify Government that "they would not tolerate" interference against us. I can assure you this sort of movement is as alarming here as a slave insurrection would be in the South, and we have our hands on the springs that can raise or pacify such agitators, at least as regards our own affairs, they making common cause with us. I never quite appreciated the "moral influence" of American democracy, nor the cause that the privileged classes in Europe have to fear us, until I saw how directly it works. At this moment the American question is organizing a vast mass of the lower orders in direct contact with the wealthy. They go our whole platform and are full of the "rights of man." The old revolutionary leaven is working steadily in England. You can find millions of people who look up to our institutions as their model and who talk with utter contempt of their own system of Government. Within three months this movement has taken a development that has placed all our enemies on the defensive; has driven Palmerston to sue for peace and Lord Russell to proclaim a limited sympathy. I will not undertake to say where it will stop, but were I an Englishman I should feel nervous. We have strength enough already to shake the very crown on the Queen's head if we are compelled to employ it all. You are not to suppose that we are intriguing to create trouble. I do not believe that all the intrigue in the world could create one of these great demonstrations of sympathy. But where we have friends, there we shall have support, and those who help us will do it of their own free will. There are few of the thickly populated districts of England where we have not the germs of an organisation that may easily become democratic as it is already anti-slavery. With such a curb on the upper classes, I think they will do little more harm to us.

The conduct of the affairs of that great republic which though wounded itself almost desperately, can yet threaten to tear down the rulers of the civilised world, by merely assuming her place at the head of the march of democracy, is something to look upon. I wonder whether we shall be forced to call upon the brothers of the great fraternity to come in all lands to the assistance and protection of its head. These are lively times, oh, Hannibal.

CHARLES FRANCIS ADAMS, JR., TO HIS FATHER

Camp near Potomac Run, Va.
January 28, 1863

. . . .

THE fine weather seems fairly to be over and the wet season to have set in. In addition to the week of rain before, which played Burnside out, it rained steadily all last night and this morning set in from the N.E. with sleet and snow, and is at it now very lively. The results of this you may imagine, but I dare not. For myself it is of little consequence. My tent is logged up, I have a good fire-place, a pretty complete outfit and am as comfortable as I have any wish to be; but I feel for my men and dare not go and look at my horses. I know just how they look, as they huddle together at the picket-ropes and turn their shivering croups to this pelting north easter. There they stand without shelter, fetlock deep in slush and mud, without a blanket among them, and there they must stand — poor beasts — and all I can do for them is to give them all the food I can, and that little enough. Of oats there is a sufficiency and the horses have twelve quarts a day; but hay is scant, and it is only by luck that we have a few bales just now when most we need them. I have them fed four times a day — at morning, noon, night and midnight — and if they have enough to eat, they do wonderfully well, but it comes hard on them to have to sustain hunger, as well as cold and wet. It is all over, however, with any horse that begins to fail, for after a few days he either dies at the rope, or else glanders set in and he is led out and shot. I lose in this way two or three horses a week. The men do better now, as they too have logged in their tents and built fireplaces, and, as a rule, they are well clad and shod; but, after all, it comes hard on them, this being wet and always sleeping on damp ground, and we have had five funerals this month, one from the fall of a horse and four from sickness, one of which was in my company — a boy, named Pierce, from the central part of the State.

I had two men desert the other day also, and under peculiar circumstances. They were two of our recruits and did not properly belong to my Company, but were assigned to it for duty. They had cost the Government some three hundred dollars each and were good for nothing, as by far too many of these "bounty-boys" are. They were sent out as part of a detail for picket duty from my Company, under Lieutenant Merrill. On the night of the 8th of January they were posted at an important point on the extreme front of our lines, and in the immediate vicinity of Hartwood Church. When the patrol came round they had disappeared. The case was reported and I supposed that they had grown cold and drowsy and been ingeniously spirited away by guerrillas — for such things are done. At the end of ten days however one of our men accidentally found their horses tied to a tree in the woods near their posts, all saddled, just as the men had left them, and on the saddles were hanging all the men's arms, except their pistols. There the poor brutes had stood for ten days, without food or water, until one had died in the agonies of starvation, and the other, having gnawed up all the trees around him, was reduced to a walking skeleton. This last, however, is alive and now at my picket-rope. (P. S. He died of exposure the next morning after I wrote this.) Meanwhile the human brutes, this brace of $300. men, had, I find, quietly deserted their posts as videttes and walked off, enquiring their way to Warrenton and leaving their horses and arms, except pistols, as too likely to lead to their being caught — their design evidently being to get through our lines near Alexandria and so North. Meanwhile I am doing all in my power to catch them by notifying the authorities in Washington and at home. Should I succeed, their fate is not to be envied. They will be court martialed and probably shot. If not shot, they will suffer some terrible military punishment at the Tortugas. . . .

Meanwhile peace reigns once more in our domestic affairs — a very lively storm has purified the air. Colonel Sargent went on in his career until one day he put Lieut. Col. Curtis under arrest and then the storm burst. I rode over and stated our case to General Buchanan and he advised me as to the proper course to pursue, and the next day Sargent found his head in a hornet's nest. Curtis forwarded a complaint on his

MAJOR HENRY LEE HIGGINSON

arrest to General Averell. Major Higginson as next in command forwarded a paper in behalf of his brother officers to General Hooker, through Colonel Sargent, setting forth the Colonel's utter ignorance and glaring incompetence, and prepared a similar paper for Governor Andrew; and Dr. Holland was brought up to the point of preferring charges against him for unwarrantable interference with the sick. At first the Colonel showed signs of bulling ahead to his destruction, but General Averell sent for him, Curtis and Higginson, and the last two stated the regimental grievances to General Averell in Sargent's presence, glossing nothing. Sargent asked: "On account of what vice am I incompetent to command this regiment?" To which Curtis answered: "On account of no vice, Sir; you are simply utterly incompetent," and so on, and referred him as authority to the Company officers. Averell was very anxious that "an arrangement" should be effected, and requested them to consult together. Sargent came back to camp and sent for some of the officers — his peculiar favorites. They all came up to the mark and plainly informed him that he was not able to run the machine. He then sent for Curtis and Higginson and the three had a long discussion, the result of which was that Curtis was released, Higginson withdrew his papers and peace was restored. . . .

Friday, the 30th

I think you may as well make up your mind to passing the remaining two years of your term abroad. The war is on its last legs and it would hardly pay for

England to abandon her neutral policy now, simply to get into a quarrel and revive our dying spirit. We are playing her game better ourselves. Whatever Cabinets and correspondents may say to the contrary, I feel persuaded that *unless* we have rapid and brilliant successes in the southwest soon, and *those leading to something*, the fighting in Virginia is over. The New York Herald may say what it pleases, but the Army of the Potomac is at present fearfully demoralised. Even I can see that, small means of observation as I have. You can have no idea of the disgust felt here towards the Government. Unable to run the army themselves, they take away McClellan, and when that leads to terrible disaster, they cashier Fitz John Porter, one of the best general officers we have; and now relieve Burnside, one of our best corps commanders, ridiculously displaced by these very men; Sumner, the hardest fighter and best man to take or hold a position in the whole army, and Franklin, on the whole considered the ablest officer we have — all this that Hooker may be placed in command, a man who has not the confidence of the army and who in private character is well known to be — I need not say what. This army, now, does not know under whom it is fighting. Government has taken from it every single one of its old familiar battle names, save Hooker's. I most earnestly hope it will now break up the army, else some day it will have it marching on Washington. . . .

HENRY ADAMS TO CHARLES FRANCIS ADAMS, JR.

London, January 30, 1863

. . . .

POLITICALLY things go on swimmingly here. The antislavery feeling of the country is coming out stronger than we ever expected, and all the English politicians have fairly been thrown over by their people. There was a meeting last night at Exeter Hall which is likely to create a revolution, or rather to carry on a complete revolution in public opinion which was begun by the great Manchester Meeting on the 31st December. Last night's meeting was something tremendous, unheard of since the days of reform. The cry was "Emancipation and reunion" and the spirit was dangerously in sympathy with republicanism. The Strand was blocked up in front of Exeter Hall by those who could n't get in, and speeches were made in the street as well as in another hall opened to accommodate a part of the surplus. As for enthusiasm, my friend Tom Brown of Rugby school-days, who was one of the speakers, had to stop repeatedly and beg the people not to cheer so much. Every allusion to the South was followed by groaning, hisses and howls, and the enthusiasm for Lincoln and for everything connected with the North was immense. The effect of such a display will be very great, and I think we may expect from Lancashire on the arrival of the George Griswold, a response that will make some noise.

Next week Parliament will meet. Of course it will bring hot water, but the sentiment of the country will not tolerate any interference with us. I breath more easily about this than ever. My main anxiety is about the Alabama case, which has been the subject of the sharpest kind of notes between the Chief and Lord Russell. As these notes will probably now be published, I can say that in my opinion my Lord has been dreadfully used up, and if you don't howl with delight when you read the Chief's note to him of 30th December, you won't do what I did. But our cue is still friendship, and we don't want to irritate. The strong outside pressure that is now aroused to act on this Government will, I hope, help us to carry through all we want in time and with patience.

HENRY ADAMS TO CHARLES FRANCIS ADAMS, JR.

London, February 13, 1863

. . . .

THE last week here has been politically very quiet. I am surprised at it, for I thought that the meeting of Parliament would set the floods going. Lord Derby, however, put his foot on any interference with us, on the first night of the session, and so we have obtained a temporary quiet. But the feeling among the upper classes is more bitter and angry than ever, and the strong popular feeling of sympathy with us is gradually dividing the nation into aristocrats and democrats, and may produce pretty serious results for England.

Society is beginning. As it is almost certainly the last season I shall pass in London, I intend to see all I can. Society in London certainly has its pleasures, and I found an example of this, the other evening. We

THE DUKE OF ARGYLL

were asked to dinner at the Duke of Argyll's, who is a warm friend of ours, as well as the Duchess who is daughter of the anti-slavery Duchess of Sutherland. The party was evidently asked on purpose to meet us. There was Lord Clyde, who always has his hair on end and never seems to talk; Charles P. Villiers, a friendly member of the Cabinet; Charles Howard, a brother of Lord Carlisle; John Stuart Mill the logician and economist, a curious looking man with a sharp nose, a wen on his forehead and a black cravat, to whom I took particular pains to be introduced, as I think him about the ablest man in England; very retiring and embarrassed in his manner, and a mighty weapon of defense for our cause in this country. Then there was the famous physician, Dr. Brown-Séquard; then Professor Owen, the famous naturalist, geologist, palæontologist and so on, whom I have met before. Then came Lord Frederick Cavendish whom you know. . . . You know your friend "Lord Fwedewick's" style of costume in America. It's not much better here. If a man chooses to neglect rules he can do it in London though not with impunity. As for example, our friend and cousin the phenomenon who has just graduated at the university with much lower honors than we had hoped for him. . . .

CHARLES FRANCIS ADAMS TO HIS SON
London, February 27, 1863

. . . .

HAVE you ever seen the narrative by the Prince of Joinville of the events of the campaign of McClellan against Richmond? It seems to me remarkably well done. I think he touches as with a needle's point the radical defect of our military system. They have always impaired the efficiency of our troops. I can see clearly the reason why we have not made an adequate use of the multitude we have summoned to the field. Two armies of a hundred thousand men each, properly officered, would have done more than our million.

In the meantime the people of this country have so far changed their views as it respects our share in the strife, as to give me a fresh source of occupation in the work of transmitting addresses and resolutions of crowded meetings everywhere. The anti-slavery feeling has been astonishingly revived by the President's proclamation and the kindly disposition by the supplies furnished to Lancashire. It is however to be noted that all this manifestation comes from the working and middle classes. The malevolence of the aristocracy continues just as strong as ever. Every item of news that favors the notion of division and disintegration is eagerly caught up. I only wish our people could be here a little while and see what is hoped from their differences of opinion. If it did not have the effect of smoothing them all down into the pursuit of a common object, then there is not a particle of patriotism left among them. . . .

CHARLES FRANCIS ADAMS, JR., TO HIS FATHER

*Camp of the 1st Mass. Cav'y
Potomac Bridge, Va., March 8, 1863*

. . . .

AT nine o'clock on the 25th we set out for Hartwood,[1] which is the somewhat famous centre of our Brigade picket line, and some ten miles from here. Our lines run from the Rappahannock to Acquia Creek, a length of some eighteen miles and covering the whole right flank of our army. The morning was bright and sunny, the roads very heavy and the snow melting fast. We looked on our business as rather a lark and rode leisurely along enjoying the fine day and taking our time. At half past twelve we entered the woods within half a mile of our picket reserve, and just then Major Robinson of the 3d Penn., who, with Captain Blood, a curious nondescript from the 4th Penn. made up of whiskey and dullness, and myself, constituted our board, said: "Oh! there's a carbine shot," and we trudged along. Like Bull Run Russell, I am now about to tell you things which I myself saw. A few paces further on we were challenged by a vidette and Robinson rode forward and explained our business. He spoke to the man, and just then I heard a few more shots and Robinson shouted to me: "Hurry up, there's a fight going on," and began to press on through the road, knee deep in mud. I was picking my way through the woods and, in my disbelief, replied: "Well, I can't hurry up in these roads, even if there is." The words

[1] To assess damages done to property of loyal men near Hartwood Church. Three officers constituted the board.

were scarcely out of my mouth when I saw good cause to jam the spurs into my horse and hurry up indeed. Pell-mell, without order, without lead, a mass of panic-stricken men, riderless horses and miserable cowards, our picket reserve came driving down the road upon us, in hopeless flight. Along they came, carrying helpless officers with them, throwing away arms and blankets, and in the distance we heard a few carbine shots and the unmistakable savage yell of the rebels.

We drew our sabres and got in the way of the fugitives, shouting to them to turn into the woods and show a front to the enemy. Some only dashed past, but most obeyed us stupidly and I rode into the woods to try and form a line of skirmishers. But that yell sprung up nearer, and in a twinkling my line vanished to the rear. Nor was this the worst. The panic seized my horse and he set his jaw like iron against the bit and dashed off after the rest. Oh! it was disgraceful! Worse than disgraceful, it was ludicrous!! My horse dashed through the woods — thick woods — both feet were knocked out of the stirrups, I was banged against the trees, my hat was knocked over my eyes, I could not return my sabre, but I clung to the saddle like a monkey, expecting every instant to be knocked out of it and to begin my travels to Richmond. This went on for a couple of hundred yards, when at last I got my horse under, and out of the woods into the road, when I found myself galloping along with the rear of the fugitives, side by side with Major Robinson. "My God! Adams," said he, "this is terrible! This is disgraceful." "Thank God," I replied, "I am the only man of my regiment here today." "Well you may," said he.

Something had to be done to rally the men however at once, else we should soon find ourselves rushing, a mob, onto the infantry pickets two miles behind. I said I would go ahead and try to stop and rally the last of the column, and I let my horse out. The fresh powerful animal shot by the poor worn out government brutes and did some tall running through the Virginia mud and soon brought me out of the woods into a broad field. Here I turned and blocked the road, and pulled and stormed and swore. Some hurried by through the woods and across the fields, but a number stopped and Robinson began to form a line, such as it was. Here at once I learned the cause of the panic. Nearly all the men belonged to a new and miserable regiment, the 16th Penn. They had never been under fire before, were Pennsylvanians and — ran like sheep. We got some thirty men in one line and I was busy forming another, but what lines! No two men knew each other, their officers were gone, God only knew where! Not one face had I ever seen before, and a glance showed me not one man could be relied on. They were all squinting behind them. In less than two minutes the enemy was on us.

Meanwhile Robinson had sent Lieut. Colonel Jones, an old incompetent of his own regiment who had had command of the pickets, to the rear to rally the fugitives and had taken command. I had sent Blood off on the same errand. Meanwhile the hompesun coats dashed out of the woods, or we could see them riding through them, and instantly Robinson's line began to vanish, to dissolve. He shouted to them to fire and an abortive volley was the result. Poor as it was it did the work. A few saddles were emptied and the rebs grew at once more prudent. But alas! If it scared the rebs, it scared my line also, which was forming a little to the right and rear and I saw the rascals wavering on the verge of a panic, while I heard Robinson calling on them to come up, for his men were leaving. "I clearly can't drive them," thought I, "perhaps they'll follow me," and I spurred my horse forward and shouted, "Come on, follow me, there they are," waving my sword — all in the most improved patterns; but the disciples of Penn did n't see it in that light, and as I looked over my shoulder I saw my line vanishing from both flanks and the centre on the road home. Then wrath seized my soul and I uttered a yell and chased them. I caught a hapless cuss and cut him over the head with my sabre. It only lent a new horror and fresh speed to his flight. I whanged another over the face and he tarried for a while. Into a third I drove my horse and gave him pause, and then I swore and cursed them. I called them "curs," "dogs," and "cowards," a "disgrace to the 16th Pennsylvania, as the 16th was a disgrace to the service," and so I finally prevailed on about half of my line to stop for this time.

Meanwhile the firing had ceased and no more rebs were in sight. I joined Robinson and we debated what was to be done. The enemy's fire had done us no harm and one dead body was in the road before us. Our men were utterly surprised by the effect of their one wretched volley, but alas! they were no more reliable, and as I glanced at those feeble undecided faces, I trembled lest the enemy should attack us again. Oh! thought I, for my own company! I felt rejoiced that they were out of that scrape, but I realized how good and reliable they were. In a few minutes we had settled on a sort of plan and I went into the woods with a dozen men to cover our flank and skirmish. I scattered my men along and encouraged them with the information that at the first sign of wavering I should shoot the first man I came to, and I portentously flourished my pistol. In fact I think I should have done so then, for it could have done no harm at this stage of the game. Before I had not dared to, as I felt that if I did, these men, so green and undisciplined, would only run away from me as well as the enemy, and what we wanted was to get them to stand and stop running. Anyhow I deployed my skirmishers, such as they were.

We saw nothing of any enemy and presently I returned to Major Robinson to settle on some plan of operations. I told him I was ready to take the offensive and charge of the skirmishers, if he was ready to advance, and finally he gave me some more men and we began operations. I extended my line through the woods to the open fields beyond and began to advance. The ground was covered with snow, but the woods were so thick that I could not see more than a third of my line at once. However I pushed steadily forward and in a short time heard some one calling to me. I rode up and found two or three of my men standing round a veritable grey coat, with an officer's chevrons on, near a tree, by which two horses were standing and at the foot of which lay a man, one glance at whom satisfied me that his course was run. As I came up the unhurt man approached me and told me he was a Captain and my prisoner; that the wounded man was his Lieutenant and friend, and that he had remained to look after him, and, adding with much agitation: "We have always tried to have your men who have fallen into our hands well treated, and we hope you will do the same. At least, let me have a surgeon for my friend." The poor fellow was lying in the snow at the foot of the tree, shot through the abdomen and now and again writhing in pain. And how could I look on him wholly without feeling? And yet I did just that. No one who has not felt it knows what a brutaliser war is! My duty was clear and I did n't feel an instant's hesitation. I assured the prisoner that I did not doubt he had always behaved with humanity, that his friend should receive all possible care; asked him a few hurried questions and then told him he must leave his friend and go to Major Robinson as a prisoner. I took away their arms and parted them. They shook hands, the dying man begging his friend to tell his family of his death, and his friend almost crying as he wrung his hand and left him expiring there on the snow in the woods — alone — for my men could not stop. I went back to Robinson with the prisoner to see how his information would affect our plans, and in a few minutes went back to my men in the woods and have not seen the prisoner or the wounded man since. The last Robinson had carried into a neighboring house where he died in a few hours, I believe and hope with his Captain by his side; but I have since often thought of that scene in the woods and it has brought very near to me the horrors of war.

Now however I was very busy pushing forward my line and trying to discover where the enemy were. We could see them in force on the left across some fields, but not in the woods in front. I sent Blood into the fields with six men to observe them and cover my flank and have n't seen him since. Somehow, no one knows how, the cuss contrived to get captured about an hour later. I can't imagine how he did it, but he has n't been heard of since. Well, I pushed steadily on and presently came to our old line of picket and found myself with about twenty men left. I sent three by the road to the right, three to the left, leaving the rest as reserve. I went a few hundred yards and saw a body of men drawn up on the skirts of the woods. Were they friends or foes? I halted my men and rode forward and called to them, but they made no answer. My men insisted on it they were rebels. If so, I was way ahead of our forces and in a dangerous place, but I could not believe it. They soon settled my doubts, for I heard an order given for a party to go down and drive me back, and down they came. They had carbines and we had not, and they called on us to surrender. As they approached I told my men to fall back, and two of them at once vanished into the woods, while one advanced, stood stock still, as if fascinated, and, I suppose, surrendered.

As for me, finding myself alone, after in vain calling

on the man to fall back and not shooting him at once,
as I should have done, I fell back myself. I knew I
could rely on my horse and cared little for the enemy,
keeping just so far in front watching them. Presently
the one in advance of the rest saw my reserve and pulled
up, and then took a long, deliberate aim and sent a
bullet after me. I had never had a bead drawn on
me before and the sensation was now not disagreeable.
I was cantering slowly along watching my well-wisher
over my shoulder and, as he aimed away, I pleasantly
reflected: "You're mounted, I'm in motion, and the
more you aim the less you'll hit"; and then the ball
whistled harmlessly by, and we both stopped and he
went back and molested me no more. Then came moments of doubt. A skirmish began with yelling and
shooting where he came from. Who could be there and
fighting? And I saw skirmishers coming up in my rear.
Oh Lord! thinks I, I have got ahead of our forces with
twelve men and here are the rebels in my rear. Where
is Blood? and I cast anxious glances into the woods for
a line of retreat and began to fall back. But the advancing line proved to be the 1st Rhode Island and
at last light began to dawn on me. Our picket reserve
had been divided and I had fallen in with one portion,
while of the existence of the other on my left all day
I had been wholly ignorant and had so blundered
ahead of them and onto the enemy's flank. Now they
had come up and a skirmish was in progress. I turned
back and again advanced, but when I reached my old
place the skirmish was over. Fitzhugh Lee had accomplished his object, left us his compliments by the

widow Coakley, and gone off with, as it now appears, about 120 horses and prisoners. I rode forward and again had a prisoner announce himself as at my disposal. This one had been left behind with two more wounded men at the widow Coakley's, and from her fair daughters I grimly received General Lee's compliments.

It was now evening and my thoughts fondly turned on home and the delights of my tent. I saw the officers who had that day come out on picket, and deeply compassionated them, but did n't offer my assistance for the night. I found Major Robinson and, at last, as night was falling persuaded him that it was just as well to go home and not to pass the night there, meddling with other people's business and giving orders to our superior officers, and so we started back. The weather had changed and the sky was full of rain, and we met the brigade coming out, now that the bird had flown and was hours away. We wished them joy of their thankless job and got home to a late dinner and that night you may well believe I revelled in my blankets, as I reflected how my share of this job was over, and the next morning I revelled the more as I thought of that miserable brigade when the patter of the rain on my tent woke me and I folded my hands for slumber anew. . . .

In coming in [on the 4th] I found myself Judge Advocate on a Court Martial called to try the fugitives of the 25th and that has busied me ever since. My only variety has been morning drills and on Sunday last a Brigade review, at which our regiment by its appearance and general excellence, not only called forth much remark, but alone in the Brigade was most highly commended by the Division Commander. In fact, at last we are coming up and winning that place in public estimation which we have always felt belonged to us of right. We have long been under a cloud, but at last we have been found out and now every day adds to our reputation. . . . I am high in favor with all the remaining powers that be, and, having confidence in me, they allow me full swing with my Company and never molest me and, though I say it who perhaps should not, there are few better companies in this regiment or army. Promotions with us are rapid and already I find myself one of the four senior Captains, and consequently a chief of Squadron, which command I, a short time since, considered as filling the measure of my ambition; but we are never contented and now I find myself lusting after a staff appointment with its increased rank on a larger sphere. . . .

CHARLES FRANCIS ADAMS, JR., TO HENRY ADAMS

Camp of 1st Mass. Cavly
Sunday, March 22, 1863

. . . .

I AM glad you have come to my conclusion as to the best basis for an end to this war. Virginia, Kentucky, Tennessee and all west of the Mississippi was my theory, I think, in my letters from Hilton Head last July and was, I recollect, stigmatized by you as "English." I am glad you have come round to it and wish the Administration would do the same. Meanwhile things are improving here, though the weather continues abominable, beastly, unbearable. I wish I could go to Boston just to get rid of the east winds, which are increasing and bring with them almost daily snow, rain and sleet, or, now and then, watery, cold, blue sky. But the army is *decidedly* improving, and is, I imagine, in a far better condition than ever before. It will improve daily too, and if Hooker acts as judiciously as indications would warrant us in hoping, we shall, I think, by the first of June be again within sight of Richmond with no very serious loss. The plan of the campaign, I think I see, and, if I do, it is only the execution of McClellan's mutilated scheme of a year ago. When the roads permit, a large column will be rapidly pushed forward from Fortress Monroe, to cut off the army on the Rappahannock from Richmond, thus necessitating its capture or the abandonment of the line of the Rappahannock. But Lee will not be caught; he will fall back on Richmond and, perhaps, on his way, try to crush the army of the Peninsula. This army here will push him back with great rapidity and regardless of loss and try to force an engagement, and will crush him if it succeeds. If it fails, as I think it will, it will join the Peninsula column and push on Richmond, and be before that city in one week after leaving its camp here. None of the delays of last year will be tolerated. The march on Richmond will be such a rush as was ours of last fall to Antietam. The distances are about the same, and now all preparations are made before hand, which they were not then. At Richmond will come the tug of war, and God spare the

Infantry! As for the Cavalry, I think that we shall do one of two things: either push after Lee, if he allows himself to be caught in a tight place; or, which to my mind is more probable, if he slips off, be sent up towards Culpepper to operate on his left flank and annoy him. Anyhow we shall have work enough and fighting enough, and you may well wish us well through with it. Such are my views and theories and time will show how correct they are. As I understand it, they cover only McClellan's old plans corrected in the light of a year's experience. Of course the army will do something else, and meanwhile we'll see how wrong I am.

As to your and my futures, they will probably work themselves out in their own way, and I trouble myself little about them. You a little misunderstand me however. My plans for life are altered little if any; it is only my way of coming at them. All my natural inclinations tend to a combination of literature and politics and always have. I would be a philosophical statesman if I could, and a literary politician if I must; but to command attention as either I must have a certain position of my own. A lawyer's would have done, if I could have won it, but I failed in that and that is all over, for I *could* not go back to it. I must look about for another. Why should not the army serve my turn — if I hang to it? Here is support, leisure for reflection and promotion — two years would make me a Colonel almost surely and my very faculty with the pen will give me reputation as such, besides my chance of distinction as a soldier. Here then would be support and position for ten years, and then, at thirty-seven

I may hope to have reached that position of my own which will enable me to leave the army and to devote the rest of my life to those pursuits in which I can best play my part in the plan of the universe. This is all that my "avowal of belligerent intentions for life" amounts to, and why is not the plan a good one? You do not say it is not. So far as I *now* see, it is my only alternative with a long period of aimless indolence. I can't think of coming abroad to stay without some definite plan for the future. I see only this. I am twenty-eight years old in two months and at that age a man cannot afford to say "I will devote four years to seeing the world and thinking of what I will do." At that age my father had a son named Charles. . . .

I begin to realize that I have made a mistake in not getting a furlough, for I find myself most thoroughly played out with the army and camp life — out of spirits, desponding and blue, and all for the sake of a few days' change. It is in this mood, always brought on me by monotony and camp life, that I continually imagine that I am going to be hit in the next fight. When we move the mood passes away and my faith in my luck and future revives. . . .

CHARLES FRANCIS ADAMS, JR., TO HENRY ADAMS

Camp of 1st Mass. Cav'y
Sunday, April 5, 1863

No wonder that I began to write March instead of April, for there is nothing of April in the weather. Your last told me of the delightful weather you were having in London. Here it has been and still is beastly and unbearable. Last night, or April 4th and in Virginia, we had a violent and pelting snow storm and this morning the country is again under water, and hills, forts and camps are white with snow. Yesterday the wind was north all day and cold and violent — such as we remember in early March in Washington — accompanied with clouds of dust. I was out in it all day, for I was sent out to inspect the pickets, and starting at nine A.M. did not get in until half past three P.M. Cold, dreary, uninteresting work, riding from post to post and putting the same questions and receiving the same answers from all manner of stupid men. My escort, as is usual in such cases, consisted of twenty-five men, who served finely to impede my progress, were of no use to any one; and also my bulldog Mac, who frisked along with the column in a state of high enjoyment — in fact he would n't fight and submitted to insults from divers curs, great and small, with almost abject deprecation of a row. You see Mac's only idea of fighting is taking hold and then holding on, and as he stands in great fear of being left behind he calculates he won't have time to finish up the job and make a really neat piece of work before I'm out of sight. So he dares not take hold at all. We finished our work at half past three and at four o'clock Major Higginson and myself rode off to dine with General Griffin and George Bancroft (Tacitus). And hereby hangs a tale.

Friday evening last, as Colonel Curtis, Major Higginson and myself were crooning over the fire in their tent and mourning over the loss of so many old friends, and wondering dismally what was to become of us, I was called on by Captain Bliss — George Bancroft's step-son — and took him into my tent. He was in company with a Captain Batchelder and soon opened his business. He was sent by General Griffin, on whose staff they both were, to offer me the position of aid on the same staff. General Griffin is a well known officer of the old army, a Brigadier now in command of a Division, a young man and highly reputed. An officer of the old army, he never drinks, and he married one of our old Washington acquaintances, the Carrolls. So much for General Griffin, whom I had never seen but whose staff I should consider one of the most desirable in the army. I intimated to Bliss what my answer would be, and told him that I would express my acknowledgments to the General in person next day. Accordingly Major Higginson and I rode over at four o'clock to dine. Before dinner I had my audience and politely declined the proffered situation. I found Griffin a young, rather handsome man, with a face expressive of a good deal of resolution and energy, pleasant manners and a good deal of conversation. I told him that I was fully sensible of the great advantages and yet greater comforts which the proposed situation offered me. I did not deny that I was uncomfortable and ill at ease where I was, and that my chances of rising and of knowing what was going on would be much greater with him; but I told him I could not accept his offer for two reasons. First, if I did so I must yet retain my commission in my regiment. For a captain to do this I did not consider right. He knew what cavalry service was and how it differed from the other arms. In it all officers had to act for themselves and on their own responsibility. We were always in the face of the enemy and generally in small force. Our responsibility was great both for men and property and we were paid additionally for assuming it. I could not think it right that I should retain my rank and commission, receive the pay and stand in the way of those below me, while I shoved onto them the danger and responsibility, left my men to take care of themselves and went off and enjoyed myself looking only to my own advancement. This objection might however be removed by my receiving a new commission as aid. This he could not offer me, but even if he could, my second objection would still be in the way. He knew how essential in the cavalry officers of experience were and I told him how in our regiment our officers had been weeded out, so that now actually we could not boast of one officer, considered really reliable, to each of our four squadrons and that I was now the third line officer in this part of the regiment. I could not tell him of the sort of indirect appeal Curtis had made to me a few days before when Clapp had decided to leave us. I sustained Clapp in his course and said, that so far as the good of the regiment was concerned no officer had a right to consider himself so valuable to it that he ought to stay. Curtis replied: "That is very well to say, but you *know* the facts. You know whom we have and you *know* that if I went, and Higginson went, and yourself and one Captain more, the regiment would be stripped of its reliable officers. You know well enough that we can't officer our companies, and then what do you want us to say?"

Now I do know all this and unfortunately for me I have not only the highest opinion of Curtis' judgment and common sense, but the greatest admiration for his pluck and courage and the greatest fear of his censure. I know that he values me more than any line officer he now has left, and, finally, he fairly set it before me as a question of duty. Did I pretend that I could be of more use and service in this war on a staff than in my present position? If so, he disagreed with me. Would I allow myself to be driven from the post of usefulness by a man as radically wrong and dangerous as ———? If so, he could not sympathize with me. Did I go into this war as a soldier to enjoy and benefit myself or to contribute all in my power to a great result? If the last, would I not contribute most by remaining where I was, where I was of use and really essential and respectable in rank, rather than by appending myself to a General, no matter how agreeable or able? He argued in this way, and, while he preached, I felt that he himself was living up to his doctrine. I knew that he was the life and soul of this regiment, that he was doing his share in the war in his place; that Sargent could not drive him from it, and that he himself would not leave it. I felt that among us all he was the one strong, determined, formidable man. All this had its influence on me. Four months ago I should have felt differently and replied that there were better men than I here and my loss will not be felt; but now they are so all gone that I felt that the loss of each one was irreparable.

All this I could not tell Griffin without appearing conceited, and as I spoke in a general way, saying that, under existing circumstances, I felt that I was of more service in this stage of the war where I was than I could be with him and so — a miserable sense of duty triumphed over pleasure, comfort, advance, knowledge and excitement, and I gave up in favor of exposure, discomfort, danger, a contemptible superior, tyranny and hopeless obscurity, all the wished for pleasures and advantages of a Head Quarters' life. I hope I decided wisely; I know I did honestly, unwillingly and according to my lights. It will cost me all my comfort and most of my pleasures; it may cost me my life, and that too grossly blundered away. It certainly consigns me to hopeless obscurity in this war, but I meant it for the best. When the moment came I did not want to leave my post and I have thought to remain where I believed I could be of most use. Certainly I ought to love this regiment, for certainly first and last I have undergone and sacrificed enough in its behalf.

Such was my decision. Griffin listened and agreed to the force of my reasoning and did not try to dissuade me. He only expressed regret, as he assured me that he had been in it and was well enough aware that mine was the hardest, most trying and most thankless branch of the service in existence. Colonel Williams, he told me, had recommended me to him strongly and had induced him to make the offer; but apart from all I said he evidently considered that he rather offered me a fall from a senior captaincy of cavalry to a position as personal aid to a Brigadier.

Having finished business we went in to dinner. Ah! is n't it pleasant, this dining at Head Quarters! Line life is indeed beastly and one learns to appreciate glass, crockery and a table cloth. Old Bancroft was there and, as usual, I thought [him] a bore. The General was immensely civil to me and altogether I enjoyed myself very much. It was well I did, for some enjoyment was needed to compensate me for a ride home at nine o'clock, through a pelting, driving snow storm. . . .

HENRY ADAMS TO CHARLES FRANCIS ADAMS, JR.

London, April 23, 1863

TROUBLED times! troubled times! My own opinion is that our bed here is getting too hot for comfort and I don't much care how soon we are out of it.

The last storm really amounts to very little, but serves to show the temper of the people here, or rather, of the business men. I had not sent my last to you when it burst, and you would have thought the devil was loose. Ecoute, mon chéri.

The cursed blockade-runners got up a lovely scheme of trading to the Rio Grande, a few months ago, and to insure success they made a contract with J. D. at Richmond to furnish cotton at half price on the spot, etc., etc., and in accordance with the program, a steamer called the Peterhoff was sent out, which Admiral Wilkes very properly bagged, and deserves the thanks of the Government for doing so. But the owners had covered the transaction under the appearance of a trade with Mexico and Matamoras, and finding their whole game spoiled and the officers refusing at any price to insure their ships or any ships to Matamoras, they set up a tremendous cackle, and the Times and the Telegraph and all the newspapers cackled, and deputations of blockade runners went to the Foreign Office and in short the whole blockade-breaking interest, the insurance Companies and underwriters, the ship-owners, and all and every their relations, friends and acquaintances, were exasperated and acrimonious.

Meanwhile two Americans named Howell and Zerman had been some time here engaged in purchasing articles on account of the Mexican Government, but mostly with British money. The capture of the Peterhoff suddenly destroyed their chance of insurance. In great disgust they went to the Minister and asked him for a certificate of loyalty, on which they might act. The Minister saw his chance of hitting the Peterhoffers a hard blow, and at the same time of helping Mexico, and so wrote the letter which you have probably already seen in the newspapers. Of course it was secret, for its publication would necessarily destroy the insurance, but it was intended for the gentlemen at Lloyd's. It had the intended effect. The policy was to have been executed the next day, when one of the very underwriters made public a copy of the letter which his clerk had surreptitiously taken in short-hand as he himself read it aloud to the other four underwriters; within an hour a deputation had gone up with it to Earl Russell; the Exchange was raving mad; the Times next day thundered at the Minister for his insolent attempt to license British trade; the Standard cried for his dismissal; the public cursed and threatened; even our friends were frightened, and all thought that at last salt had been deposited upon the caudal appendage of a very venerable ornithological specimen.

The Minister was grand. I studied his attitude with deep admiration. Not all the supplications of his friends could make him open his mouth either to put the public right on his letter or on the gross falsehoods told about the Peterhoff. The time had not come. Of course he was cursed for his obstinacy, but he is used to that. We remained perfectly silent while the storm raged and laughed at it. But you can't conceive how bitter they were in the city, and the matter was twice brought up in Parliament, though nothing was said there, nor shown, except a strong desire to get hold of the Minister. Luckily Lord Russell was firm and his course irritated the Peterhoffers so as to draw off a large portion of indignation upon him. Meanwhile the man who betrayed the letter in the hope of getting revenge for being called "dishonest and fraudulent," and of stirring up hostility to our Government, honorably refused to proceed with the insurance and was blackguarded in his own office like a thief by Howell. To complete their discomfiture, a letter of the Minister to a London firm is published this morning, coolly putting it right as to the licensing business, and referring British subjects to their own Government for protection. When the whole Peterhoff story is told we shall reverse everything and overwhelm these liars, I hope, but meanwhile the storm seems to have blown itself out and we are still steady and going straight ahead. But England is not comfortable with such Irish rows.

April 24

You may judge the state of feeling here by the debate in Parliament last night, where much bad temper was shown, but no case. You will observe that our friends kept silence and left the Government to manage the matter. As to Lord Russell's declaration about the Minister's course and the complaint at Washington, it is of course annoying and hurts us here, but I believe it to be only the result of the outside pressure, and I do not believe he expects really to affirm that the American Government has no right to protect its own citizens against its own fleets. One thing however is certain. There is great danger in this feeling of irritation on both sides and a rupture is highly probable. But then, if we can weather it and turn the current, as I hope we may do, if the Peterhoff case is a strong one, we shall have plain sailing for another spell. Meanwhile we still bear up and steer right onward. Another debate comes on tonight and our friends will have their innings on the Alabama case. You will probably see this in our papers, but I shan't be able to send it to you. . . .

CHARLES FRANCIS ADAMS TO HIS SON

London, April 24, 1863

WE go here much as usual. The American question excites more fever than ever. The collisions that inevitably take place on the ocean in the effort to stop all the scandalous voyages to help the rebels, that are made from this island, necessarily created much bad feeling. I have got a little mixed up in it of late, so that my name has been bandied about rather more than I like. But such is the fate of all men who are in situations of difficulty in troubled times. I hope and trust I shall survive it. My rule is, so far as I know how, to follow a strict rule of right. As long as I keep myself within it, I trust in God and fear no evil. My endeavor will be to prevent things from coming to a rupture here, not from any particular goodwill to the English, but from a conviction that quarreling with them just now is doing service to the rebels. So far as I can judge from their own reports of their condition, the suffocating process is going on steadily to its end. On the other hand the position of the loyal part of the country is more dignified and imposing than ever. In spite of lukewarm generals and a defective and uneven policy, the great body of the people and the army are true to their duty which is to *save the country*. I feel more hopeful of that result than ever before. Presently our people will fight with the same energy that animates the rebels. Whenever that happens, the struggle will be soon brought to an end.

We have of late quite an influx of Americans, more than have been here all the winter before. First, there is Mr. Robert J. Walker, the quondam Secretary of the Treasury and Governor of Kansas. I am amused to find him changed into a thorough anti-slavery man, determined upon emancipation as the only condition of pacification. Then we have Mr. W. H. Aspinwall of New York and Mr. John M. Forbes. And in addition, Mr. John A. Kasson of Iowa, late Assistant Postmaster General, and now member of the next House of Representatives, who is out here as a delegate to a convention to settle postal matters between nations. I wish he could succeed in getting a reduction of ocean postage. Over and above these we have my old colleague in the Massachusetts Legislature, Mr. Alvah Crocker of Fitchburg, and George Morey, whilom the great factotum of Whig politics, in days of yore. So we cannot be said to be solitary or without sympathisers. . . .

HENRY ADAMS TO CHARLES FRANCIS ADAMS, JR.

London, May 1, 1863

. . . .

AND so two years have passed over and gone, and still I am abroad and still you are a Captain of cavalry. You meanwhile are near twenty-eight years old. I shall never on this earth see my twenty-fifth birthday again. Does not this fact suggest certain ideas to you? Can a man at your time of life be a cavalry captain and remain a briefless solicitor? Can a man of my general appearance pass five years in Europe and remain a candidate for the bar? In short, have we both wholly lost our reckonings and are we driven at random by fate, or have we still a course that we are steering though it is not quite the same as our old one? By the Apostle Paul, I know not. Only one fact I feel sure of. We are both no longer able to protect ourselves with the convenient fiction of the law. Let us quit that now useless shelter, and steer if possible for whatever it may have been that once lay beyond it. Neither you nor I can ever do anything at the bar. . . .

You don't catch me entering the army now. It would be like entering college Freshman when all one's friends were Seniors. I have a trick worth twenty of that. My friend General Zerman, who has been the means of kicking up such a row around us here, and who is an old Dugald Dalgetty; a midshipman under the French at Trafalgar; a *sous-officier* at Waterloo; a captain at Navarino; a Russian admiral; a Turkish admiral; a Carbonaro; a companion of Silvio Pellico in the prisons of Spielberg; a South American officer by land and sea; and lately a general in the army of the United States; now a Major General in the Mexican service; and I've no doubt a damned old villain, though a perfectly jovial old sinner of seventy odd; this distinguished individual offers to take me on his staff with the rank of major to Mexico. Would n't I like to go! The chances are a thousand to one that my bones would bleach there, but for all that the chance is worth having, for it would be a great step for a young man to secure for himself a control even to a small extent over our Mexican relations. But such magnificent dreams, worthy of the daring of those heroes, Porthos, Athos, Aramis and D'Artagnan, are not for me. By the by, though, what a good Porthos Ben Crowny would make; you could do D'Artagnan, I would put in for Aramis, and no doubt you could hunt up some one that might pass equally badly for Athos. Then we could all go to Mexico together. . . .

I left off by sending you the debate of last Friday night which contained Earl Russell's brilliant remarks on the celebrated letter of our Minister to Admiral Dupont. In those remarks Earl Russell was indignant at the idea of his speaking to Mr. Adams about it. No! No! He should go straight to Washington! But my Lord, having thus pledged himself in order to please the English copper-heads, to go straight to Washington, amused himself the next morning by sending straight to Mr. Adams. Of course I know nothing of the conversation that followed. That is all a secret with Mr. Seward. But I think it is not difficult to guess. It had suited Lord Russell to yield a little to the copper-head pressure on Thursday night; it suited him to allow Mr. Adams to triumphantly purge himself of misdemeanor on Friday morning. It suited him to make the American Minister think that he (Lord R.) thought him to be in the wrong — moderately. It also suited him to make the British public think that Mr. Adams had confessed his error and contrition and had received pardon. English statesmanship consists in this sort of juggling and huckstering between interests.

Such was the position when I wrote to you, or rather, immediately after I wrote to you. Since then nothing has been heard of complaining at Washington. But now see the resources of a British Minister. Last Tuesday morning the *City Article*, what we call the money article, of the Times, in which most of the attack has been directed, contained the following paragraph:

"The public will be glad to learn that the difficulties occasioned by the recent issue by Mr. Adams of the certificate or pass to Messrs. Howell and Zerman, are likely to be smoothed down. It is reported that Mr. Adams is conscious of having acted in the matter upon imperfect representations and with undue haste, and that consequently he raises no pretensions such as would necessitate any absolute protest from one Government to the other on the subject. It is therefore believed that the relations between our Cabinet and the United States Legation in London will continue on a friendly footing — a result which in a personal sense will afford unmixed satisfaction, since the individual and historical claims of Mr. Adams to respect and esteem have never been disputed in any quarter."

Now, is not this a remarkable State Paper? Did you ever see a case in which the butter was laid on so curiously over the interstices of the bread? The real fact is that you should read "Earl Russell" instead of "Mr. Adams" in the fifth line. That would be the correct thing. But this statement has received universal currency and is accepted as a conclusion of the difficulty. It now remains for Lord Russell to make the explanation which no doubt Mr. Adams must demand, at some time when the whole affair shall be forgotten, and then I hope this curious chapter will be closed. . . .

Our own position here does not change. We lead a quiet and not unpleasant life, and I pass my intervals from official work, in studying De Tocqueville and John Stuart Mill, the two high priests of our faith. So I jump from International Law to our foreign history, and am led by that to study the philosophic standing of our republic, which brings me to reflection over the advance of the democratic principle in European civilization, and so I go on till some new question of law starts me again on the circle. But I have learned to think De Tocqueville my model, and I study his life and works as the Gospel of my private religion. The great principle of democracy is still capable of rewarding a conscientious servant. And I doubt me much whether the advance of years will increase my toleration of its faults. Hence I think I see in the distance a vague and unsteady light in the direction towards which I needs must gravitate, so soon as the present disturbing influences are removed.

We are surrounded by assistants. Mr. Aspinwall, Mr. J. M. Forbes, Mr. Robert J. Walker and Mr. Evarts are all here.

CHARLES FRANCIS ADAMS, JR., TO HIS FATHER

*Hartwood Church, Va.
May 8, 1863*

THIS is indeed a twice told tale and of the weariest at that. Here am I once more picketing Hartwood Church after another battle of Fredericksburg, just as I did last December! I did on the fifteenth of last month confidently hope never again to see this modest brick edifice, but the wisdom of Providence differently ordained and here I am once more and, from here, go on with my broken story.

I left off with Sunday, 26th April, and an order to send me out on picket. I got off at about ten o'clock and reached my position on the road to Sulphur Springs at about four. I had only about sixty men and my line was very long. The officers whom I relieved looked disgusted enough when I told them what my force was, and said that they had twice as many and had sent for more. However I was sent to relieve them and went to work to do so. There are few things more disgusting I imagine than being called upon to establish a line of pickets at night and in a strange country, and then having night shut down on you just when you realize how difficult your task is. It took me four hours to ride over my line, and when I returned I was in an awful maze. Major Covode, whom I relieved, had taken me through the fields instead of over the roads, and I no longer knew where the river ran, which was north or south, or indeed where I was. My mind was a jumble of fords, hills and roads, with a distinct recollection of a rapid brook called "the river," and the immense desolate ruins of the huge hotel at the Springs, burnt by Pope last summer and through which I had ridden by moonlight. Major Covode left me with the encouraging information that I need n't fear much until the river went down, but then I'd have to look sharp and I proceeded to secure myself.

As for guarding the army, I gave that idea up at once and perforce ran for luck; but I was n't going to be surprised myself, so I made my arrangements to protect myself and concluded that they were eminently unsatisfactory. Flint with twenty men was posted about four miles to my right and in a very exposed and dangerous place, and my force was too weak to keep up communication with him. He might be swallowed whole and I not know it. I was near Sulphur Springs and tolerably secure until the river fell. The enemy left us alone, however, and in the morning one of my men crossed the river and found it fordable. I sent in my report and at nine o'clock — as I was not likely to be on duty three days — went out to study the country. At two o'clock I had gotten through and set my mind at ease, for I understood the position and knew how to go to work for the next night, and at three o'clock I was notified that I was relieved. Our picket duty is made immensely more difficult here by the state of the population. The enemy know the country and we don't, and every man is a citizen or a soldier, as the occasion offers. We feel no single man is safe and so our posts have to be double, and we feel at any time that these may be picked off and thus our reserves and the army exposed to surprises. I was glad to be relieved, although now I felt that I knew what I was about, and at seven o'clock got off and got into camp at nine. At eleven Flint got in and we turned in for a good night.

Monday the weather had changed again and all day it rained and was threatening rain, but we nevertheless went to work and made ourselves very comfortable. We moved our squadron camp to the top of the hill and had the tents pitched in line and our own head quarters fenced in with brush. When evening came all was finished, swept up and clean, and I looked round on the pleasantest camp I had ever seen in a bivouac. Teague, Flint's 2d Lieutenant, had constructed a rustic bench and the bright fire in front of it threw its light into the shelter tents where Mac had ensconced himself on our blankets. It was very pretty and Flint and I sat down to a pipe of deep contentment, preparatory to a sleep of supreme comfort.

While we were simmering over these pleasant sensations an orderly blundered by inquiring the way to Colonel Curtis' quarters, and a cold shiver went through me. In a minute more orders came for me to get ready to march at once. It was then eight o'clock, and a night march was before us, and we so comfortable and tired! It went very hard, but it had to go, and at nine o'clock we were in the saddle and our comfortable camp was nowhere. It was a general move. We marched down to Bealeton and struck the railroad and kept along until we came to within a mile of the river when we turned off into the woods, and Mac lost us and disappeared. It was then about two o'clock in the morning. We dismounted, unsaddled, built some fires and went to sleep before them. The night was cloudy, damp and warm. We were called and saddled at daylight and the men got their breakfasts — mine being a cup of coffee and at eight we started. In vain had I whistled and inquired for Mac. He seemed gone and I gave him up; but just as our column was formed out in the fields my heart was rejoiced by seeing him poking down the ranks, evidently looking for me. He caught sight of me at last and evinced his satisfaction by at once laying down and going to sleep. Since that he has pegged steadily along with the column and is now placidly sleeping in my tent. I did n't expect to keep him so long, but now I think he's got the hang of it and has a chance of coming through.

We marched towards the river and halted. It was a cold, cloudy, dismal east wind morning. Apparently the ford there was impracticable, for presently we started again and moved rapidly down the river. I now felt pretty sick of this running round after a ford and began to doubt whether we ever should get across that miserable little river. My doubts were solved, however, when at noon we got down to Kelly's Ford and I saw a pontoon bridge thrown across and the cavalry fording. Here at last we crossed the river at a point which we reached at the end of our first day's march, and we left camp on April 13th and this was April 29th. After crossing we dismounted and let our horses graze and lay there, doing nothing, or mounting, moving and accomplishing nothing, until nearly evening, when just as we were thinking of going into camp, the column began to defile into the woods and we followed in our turn. We had had nothing to eat since the evening before and were getting cross; but luckily, just then Flint's man came up with a canteen of coffee and a plate of meat, and at the same time the skirmishing began in front. So we rode forward feasting and ready to fight.

We pressed rapidly forward in line of battle through the woods with a rapid skirmishing fire in front and a few shells now and then going or coming and, presently, about sunset, emerged onto an immense open country, on the farther side of which could just be seen the enemy's cavalry. Here we formed line, but it was too late to attack and so presently we fell back to the edge of the wood to pass the night. Of course we could have no fires and our ranks were not broken; but the men dismounted, the horses were fed part at a time, and the men lay down and slept in front of them, holding the bridles. Presently it began to rain and kept it up smartly pretty much all night, but we slept none the less and I know I slept well. We certainly calculated on a fight that morning, but when morning came the rumor crept round that the enemy was gone and so it proved. It had stolen away like a thief in the night and left open to us the road to Culpepper. This we took at once and again breakfasted in the saddle, glad enough to see Davis, Flint's man, with his coffee and tin dish of fried beef.

This was Thursday and we had one of the most delightful and interesting marches I ever enjoyed. The morning was cloudy, but it cleared bright and warm at noon, and the afternoon and night were charming, with a few slight drawbacks. The country towards Culpepper is open and we approached the town in order of battle — five columns or squadrons, marching straight across the country and all manœuvring together. We saw nothing of Lee or Stuart, however, except his dead horses, which lay along our course thick and unburied, and by noon we were close to Culpepper. The country looks old, war-worn and wasted, but not so bad as the other side of the river. Most of the houses along the road were deserted and apparently had been so for a long time. Some of them were evidently old Virginia plantation houses, and once had been aristocratic and lazy. Now they are pretty thoroughly out of doors. We marched rapidly through Culpepper and out on the other side, exciting the especial notice of the negroes and curs of the town and the lazy attention of the few whites left. It's quite a Yankee looking place and, with Warrenton, very unlike most Virginia towns. Hardly were we dismounted when I was sent scampering out to the front to attend to a party of rebels who were said to be threatening our advance guard, but when I had pounded my horses up hill and down dale for a mile and a half, I found no enemy to attend to and was told I might come back and feed my men and horses. I did so and we lay off for a couple of hours in the woods. Presently the column came up and we fell in and continued our march until we came to the battlefield of Cedar Mountain, where we halted while the column was passing an obstacle in the road. Here you know our 2d Regiment was so cut up and Stephen Perkins was killed. We looked over the field and saw the graves of our troops, but there are few signs of a battlefield left. I noticed that our horses would not eat the grass and, as we passed one ditch, some of my men hit upon a skull, apparently dug up and gnawed by the swine. Such it is to die for one's country!

While resting here a tremendous shower came up and, before it was over, we were again on the road. As night came on and we approached the Rapidan things got worse. The afternoon was clear and was followed by a full moonlight evening, but the roads were heavy enough and the head of the column passed on at a gait very unmerciful to the rear. I once got a mile to the rear of the squadron in front of me and was kept at a trot the whole time. At sunset we entered a thick marshy wood of heavy timber, between Cedar Mountain and the Rapidan, and pressed on, through perfectly fearful roads, until about eight when the river brought the column up standing. Then came one of those nights which try the temper and patience. After dark, with exhausted horses, tired, wet and hungry, we were first kept waiting and then marched into the woods, and then more delay, and then marched back in search of a camp. But the whole wood for miles was literally a marsh, and so after bungling round for some time, at ten o'clock we were dismounted and told to "make ourselves comfortable." It was the worst camping ground I ever saw. The mud and water stood everywhere up to the horses' fetlocks and our ankles and it seemed a dead flat; but the moon was in our favor. Had it rained, it would have been very trying. The men picked out the dry spots, or those least wet, and Flint, Teague and I had some young trees cut and, resting one end on a dead trunk and the other in the mud, made a sort of inclined plane bed on which we spread our blankets, had some coffee and beef and went to sleep.

The next day was the 1st of May — the day two years that you sailed for Europe, as I did not fail to remember. It was a delightful day, bright and sunny. We did not leave our charming camp, christened by the men the water-cure establishment — until about nine, and then went slowly forward to where we could hear some skirmishing and artillery practice along the line of the river. Presently we halted and our carbineers went to the front and there we waited all day. I don't know what the plan was, but I cannot think that it included our crossing the river. The enemy had a few pieces of artillery on the hills beyond and the sharpshooters lined both banks. No attempt was made by us to cross and our plan seemed rather to be to make a feint and to distract the enemy's attention from some other point. Once or twice during the day we changed our position, but otherwise we killed time only and finally when evening came and when we were in a very comfortable position orders came for us to go into camp and to our unspeakable disgust we were marched straight back to the water-cure establishment, and dumped down into the mud again. This time I could n't stand it and at eleven o'clock, after wading round and looking at my horses wholly unable to lay down, I got permission to move my company and went to bed satisfied that men and horses were high and dry.

Saturday we started at eight o'clock and, to our immense surprise, found ourselves on the back track. They said that we had accomplished all we came for, but we could n't see it, and we did n't relish our march. As for me, I did n't relish the reticence about high quarters. There seemed to be an air of solemn silence which omened badly and I felt sure that evil tidings had come from Hooker. Still the day was very fine and the spring young and full of life and at this season, in this open air life, one can't be dull long, so I soon brightened up and was all ready for the first rumor which told us of a battle and a great victory of Hooker's the day before. After that we lived in anxiety and rumors, now victory, now defeat, now all up and again all down, until the final acknowledgment came. We did not hear the guns of the battle until that afternoon, but as we approached the Rapidan near Ely's Ford they began to boom faintly up and when we reached the ford at sunset they sounded loud and fast. Here we halted and went into camp with a notice that we should go on again at midnight; but just as we were getting ready to lay down there came a most tremendous volley of musketry close to us, causing us to saddle with the least possible delay. Our camps were knocked to pieces and the regiments moved off as soon as possible and my squadron was ordered to support Tidball's battery. I reported and all the dispositions were made and things were prepared for a night attack, and then our commanders concluded that there would n't be any after all. It proved that a rebel regiment had fired across the river into our camp and had then subsided into silence. So I was told that I might unsaddle and go to sleep, which I did, and at one o'clock we lay down in the hospitable furrows of a corn field to be called at four.

Saturday was a lazy, anxious disagreeable day. Heavy firing in the direction of Chancellorsville, about five miles off, began at daybreak and was kept up until nearly noon without intermission. We anxiously watched the direction and distance and tried to draw inferences from it. We listened to all sorts of rumors which came flowing in, most of them encouraging, and tried to believe them, and, in fact, we did and that afternoon I, for one, was sanguine and confident. At noon the battery left and I was relieved, so, to pass the time, I was ordered to go and strip an old secesh farmer of his corn, for our horses were well-nigh starving. I did so in most approved style and in reply to his long story of losses, plunderings and impending starvation turned the deaf ear of duty, and, as I swept off his last ears of seed corn, told him that Virginia had brought this on herself and need expect no mercy. I think that that old pod realises that the ordinance of secession was a mistake. After finishing this job I took my squadron into the woods and we lay off for a few hours under the trees in the pleasant spring afternoon until the column started to cross the river, when I fell in.

We crossed and came into our lines a couple of miles on the other side. Though I did not know it, those two miles were very dangerous to us, for it was through thick woods, of which we did not hold possession, and in which a few felled trees and a small force of infantry could have driven us back. We got through safely however and came into our lines. We found our forces throwing up defences, as busy as bees, already strongly protected and apparently in excellent spirits. They looked fresh, clean and confident. We went on to U.S. ford and soon struck the main road with its endless confusion — reinforcements, supply and ammunition trains and messengers going to the front; stragglers, ambulances and stretchers with the loads of wounded and dying men toiling to the rear; cattle, horses and mules; wounded men resting, tired men sleeping, all here looking excited and worn out with fatigue. The news here was not so good, but the 11th Corps had fought here and had not fought well, and we thought it was probably colored by their reverses.

We got to the ford at dusk and encamped, and in the evening we had a shower or two and in the morning we woke by a brisk discharge of artillery and bursting of shells. At ten o'clock we moved and came across the river and encamped on this side in a wood, a mile or so from the river, and received a new issue of forage or rations. The rumors were very good and very bad. At first, the enemy was surrounded, Sedgwick held the heights and we were getting ready to follow in pursuit. Then Sedgwick had lost the heights and Hooker was coming to grief, and night fell on rumors of an unpleasant aspect. Still our quarters were comfortable and we turned in for a good night's sleep; but at two o'clock we were called and ordered to be ready to move in ten minutes and three found us on the road. We marched down towards Falmouth, utterly ignorant of our destination or of what was going on; but as day broke through a thick heavy fog we found various stragglers, etc., and picked up scraps of news. It was all bad, not decisive, but bad; things evidently were going wrong. At last I met a Captain from Sedgwick's Corps who gave me the gross results, and in a few minutes I rode through Falmouth as dejected a man as you would care to see. I felt sick of the war, of the army, almost of life. I thought of you and of this result abroad; it seemed too much and I felt despairing. We presently halted beyond Falmouth and there passed the day trying not to believe news which we felt to be true. The morning was very hot, but in the afternoon a tremendous rain-storm came up ending in a northeaster, wetting us through, driving us out of our tents and freezing us nearly to death, and in this we passed the night.

Wednesday was cheerless to a degree. Wind northeast, cold and rainy, and we wet and shivering; but it wore away by degrees and our spirits kept rising, until at last we actually believed that the army had not retreated; but in the afternoon came the crusher. The news of the retreat of the army came upon us at once with the order to saddle and return to our old camp. We did so and returned to Potomac Run Bridge. It was a cold, cheerless afternoon. The rain fell by showers in torrents and we had been wet through twenty-four hours. We found our old camp deserted, burned up, filthy and surrounded with dead horses. We tied up our horses and stood dismally round in the pouring rain. Presently shelters were rigged up and we crawled into them and passed a supperless, wet night, by no means uncheerfully, for things were too bad to be trifled with now and woe to a grumbling man, or one who intimated that things might be more agreeable.

Thursday, just as we were getting ready to clear away the wreck and to discover what our four weeks of active service had left of our companions an order came for us at once to go out on picket. I was not sorry to do it, for the old camp is not pleasant. We did so and here I am now, doing the lightest possible picket duty and sitting in the woods. To be sure it rained again last night and we are still wet; but we are out of that confounded filthy camp which oppresses us with defeat.

Potomac Bridge, Va.
May 9, 1863

BACK at Potomac Run and so ends today the four toughest weeks campaigning that I have ever felt — mud and rain, rain and mud, long marches and short forages. It is strange how I like the life though, in spite of its hardships and beastly slavery. I no longer care for a leave of absence, or wish to go home. I am satisfied to stay here and see the thing through. Still we are now clearing away the wreck and can see what damage is done. We got in from picket last night at nine o'clock, and today it has cleared off and we can take account of stock. The trip has used up about twenty of my sixty horses and done no good to the men, but we have seen no fighting. Our regiment has lost one officer, poor Phillips, picked off by a sharp-shooter on the Rapidan. He was a promoted sergeant and came from Springfield. Our division has lost its General — Averell — placed under arrest, why, I do not know. I think they'll have to release him, as, good or bad, he's the best we have. Stoneman turned up last night and what he has done the newspapers will tell you; I can't. As for the Army of the Potomac, it's loss is great, but not irreparable. The men do not seem cast down or demoralised and the enemy cannot afford to diminish their forces opposite. The real trouble, I imagine, is the mustering out of the two year men. If it were not for that I should feel confidence in immediate movement. As for Hooker, I think the army feels confidence in him. He ran his head against a stone wall here, but that is his tendency and the lesson will be of great service. I think he'll do much better next time. On the whole things might be much worse; but the army must be kept in motion and the enemy engaged. If Hooker rests, he's lost, and so I look to being in the field again at once. . . .

HENRY ADAMS TO CHARLES FRANCIS ADAMS, JR.

London, May 8, 1863

MY bulletin is calmer this week than has been usual of late. The little squall has passed and instead of pressing on the Minister, people here feel that Lord Russell was in the wrong in his attack that I sent you some weeks ago, and the Times has this week administered a second pacifyer in the shape of a flattering leader on Mr. Adams' speech to the Trades Unions delegation. I send you a newspaper containing this speech. Notice also the Royal Academy dinner and Lord Palmerston's remarks. They are not political, but are a noble specimen of lofty sentiment and brilliant rhetoric, worthy of the experienced statesman to whose power and wisdom this vast nation bows. And these men call Seward shallow and weak!

A much quieter feeling and a partial reaction against the blockade runners have generally prevailed here for a week past. Our successes on the Mississippi, too, and the direct advices from the South are having a quieting effect here on the public, and the Polish question is becoming so grave that we are let up a little. On the whole we have made progress this last week.

Meanwhile we have a complete Cabinet of Ministerial advisers and assistants. I wrote you their names in my last. Of them all Mr. Evarts is the only one whom I put very high. Dana too has written to call on my services for him. So I have done and shall do everything I can to make him comfortable and contented. Last Sunday I took him down to Westminster Abbey in the afternoon, where we listened awhile to the services, and then trotted off and took a steamboat up the river. We had a two hours' voyage up to Kew, where we arrived at half after five, and had just time to run over the gardens. Then we took a cab and drove up to Richmond Hill, where we ordered dinner at the Star and Garter, and then sat in the open air and watched the view and the sunset until our meal was ready. Much conversation had we, and that of a pretty confidential nature. We discussed affairs at home and philosophic statesmanship, the Government and the possibility of effectual reform. He is much like Dana in his views, but is evidently a good deal soured by his political ill-luck.

Another evening I took him out to see London by night. We visited, as spectators, various places of popular resort. He was much interested in them, and seemed to enjoy the experience as a novelty in his acquaintance with life. London is rather peculiar in these respects, and even an experienced traveller would find novelty in the study of character at the Argyll Rooms and at Evans's. At any rate, I consider that I have done my part there, and you may imagine that I do not much neglect opportunities to conciliate men like him, like Seward and like Weed. I would like to get further west, but the deuce of it is that there are so few distinguished western men.

With this exception I believe the last week has been quiet. I was rather astonished last Monday by one of Seward's jocose proceedings. The Minister had sent me down to the Trades Unions meeting three weeks ago to make a report on it to him, for transmission to Washington. I did so and wrote a report which I had no time either to correct or alter, and which was sent the next day to Seward officially, appended to a despatch. Now Seward writes back as grave as a Prime Minister a formal despatch acknowledging the other, and thanking "Mr. Henry B. Adams" in stately and wordy paragraphs for his report and "profound disquisition," etc., etc. I propose to write a note to Fred Seward on his father's generosity. . . .

END OF VOLUME I

www.ingramcontent.com/pod-product-compliance
Lightning Source LLC
Chambersburg PA
CBHW032017230426
43671CB00005B/117